T0106942

# Points OF Difference

············•·····•·············•·············•·······

# Transforming (HORMEL)

## RICHARD L. KNOWLTON
### with Ron Beyma

MORGAN JAMES PUBLISHING • NEW YORK

*POINTS OF DIFFERENCE* is neither a company history nor an autobiography. It is, instead, a perceptively illustrated and highly readable account of the principles of business transformation. Because of its vast diversity, Hormel Foods' significance in the American business community is somewhat underestimated. This book reveals how an "invisible giant" occupies the #1 or #2 rankings in 34 food categories. The author also explains the often elusive management principles underpinning its impressive success.

# Points of Difference

Copyright © 2010 Richard L. Knowlton

First Edition

No part of this publication may be reproduced or transmitted in any form or by any means, mechanical or electronic, including photocopying and recording, or by any information storage and retrieval system, without permission in writing from author or publisher (except by a reviewer, who may quote brief passages and/or show brief video clips in review).

All of the author proceeds from this book will go to the Austin Public Education Foundation, Inc. benefiting the Austin, Minnesota school system. At this decisive time in our history, there is considerable pressure on all forms of public expenditure. There is no other single investment that will serve the well-being of our nation – both its competitiveness and its strength of character – than the investment we make in the quality of our educational system.

ISBN: 978-1-60037-674-0 (Paperback)
ISBN: 978-1-60037-698-6 (Hardcover)
Library of Congress Control Number: 2009931497

Published by:

MORGAN · JAMES
THE ENTREPRENEURIAL PUBLISHER ™
www.morganjamespublishing.com

Habitat
for Humanity®
Peninsula
Building Partner

Morgan James Publishing, LLC
1225 Franklin Ave Ste 32
Garden City, NY 11530-1693
Toll Free 800-485-4943
www.MorganJamesPublishing.com

Cover/Interior Design by:
Rachel Lopez
rachel@r2cdesign.com

# DEDICATION

**THIS BOOK IS DEDICATED TO** the wonderful people of Hormel Foods in forging one of America's truly great companies through realizing meaningful points of difference.

And to my wife Nancy, my indispensable partner, my wisest counselor, and my very best friend.

# TABLE OF CONTENTS

# INTRODUCTION

## *Hormel Foods: A Timely Model for American Industry*

### by Jeff Noddle

*Jeff Noddle is executive chairman and former chief executive officer of Minnesota-based SUPERVALU INC., the third-largest grocery retail company and leading food distributor in the United States.*

FEW TOPICS CAPTIVATE AS MUCH ATTENTION on the world stage these days as food. Efficiency, quality, product innovation, changing consumer tastes and food safety are constant challenges for food manufacturers and grocery retailers alike. To meet these challenges, the food industry must also have strong leadership that embraces technology, change and the enigmatic vagaries of marketing in a rapidly changing consumer marketplace.

In *Points of Difference*, Dick Knowlton has written a penetrating account of how Hormel Foods has become a technological and marketing leader in the food industry. Knowing Dick as I have, both personally and professionally for many years, I believe him to be uniquely qualified to weigh in on the issues facing today's food industry. But even more than that, he is a talented business executive with the kinds of experience, integrity and savvy that bring value to the discussion of successful, innovative business management across any industry. No matter what our product or service, we all have the same challenges: increasing competition from new quarters, ensuring a culture of ethical and focused leadership, responsibility to an increasingly vocal shareholder constituency, and acting as a responsible steward of a company for its current and future workforce, customers and investors. In *Points of Difference*, Dick blends the Hormel story with these resonant points in his own inimitable voice. His book, frankly, couldn't have appeared at a more timely moment in American business history.

At the core of a business like Hormel – or the food retailing company I've led for the better part of a decade, SUPERVALU – is understanding and meeting the needs of your customer. At SUPERVALU, we talk a lot about customer centricity, ensuring that our stores provide our shoppers with the right mix of product, value and superior experience. It's not so different with a company like Hormel – and without visionary companies like Hormel, a SUPERVALU couldn't deliver to its consumers.

In *Points of Difference*, Dick describes a particularly prescient moment during a meeting of the American Meat Institute in 1979. During the course of discussion, a consultant from McKinsey made the prediction that none of the contemporary giant meat companies would be around in the future unless they made fundamental changes to their businesses. As Dick notes, the consultant was met with guffaws. The consultant, however, had the last laugh – he was right.

At Hormel, these fundamental changes were broad, but based in the strong traditions that had laid the success for the company since its inception in 1891. Hormel committed itself to product innovation, sensitivity to consumers, retailer and market trends, building a responsible and ethical leadership team, and careful financial stewardship.

Very few manufacturers find long-term success in making the same product, year after year, without change. This is particularly true for food, and a principle thoroughly embraced by Hormel. Although its earliest years were in pork processing, today the company dominates many categories across the food spectrum. Two particular shifts come to mind with Hormel – the demand for increasingly convenient foods and an expanded appetite for proteins in recent years. Both have given rise to the opportunity to develop myriad new products, to re-energize existing product lines, and to find innovative solutions that help today's consumer create healthy, substantial meals for their families.

Not that long ago, who would've anticipated shelf-stable microwaveable dinners or refrigerated luncheon meats without preservatives? The answer? Hormel.

Hormel's dedication to innovation is evident across its product lines. The company has been a leader in convenient prepared microwaveable products, a category that they continue to expand and improve. During the 1990s and early 2000s, Hormel Foods' new, internally developed, packaging technology pioneered a vast line of microwaveable products that was compatible with the company's traditional consumer-branded fresh meats and with fully prepared entrées within its Refrigerated Foods Division. Many of these products are found across SUPERVALU's grocery stores from coast-to-coast, and are category leaders.

Hormel is, of course, home to some of the most recognized and, in some cases, iconic, brands. Who isn't familiar with the SPAM family of products? Millions of families have grown up with this time-tested favorite, helping the product to win its own place in the popular cultural consciousness. No small feat.

Along with SPAM, the company had developed further market share with HORMEL Chili, DINTY MOORE beef stew and MARY KITCHEN corned beef hash, to name just a few. These lines are bolstered with shelf-stable, microwaveable versions.

The company continues to make breakthroughs through research and collaboration. For example, the Foodservice Group, which serves the industrial and hospitality trade, was able to accelerate advances in product development for home consumers – including microwaveable pre-cooked bacon. And through acquisitions outside of the meat area, Hormel continues to build its position by adding entrants in new food and health concepts. This awareness of market trends and opportunities has been a boon to the company. Hormel Foods is one of the top three marketers of branded salsa. The Hormel Health Labs line of products focuses on the senior market, having become the second-largest supplier of nutritional foods to the managed health care industry.

Hormel's success in taking these and other products to market depends on understanding consumers, building strong relationships with retailers and wholesalers, and being keenly aware of market trends.

The examples I've cited have helped to revolutionize the concept of "home cooking" for busy families. By leveraging the incredible prevalence of the microwave as an integral part of the contemporary kitchen, Hormel has anticipated – and kept up with – the consumer needs for fast, simple and satisfying meal preparation.

At the same time, these kinds of product innovations help grocery retailers like SUPERVALU ensure that we are meeting the needs of our customers. Hormel has long been a vital business partner for SUPERVALU, and we've built a relationship that is mutually beneficial – from new product launches to exploring new market opportunities. While I like to think of our business relationship as particularly unique – as two home-grown Minnesota companies that have grown up together – I know that Hormel is an equally valuable partner to food retailers worldwide in anticipating consumer needs, and this skill has been a major factor in the company's success.

However, all of this innovation and relationship building does not happen without a strong, responsible and ethical leadership team and the support of one of the strongest workforces in food manufacturing. During Dick's tenure, Hormel made numerous acquisitions; leveraged itself at some very high levels and repaid those debts; and has outlasted much of its competition. During the mid-1980s, Dick also faced one of the most bitter labor strikes in recent history, continuing to lead the company despite a very hostile atmosphere and a union action that is considered one of the most significant strikes in labor history. Through it all, the company has remained well-managed.

The Hormel model of leadership development during these years focused on developing a reservoir of management talent. A key to this is lateral career development and staffing, a method embraced by SUPERVALU as well. By moving high-potential managers around the company, giving the breadth of experience and exposure to the deeply held values of a success-ful company, you build an enviable degree of organizational depth that will see it through change and cultural evolution. This model became an exceptional proving ground for many executives, including Dick's immedi-ate successor, Joel Johnson, one of numerous successful Hormel executives who benefited from Dick's mentorship and would go on to implement many aspects of the long-term vision Dick held for the company.

One of the key accountabilities of a corporate leadership team is responsible financial stewardship. And, for a publicly held company like Hormel, this is more than a responsibility, it's an imperative.

Driving this imperative for Hormel and other food industry companies is the fact that the grocery industry operates on the tightest of margins, yielding about one penny per dollar in operating profits as a percentage of sales. For that reason, many companies in this sector, including Hormel and SUPERVALU, are steeped in a tradition of conservative financial stewardship. These razor-thin margins make Hormel's long-established track record of financial success all the more compelling.

Many companies profess a commitment to investment performance. Few have achieved that performance with the astonishing consistency of Hormel Foods. Aided by seven two-for-one stock splits since 1968 (four between 1980 and 1990), the company has experienced considerable appreciation from $154 million in 1979 to nearly $5 billion today. The continuity of Hormel's financial results is as remarkable as its steep upward slope of growth. Since becoming a public company in September 1928, the company has had 43 consecutive years of annual dividend increases, paying its 322nd consecutive quarterly dividend in February 2009. The company's profits have risen from modest levels of around $27 million in the late 1970s to more than $285 million in 2008.

Like any company, Hormel has had financial ups and downs, and times when it has wrestled with the balance between growth and debt. This is a balance SUPERVALU knows all too well, taking on $9 billion in debt with our acquisition of the key retail properties of ALBERTSONS INC. in

2006. The acquisition was controversial in some quarters, but gave us the opportunity to reach our business growth goals in one fell swoop. Overnight, we became the third-largest grocery retailer in the country, with nearly 2,500 retail locations and 190,000 employees. It's an incredibly exciting moment in our growth, but that kind of debt is apt to keep a CEO up at night.

It's no different, I'm sure, for Dick. Between 1980 and 1985, Hormel had at times borrowed more than the value of the entire company – at 17 percent interest! The borrowings were necessary as the company updated facilities, including replacing the old Austin, Minnesota, plant and building several mid-sized plants. These were unavoidable expenses, but that didn't make the figures any easier to digest. However, by the mid-1980s, Hormel had repaid its sizable borrowings, and the company was able to embark on a series of acquisitions in the subsequent two decades with little debt. Many of these were very wise moves – case in point, the company acquired JENNIE-O in 1986 for cash. Today, the business is a revenue contributor to the tune of more than a billion dollars annually.

At the end of the day, the Hormel Foods team has accomplished a real feat of reinvention, transformation and management that is the basis of an insightful guidebook for managers across any business: how to transform a company in an ailing industry and place it at the cutting-edge of a vibrant industry sector. Even more importantly, *Points of Difference* describes the tools and methods Hormel Foods has used to constantly revitalize itself, retaining its position as a leading business performer.

Remember that consultant from McKinsey at the American Meat Institute meeting? Maybe more of those people laughing would've done well to heed his comments. Dick and his team did – and today, through diligent attention to the dynamics of the industry and the changing needs of the consumer, Hormel Foods, with its roots deeply anchored in meat processing, has become a dominant survivor in an industry where its major competitors have virtually vanished.

Hormel Foods' transformation was so impressive that it had been the subject of two highly regarded Harvard University case studies and its management highly sought-after presenters at any number of prestigious institutions. Under Dick's leadership, Hormel was alive with points of difference during a period of dramatic growth and change.

***Points of Difference*** is an inspiring statement with an uncommonly effective approach. Much like Dick himself, his Hormel story links strong viewpoints with a soft-spoken style. The recollections express tremendous conviction and commitment to a business that has grown steadily, despite the tremendous challenges of having been in a troubled industry. It is a chronicle of key events on behalf of a remarkable team, whose exceptional success continues to this day – in many ways a testament to the culture built by Dick in this time of incredible evolution.

This analysis will be indispensable for middle and senior managers and opinion leaders looking for pragmatic, tested guidance.

- Managers wanting to innovate and restructure – simultaneously.
- Managers who have a passion for change, especially in technology and marketing, with a particular eye to developing new processes and concepts.
- Managers wanting to better their grasp of labor relations and the essentials of handling crisis situations.

The sure footing of Dick's views is squarely anchored on putting the customer first. The simultaneous pursuit of both technological innovation and major strategic changes strikes another familiar chord, particularly in today's environment, where technology is no longer just a tool, but a vital partner. A vibrant organization must be agile and flexible as it addresses technological and strategic change hand-in-hand.

*Points of Difference* reveals how to manage risk effectively while transitioning a large, established organization. Dick's articulation of ideas links broad concepts with specific facts in an easy, compelling manner. Hormel's management team had been extraordinarily successful while mastering huge challenges in overhauling and repositioning a Fortune 500 company.

But this account is much more than a business success story. It describes a company's dedication to touching a community's quality of life in a multi-faceted way, including medical care, education and recreation. And, although Dick has minimized his personal presence in the book, *Points of Difference* also gives revealing insights into the thought processes and decision-making considerations of a perceptive and successful chief executive.

In sum, Hormel is among the unique few in American industry through its combination of:

- A continuing commitment to superior technology that maintains a competitive edge and reduces costs.
- Exceptional, sustained financial performance.
- Evolution of a gifted, self-renewing management team.
- Profound commitment to the community – its education and general well being.

Hormel has a strong and enduring corporate culture. Some of its hallmarks include:

- Continuing commitment to innovation.
- Ingenuity in finding fresh applications and formats for established items and brands.

- A sizeable pool of internal talent with a willingness to develop people, give managers the opportunity to take risks (and even fail!), and an insistence that teams shoulder the responsibility for major operating and strategic decisions.

American technology and its innovative spirit remain important forces in today's global economy, but they do not shine as brightly as they once did. We are part of the most modern and efficient nation in the world, but we suffer from a national business climate under attack from within. The symptoms are endemic: jobs exported abroad, people drifting aimlessly from one job to another, and urban decay. We've seen what these things can do to businesses, cities and individual lives.

The story of Hormel Foods and its home base in Austin, Minnesota, is just the opposite of this dire forecast. Its dedication to basic values, a strong work ethic and ingenuity have enabled the Hormel story to be written in dramatically different terms.

American industry would be on much surer footing if it adopted the solid, responsible attitudes and transparent leadership embraced by Hormel Foods toward all of its stakeholders – customers, shareholders, employees and the communities where the company operates.

In short, **Points of Difference** shares the compelling Hormel story – a story that is nothing short of an epic among small-city success stories.

*Jeff Noddle*
*Minneapolis, Minnesota*
*May 2009*

# ACKNOWLEDGMENTS

**IF THIS BOOK HAS A** godfather, it is certainly the celebrated author, columnist, and speaker Harvey Mackay. My friend Harvey taught me the essential ropes that a first-time author is wise to learn. He steered me to Ron Beyma as a writing collaborator and introduced me to Morgan James. What professionals this outfit's founder David Hancock, publisher Rick Frishman, and director of operations Jim Howard are! Rachel Lopez's perceptive eye in cover design has rendered a clear statement. And, the project is fortunate to have an accomplished and conscientious author relations manager in Morgan James' Lyza Poulin.

Hormel has always been quick to acknowledge the significance of customers, and I echo that sentiment in particular regarding the development of this book. Joe Pichler of Kroger is a distinguished senior statesman of the retail industry, and I thank him for his thoughts. I am saddened that Bob Onstead of Randall's passed away before the book was published. At SUPERVALU, a company on whose board I was proud to serve, retired CEO Mike Wright and his colleague John Hooley gave penetrating input. I am deeply indebted to SUPERVALU's present CEO Jeff Noddle for his uplifting and thoughtful introduction. It's a real tone-setter for the book and a gracious tribute to the Hormel team.

Four stalwart colleagues on the board of the Hormel Foundation deserve recognition for participating in the research for this book: Jerry Anfinson, Kermit Hoversten, Bonnie Rietz, Mahlon Schneider, and Bob Thatcher. Jerry was especially innovative, as he always is, in helping me think through the civic objectives I wanted to achieve. Bonnie was the source of valued input before joining the Foundation board while she was mayor of Austin – one of the best we've ever had – and esteemed as an elected official within the region and throughout the state. While I single out these five directors for their help in the book, I cannot help but tip my hat to the entire Foundation board for its dedicated contributions to making the Hormel Foundation distinctive for its community and regional focus.

We have always been deeply proud of the caliber of Hormel Foods' board of directors. Two current board members, Luella Goldberg and Ron Pearson, shared top-level insights that I'm sure readers will find perceptive, if I dare say a tad flattering, too. In addition to being a director, Ron is also the guiding force for Hy-Vee, one of our most important retail customers. Among our retired directors, Dr. Woody Berg, Geri Joseph, and Dr. Bob Waller contributed generously of both their time and observations. These exceptional people are characteristic of Hormel Foods' retired directors. It's an alumni club which few other American corporations can rival in stature. I will also never be able to thank Bob Waller enough for agreeing to write the Afterword for this book. He has developed the civic and social implications I have suggested with his acumen and remarkable professional knowledge.

Dr. Zigang Dong, the distinguished Executive Director of the Hormel Institute is both Hormel-Knowlton Professor and McKnight Presidential

Professor in Cancer Prevention at the University of Minnesota as well. His assistant Dr. Ann Bode helped arrange the time among his all-important Institute leadership and research activities to be interviewed for this book. Gail Dennison, Dr. Dong's able communications aide, also helped with administrative details as she often and ably does.

Civic leaders in Austin and in Minnesota are among the best the nation has to offer. Earlier this year, America lost both a dynamic business leader and a philanthropist of awesome generosity and foresight in Carl Pohlad. Not only was he interviewed for the book, I also had the good fortune to speak with Carl three short weeks before he died. I shall never forget the conversation because it, despite his severe illness, was marked by the same lucid insight that shaped the entire civic and professional life of this remarkable man.

Another person who unfortunately passed during the period this book was being developed is the late Reverend Bob Morgan. What an inspirational figure and a true action-oriented unifier in bringing together the various faiths to address community challenges.

It's never possible for me to refer to Dr. Tim Johnson without noting he is the son of a Hormel Foods employee. During most of the writing of this book, Dr. Tim was CEO of the Austin Medical Clinic. It's Mayo-style to rotate administrative leadership, so Dr. Tim now works closely with the Austin Clinic's new highly respected CEO Dr. David Agerter. When the Clinic opened its doors for a research visit, Maryann Wolesky helped ensure we saw the latest diagnostic technology the Center has to offer. Lori Volz of the Austin Public Schools has made a most appreciated administrative contribution during the course of this book's writing. George Brophy, now retired Executive Director of the Development Corporation of Austin, shared his thoughtful insights, particularly in the book's early stages. John Morrison, now retired and one of the far-sighted leaders of the UFCW P-9 Local in the past, gave us his much appreciated insights.

Let me next turn to the retired Hormel managers, all of whom represent an important link to the cornerstone of what Hormel Foods is today. Jim Holton, my predecessor, shed revealing light on the top management perspective that drove Hormel decision-making from the era of Jay Hormel, son of founder George A. Hormel, through Jim's tenure as Hormel CEO. No manager with whom I've ever worked is a keener, more observant judge of people than Jim. In addition to thanking him for the valuable light he shed on company history, it's hard to imagine a more supportive and effective management partner for me as Hormel undertook wide-ranging strategic change.

Jim, of course, was also a Hormel director as were two other senior management contributors to the book – my successor Joel Johnson and Gary Ray, the recently retired President of Protein Products. Gary's status bridged the writing of this book in that it began while he was still a member of active management and in a position to offer important insights on company operation. First let me mention those officers who also served as company directors: Jim Hall – a pacemaker in meat and grocery products, the financial and administrative authority Don Hodapp, Operations veteran Bill Hunter, and Meat-Products Group head Stan Kerber.

Then come a series of retired company officers who were distinguished in an array of invaluable specialties. These I mention in alphabetical order: engineering expert Frank Brown, our first Foodservice Group head, Jim Cole, Dr. Forrest Dryden who pioneered a true research function for us, Human Resources VP Dave Larson, Chuck Nyberg, Senior Vice President, General Counsel, Director of Public Affairs & Human Resources.

Current Hormel Foods executives were indispensable in bridging a wonderful era of the company I knew directly with the exciting, contemporary, constantly renewing Hormel Foods of today. Without doubt, my deepest thanks must go to Jeff Ettinger, Hormel's Chairman of the Board, President, and CEO. When it comes to Jeff, not only must I express my appreciation for his comments. They reflect an astute vision of the business, and I thank him as well for his thoughtful review of the manuscript. I also must express my pride that he – carrying the baton from Joel Johnson – continues a tradition of succession which is the envy of many a corporation in America.

Other current senior executives who shared their thoughts on the present direction of the business demonstrate that Hormel Foods remains at the cutting-edge of industry thinking. This leadership team includes Steve Binder – Group Vice President Refrigerated Foods, Larry Vorpahl – Group Vice President and President Consumer Products Sales, and Jim Schroeder – Vice President of Engineering. Jim Cavanaugh, Senior Vice President External Affairs & General Counsel, gave his always astute thoughts on legal matters past and present.

Dr. Phillip Minerich – Vice President of Research and Development, Dan Hernandez – Director of Innovation Team and Jerry Whithaus – Director of Marketing Services, helped articulate our vision of the consumer marketplace. Fred Halvin – Director of Corporate Development – first gave input to the book in his earlier role in investor relations.

Jeff Nuytten and Randy Krug contributed their in-depth knowledge of the vast Austin plant facility as did Mark Coffey, the current plant manager. Hormel Foods VP of Corporate Communications Julie Henderson Craven and her staff played an important supporting role in the publication of this book. Len Schulke helped us navigate the Hormel communications archives. Matt Cizik patiently provided continuing financial information. Lori Marco of Hormel's Legal department did an especially fine job on trademark issues and text review.

Some people outside of the Hormel organization, Minnesota, and those directly involved in the book's publishing also made a contribution. Trend expert Harry Balzer gave his usual razor-sharp assessment of consumer behavior. Dr. Ray Goldberg of the Harvard Business School offered appreciated counsel. George Dahlman of Piper Jaffray is a discerning financial analyst, and it was good to be in contact with him after many years. Dr. Arne Weber, former president of both Northwestern University and the University of Colorado is a distinguished administrator and scholar who confirmed my recollections on some key matters. Concept Foods founder, Bernie Hansen – a former winner of the Knowlton Innovation Award – gave us his thoughtful views on the development of some important technology.

Several individuals generously contributed to the costs of writing this book, and their support is appreciated. They include: Mr. and Mrs. Jerry Anfinson, Mr. and Mrs. Don Brezicka, Mr. and Mrs. Rick Bross, Mr. and Mrs. Jim Cole, Mr. and Mrs. Richard Flack, Mr. and Mrs. Don Hodapp, Mr. and Mrs. Kermit Hoversten, Mr. and Mrs. Craig W. Johnson, Mr. and Mrs. Joel Johnson, Mr. and Mrs. Burton Joseph, Mr. David Kane, Mr. and Mrs. Bob Patterson, Mr. and Mrs. Gary Ray, Mr. and Mrs. Richard Robinson, Mr. Jim Rieth, Mr. and Mrs. Art Scherer, Mr. and Mrs. Earl Wright, and The Development Corporation of Austin.

The description "above and beyond the call of duty" never matched a person's contribution better than that of my Executive Administrative Assistant Kathy Bjorge in the preparation of this book. I could easily devote a chapter to the breadth and volume of her involvement. Over the years, she meticulously coordinated contact with all the supporting contributors, organized the various drafts, secured the desired visuals, maintained endless files, and anticipated every other detail as it arose. Kathy has dedicated hours and hours of her time selflessly to this book's creation, and that includes a number of stretches that were nothing less than 24/7. As usual, her judgment was impeccable and her suggestions to me were helpful time and again in keeping the project on course. So many others have gone out of their way to praise what a pleasant and effective ambassador she is for my office, not only in this role, but as my chief aide in administering the work of the Hormel Foundation.

All the photos used in this book are drawn from the archives of the Hormel Foods Corporation. Kathy Bjorge also played a major role in the process of selecting photos. Joan Hanson, Gene Lifka and Candace Miller did an exceptional job of locating photos to support points in the text and preparing the images for publication. My thanks to them.

I would also like to thank my collaborator, Ron Beyma, for providing a positive experience for a first-time author. Ron is a consummate professional writer, researcher and organizer. Over the years of this book's development, he has become a true friend. Ron's insights and instincts are invaluable and greatly appreciated. Despite his considerable diligence and the efforts of many others to support all of the details in this book, I am fully responsible for the content presented. One of the great contributors to this book, especially in our ability to put it in publishable form, is Ron's partner Jan Beyma. She has been there at every critical step in making this book possible.

This book, as with every major undertaking in my life at Hormel, could only be realized through teamwork. I have mentioned some of the

Hormel people who have been involved in its realization. There are surely many others, who contributed as well. For all of you, please know that you have my heartfelt appreciation. Indeed, this story itself could not have been written without all Hormel Foods employees' extraordinary commitment to success that has been so much in evidence in our excellent results each year.

My dear wife Nancy has endured much over the years of this book's creation. Its development has been a preoccupation which has absorbed huge blocks of time when I was at work on it, and it was often a distraction that captured my thoughts even when I wasn't actively engaged in the book's development. Making up for all those missed walks and neglected conversations will never be possible, but she should know that her sacrifices are once more deeply appreciated. Her contributions were not confined to moral support. It was Nancy who helped me streamline the title to **Points of Difference**, and it was she who crafted the needlepoint included in Chapter 8 – surely the book's most artful image and inspiring message.

# PREFACE

## *How Strategic Transformation Really Happens*

HORMEL FOOD CORPORATION'S PERFORMANCE in its industry during the past quarter century is unmatched. The company's transformation through emphasizing a value-added, points-of-difference culture has been stellar over that period. Wall Street says it is best reflected in the stock price's appreciation with the market value of the company increasing 38 times over the same time frame. HORMEL brand is an imposing guarantee of quality.

The Hormel management team is equally deserving of a trademark of excellence. Why? Hormel's sustained performance rests heavily on the quality of a well-built management team coupled with strong leadership succession and one of the top workforces resulting in some of the best performing operations in any industry. This extraordinary performance is fully evident at every level of the organization. It is this depth of talent which gave us the ability to reinvent the legacy of George A. Hormel – the firm's founder. With a cornerstone of "points of difference," Hormel has sustained its success entering new segments of the changing food business. This approach has been especially manifest in a continuing quest for fundamental, state-of-the-art advances that give Hormel technological leadership within the industry.

In any one item, a point of difference is a distinctive attribute which a manufacturer offers that is not available from other competitors for similar products. That difference may be in quality or ingenuity of the contents. It may be in packaging, in processing, in convenience, or in value. Every true point of difference creates a reliable experience – one a consumer can expect to have each time a product is purchased and used. A point of difference can be a competitive edge, but only if it is or becomes meaningful to the targeted consumer. For a given product, consumers usually react to the total array of differentiation that makes one product a superior choice over another. Points of difference also have a business significance that go far beyond products to embrace the very way business is done. Superior technology and facilities can create an imposing point of difference and certainly do in our industry. For any firm, human resource practices and wherewithal usually comprise the most decisive point of difference of all. Because of the nature of competition and progress, all points of difference – whether in products or in management – are vulnerable to being extinguished and need to be constantly refined and improved.

Hormel's management team demonstrated great fortitude in transforming its business against all odds, and it has done so through an emphasis on points-of-difference management. In 1981-1982, we borrowed money with interest rates ranging from 17-22%, in amounts often greater than the market capitalization of the company to replace the largest meat and food processing plant of its kind, while simultaneously developing new product lines to match contemporary tastes and needs. This calculated risk-taking allowed Hormel to incorporate new technology that continues to distinguish itself to this day in our industry. By bringing the promise of a value-added and points-of-difference culture within the reach of employees throughout the company, a strong, durable organization is firmly in place.

You, as readers, are likely to have the greatest interest in what can be learned from this book and can be applied to your own experience and challenges. You may not be in the food industry. You may not even be in industry at all, but in government, education or other professions. Many of my counterparts in a wide range of organizations have told me that the Hormel experience has broad application to any institution headed for extinction unless radical change is introduced. Just exactly what can such an organization do to continue to control its own destiny? How can it leverage its fight for survival to open the opportunity to excel on new strategic turf?

Any firm in ailing industries of all sorts must often make massive investments in technology and new products at a time it can least afford them. Frequently, such a business is trapped in its own past. As a result, potentially effective managers become preoccupied with routine tasks instead of directing their efforts toward fresh opportunities and new, more rewarding strategies.

My advice: ***Challenge conventional wisdom about change!*** Don't wait for a new concept, a new technology, or a new plant to suddenly 'arrive' and alter your world. Push the assets and establish points of difference to add value and to redesign those areas that will provide excellent return. At the same time, work intensely to implement every positive change until you can construct state-of-the-art facilities structured around cutting-edge processes and technologies. A laudable goal: develop new technologies to become an industry productivity leader while simultaneously paying the best wages.

Develop your people to seek change, step-by-step, exhausting ways in which you can incorporate points of difference and add value in every phase of your business.

Organized, well thought-out change is essential to any business or organization. While undertaking any short-term change, think through the optimum, big-picture 'flow' you will need to win the game. This attitude and experience will create intensity, an entrepreneurial outlook, and focused goals. The result: energized levels of discipline and the confidence to enter new businesses where it's necessary to prioritize time, talent, capital and a passion for point of difference.

***Challenge conventional wisdom about people!*** Don't assume you have to go 'outside' to rejuvenate your company's management resources. Nor do you need to routinely cull out the so-called bottom 10% of performers. When assessing an individual's performance, evaluate attitude and ability to be a team-builder while producing highly satisfactory bottom-line results. Be sure you have considered where every individual fits. Top management can rely on long-termers as the core of the transition team while injecting bright new members with positive, change-embracing attitudes. However, all managers must be energized. They must feel the responsibility to confront problems and have the motivation to do so. At the same time, an organization must face up to long-term commitments to its people with established goals. Step-by-step success will give your people the confidence and the conviction that they can do **anything**!

As the transition proceeds, managers learn that well-orchestrated change can unleash the power of people to address new priorities. Energy is redirected in a positive way toward points of difference in every aspect of the business. Managers should look at setbacks and failures as serious – always seeking the reasons, but never identifying individuals with failure. Don't let problems linger. Quickly correct them and move on by. In order to establish a dedication to entrepreneurism, as CEO, I personally signed off on every project until it became second nature to every employee that we were a team, and no one failed individually. "Change" was a byword and every employee had a passion for continuously searching for points of difference and value-added in everything we did. This remains true to this day.

To be a successful change agent, perseverance is essential. Many of our product ideas weren't successful the first or even the second time. And, necessary change can often be elusive to identify. (As an illustration, at Hormel Foods today, we are realizing sensational sales on shelf-stable microwaveable meals in an oval tray. For years, we had concealed the product's appeal by hiding it in a cardboard box rather than placing the label directly atop the tray.)

Then comes the big test. As you pinpoint new market opportunities, you bump against vastly larger competitors. Here's where the well-placed risk-taking, confidence and points of difference become essential once more. Managers with the courage and determination to create a new base of strength – like Hormel did with the turkey business and many other categories – enabled the company to excel at competing in new marketing arenas.

Hormel has not only survived, it has thrived as a diversified, value-added business. Hormel has successfully transformed itself from a meat-packer into a consumer-branded food company emphasizing turkey, food-service, and consumer packaged fresh meat – each contributing more than a billion dollars of profitable revenue. Furthermore it redefined itself with a self-developed team of predominately internal talent, thereby permitting the successful absorption and development of massive businesses such as Jennie-O Turkey Store. Best of all, Hormel provided new platforms for growth and opportunity for our people. For example, when we bought Jennie-O and later The Turkey Store, we were able to add our experienced talent to the organization to quickly streamline operations and grow the business from #8 to #1. This book details the secrets of how an organization and its people were motivated to embrace change. It also shares how a management team was built with a passion for success. It reveals how to prioritize time, talent and capital to transform a business.

Behind the Hormel success story is the re-invention of a unique culture that started with the founder. This blend of intelligent risk-taking with demanding attention to detail was championed by its founder George A. Hormel more than a hundred years ago. Our management team succeeded in energizing that sturdy base and made impressive breakthroughs by coupling state-of-the-art advances in manufacturing technology with highly innovative marketing. A change-friendly environment shunned personal blame for project failures and embraced the implementation of new technology as well as its purposeful development. A total commitment to practical teamwork made intelligent risk-taking a company norm... a norm that paid off! Time and again, Hormel has created compelling points of difference in all the ways that it does business and especially in how it has anticipated the needs of today's consumer.

Was this remarkable transformation achieved effortlessly and serenely? *IT WASN'T!* In 1985-1986, Hormel was at the peak of its momentum. Its new products and processes abounded, and the company looked sure to win the competitive game and accomplish the mission of becoming a leader in the food field and not just the meat industry. The whole industry had made a downward adjustment in wages. We knew our wages would need to surpass our competitors and they did. Our contractual agreements were signed and in place for all of our plants but one. Just then, the firm was rocked by a strike in its new 1.1 million square foot state-of-the-art plant in Hormel's hometown of Austin, Minnesota. The strike was supported by outside forces at a meeting in Indiana where many disgruntled union leaders had gathered. They were looking for a dramatic turnaround in the prospects for organized labor and in their individual status. The labor leadership's premise was that Hormel would never take a strike and therefore provide the labor movement a major victory. Creating a new success role for American labor was their obvious intent.

From the start, the strikers' own international union opposed this strike against the best contract in the industry. Further, the agitators were pitting themselves against a company that had a record of providing the highest wages and the best fringes with a continuous profit-sharing program dating back to 1941. This confrontation is now regarded as a landmark in modern labor-management relations. Fortunately, we weathered this difficult period as a stronger team. Industry analysts maintain we now have one of the finest workforces anywhere. True to our commitment, our people remain the best paid in our industry. Our future ability to be the leader in compensating them relies, we realize, on our ability to maintain being at the technological forefront of the food business.

Today all the communities where Hormel does business exhibit a constructive partnership between forward-looking goals and civic leaders. Hormel, and Austin in particular, create a vivid illustration of a contemporary, progressive "company town" that works. The Hormel Foundation has been an integral part of that success. Our intent has been to establish a viable model for achieving what can and *should* be right in American business.

Treatment of trademarks and brands in a book such as this is always a challenge. A great deal has been invested in the creation and protection of these valuable properties. They are hallmarks of Hormel Foods' innovative excellence. However, it's unfair to bore readers and to subject them to a continual barrage of trademark and registration identifications. The following book is intended primarily for business managers and students. Repetitive references to ® and ™ symbols is obtrusive for a readership focused on business principles. For that reason, the following practices have been adopted in the text of this book. For stylistic purposes, Hormel Foods Corporation may be referred to as Hormel and references to the HORMEL brand may appear as HORMEL. When Hormel is treated as a brand, it is presented completely in capital letters throughout the book. Other brands, such as DINTY MOORE and STAGG are capitalized words only in the first usage, but just the first letter of these brands is capitalized thereafter in the book. These subsequent instances conform to normal book usage. All terms are also identified according to their usage given the chronology of events.

JENNIE-O TURKEY STORE® turkey or (other descriptor), HORMEL® Party Trays, REAL FOOD, REAL FAST™, SPAM® family of products,

SUPER SELECT® pork, CURE 81® ham, DAN'S PRIZE® beef and pork products, DINTY MOORE® beef stew, HORMEL® chili, SPAMBURGER® hamburgers, STAGG® brand, JENNIE-O TURKEY STORE® OVEN READY™ turkey, HORMEL® TOP SHELF™, HORMEL® bacon toppings, HORMEL® pepperoni, LAYOUT PACK® bacon, KID'S KITCHEN® microwave meals, DINTY MOORE AMERICAN CLASSICS® meals or other descriptor, HORMEL® COMPLEATS® microwave meals, TRUETASTE™ technology, NATURAL CHOICE® branded lunch meat, CHI-CHI'S® salsa products or other descriptor, HERDEZ® salsa, products or other descriptor, Hormel Health Labs line of products, HORMEL® APPLEWOOD™ smoked bacon, HORMEL® FRESH PANTRY™ peppered bacon, CAFÉ H® jalapeño bacon, BREAD READY® pre-sliced meats line, AUSTIN BLUES® BBQ, CAFÉ H® product line, FAST 'N EASY® bacon: are trademarks and registered trademarks of Hormel Foods, LLC or one of its affiliates.

*Richard L. Knowlton*
*Austin, Minnesota*
*May 2009*

# *The New Foodscape*

## IT AIN'T JUST "MEAT-AND-POTATOES" ANY MORE!

A dramatic change in the food we eat and buy every day has escaped our attention.

Big revelations often come in small packages. . . some of them just two pounds big. One such revealing moment happened for me in a supermarket in Minneapolis in 1979, and it's worthy of comment. I had just become president of Hormel Foods. Having had an intense interest in marketing for much of my career, I had a long-standing practice of visiting supermarkets whenever I have the chance, and not just to look at products and our own presence. These visits have given me the chance to study consumers as they shop, and studying consumers in stores can be profoundly revealing. Marketers know that it pays to watch shoppers in action.

On this store visit, a young mother stood in front of the meat case. Her three-year-old was sitting in the cart playing with a box of crackers. Mom had just picked up a two-pound pork roast which I knew to be one of Hormel's. She eyeballed it, pressed the cellophane wrapper, read the label, stared at the ceiling thoughtfully, set the roast down, picked it up again, sighed, set it down a second time, and moved ahead with her shopping.

I couldn't resist. "Ma'am," I said, "Excuse me for intruding. I'm in the food business. I saw you looking at that pork roast a minute ago. I'm curious to know why you decided *not* to buy it. Didn't the quality look quite right?"

My question flustered her at first. "Quality?" she answered with a puzzled smile, "Oh, no, the quality looked first rate. . . It's that I just wouldn't know what to *do* with it. My mother made a yummy pork roast, but I'm not sure I even have her recipe. Besides, with this little charger in the cart, another in second grade, and a full-time accounting job. . . how am I going to find the time to fool around with a pork roast? Even if I had the recipe and all of the ingredients, where would I get the time and the energy?" Little did we know then that it would take 25 years to provide her with a fully-prepared pork or beef roast that she could microwave in 3-5 minutes depending on whether it's refrigerated or frozen.

Focus groups can be priceless, but this one impromptu conversation was worth a thousand of them. The image of that young mother – juggling career and kids – has stuck with me for three decades. For me, she was an icon of the revolution that had taken place and still continues in the food industry. It struck me, and I'm sure others, that there would be a day when these fresh meat products would be consumer-packaged – often shelf-stable, fully prepared, conveniently flavored, and ready in minutes. But, it took time for this to happen. It took time for the processes and packaging to evolve and to be accepted. Quite a leap was required to move beyond butchers breaking apart carcasses at the store level.

> ### STUDY CONSUMER BEHAVIOR 'ON THE GROUND' AND LEARN IF THE CUSTOMER YOU ARE TRYING TO REACH TODAY STILL EXISTS.

Marketing-driven firms must anticipate consumer desires and design products to which the present and future consumer will respond. When we think of business revolutions, we focus on grand and lofty milestones. As startling as these breakthroughs may be, I contend that *most Americans have failed to observe a pivotal transformation – the fundamental revamping of the American food industry.* Unnoticed, massive changes have been underway. Some were so sudden and others so subtle, taking place on a daily basis, that they caught giant corporations off-guard, and some of those businesses are no longer here as a result.

Here is some of the evidence:

- Not surprisingly, a 1999 Gallup study found that 45% of households surveyed believed: "It is difficult to find time to prepare meals."
- Until recent years, people had been eating out more, eating more take-out food, and they had been eating it everywhere – at work, at home, and on the go in their cars. The cost of meals bought from restaurants and vending machines had come to rival the meals prepared at home in consumer dollars spent. (In 2009, as of this book's writing, this long-standing trend may be undergoing a serious challenge as volatile energy cost fluctuations and economic upheaval continue to change fundamental consumer behavior.)

- Consumers aren't just buying prepared food from restaurants. In 1991, there were more than 20,000 delis in supermarkets. Deli penetration in supermarkets has climbed steadily. In 1989, supermarket deli sales were $10 billion. Including prepared foods, deli sales today for meat, dairy, and bakery in all retail channels amount to $25.5 billion. Of this total, $18.8 billion are in full-service sales, and $6.7 billion are in self-service.

Each of these changes presents opportunity. This is evidenced by the consumer's appetite *for* and familiarity *with* deli trays. This trend has created an entirely new market for Hormel. Store-made deli trays are created to order, but they typically have a shelf life of just 3-5 days. HORMEL® Party Trays, which reached $40 million in sales in 2007, are available year-round in the refrigerated section and have a shelf life of 120 days.

Breakthroughs in processing and packaging have enabled food to be presented in totally new formats. Today flavorful entrées are available in microwave packaging which take high-quality, convenient food to a whole new plateau. As my successor at Hormel Food's, CEO Joel Johnson put it, "Convenience is very important to consumers, but good tasting food trumps all other needs including convenience." Indeed, that's true: Good-tasting, convenient food is the goal.

What do you discover if you break down the price for any food product today into the elements that contribute to its value? A double-digit percentage of the value for most food products is the convenience they represent. As we said in the late 1980s and as Hormel's ads have put it, the consumer wants "REAL FOOD, REAL FAST™."

Other essentials have changed too, Reflect on some of the basic terms that define our understanding of what we eat and cook:

- **What *is* a meal?**
- **What *is* a recipe?**

Few concepts have more influence on our everyday lives. The reality of dual-income families and working mothers has changed the entire essence of the kitchen and meal preparation. What do these questions suggest? Consider the facts:

- In the 1960s, the family dinner consisted of seven components. Today, it is just one or two. "Cooking" dinner (or "preparing" it) has often become archaic. More and more meals are simply "assembled."

- A pizza, for example, is regarded by many to be a full meal.

- Nearly 23 percent of consumers consider a recipe to contain no more than three ingredients and 58 percent say they have a repertoire of only 8 recipes. . .

- In the 60s, a lasagna recipe contained 16 ingredients. It is now down to just 5 to 6 elements: In general, today's at-home dinner preparer would like to work with just three ingredients and would like the meat item – the "center of the plate" starring attraction – to be marinated, pre-seasoned, microwaveable, and often pre-cooked.

- Also in the 60s, a salad contained 7 ingredients. Today, it's common to buy a salad mix in a bag or a fresh salad fully prepared.

In 2008, Harry Balzer of the NPD Group provided us with an additional series of compelling facts about American food habits. Harry's observations are fresh and are clearly in sync with today's realities. Harry's direct comments are in quotes:

- "The way people eat in America is not actually well known." While health appears to be a primary factor in consumer food choices, "the real 'priority chain' centers around habits and taste preferences as well the desire to experience new things." Harry includes health values as a part of the quest for new and better options. These general priorities are followed by the desire for more convenience and greater value.

- "Convenience has long been a motivator in changing our food habits. After convenience, the next criterion in changing our eating behavior is value: a less expensive way to do something I must do every day." Value easily becomes the #1 consideration, as it has in the very difficult economy of 2009, when several of our strongly value-oriented brands such as the SPAM® family of products experienced all-time sales highs.

- Overall, a driving force for food marketers has been to supply Americans with healthier products that can help tackle the issues of wellness and weight. "Eating a truly balanced diet isn't easy because it usually requires the time to buy, prepare and store fresh foods," Harry notes.

- Responding to consumer demand, marketers have offered products to help people lose weight through changing their eating habits, although the perennial emphasis on dieting has lost ground. In 2005, 26% of Americans were on a diet and that number had stayed constant for some time. This percentage has now declined to 22%. Additionally the words "I'm on a diet" deserve caution. Studies show people "on a diet" often don't eat less, but frequently consume *more* foods that are better for them.

- Thirty-two percent of Americans believe they should be very conscious about the amount of fat they consume, and 31% believe they should have this high-level awareness about cholesterol. This is a sharp decline from the peaks of 51% having a comparable level of concern about fat in 1994 and of 56% having this thoughtfulness about cholesterol in 1989.

- There is a huge difference between what people *say* they do and what they actually *do*. Americans were eating more salads two decades ago in 1988 than we do today.[1] What *has* changed is that the salad is no longer something people *make*. It is a pre-washed and mixed convenience product.

- Due to rising food and often gasoline prices, people will report with conviction they are eating out less often. In fact, that has not been true. People are not cooking more often at home. What's the solution to the apparent paradox? Folks are not eating out less, but they are managing their eating-out budget and their total food outlay differently.

---

1     *While salad consumption isn't up, sales of precut fresh salads have increased.*

- Our #1 eating behavior in any given day? Eating a turkey or ham sandwich of one sort or another.[2] "The sandwich remains America's #1 food. We talk about the new tuna or salmon steak we had a week or two ago at a fine-dining restaurant, even though we might only go to such a place once in our next hundred dining experiences."

- "As to food, the whole question has been moving toward: **Who** will make that food for me? Not, what will I eat. . . but **who** will make it?"

- "If you can't afford to have other people make your meals, the next goal is to make easier meals with fewer items." For an entire generation, the side dish and dessert were disappearing from home-prepared dining. This latter trend has only leveled off in the last two years.

- "The last century has been all about packaged **foods**. In the current century, the focus will be on packaged **meals**."

- After an explosive and impressive start, the usage of microwaves hasn't grown dramatically. Over 90% of American homes have at least one microwave, and many have more. The new challenge in developing food products for the microwave is identifying **which** foods can create flavorful, yet convenient meals.

- Less than fifty percent of all dinner preparations today involve a stovetop. The use of the stovetop has reached an all-time low. The greatest threat to all meals prepared with in-home appliances is now the ready-to-serve takeout food offered by restaurants and retailers.

- In 2008, when people prepared their own dinner, NPD found that 18% spent less than 15 minutes doing so and 32% spent less than thirty minutes. As to preparing dinner, then, half of the public is willing to spend no more than a half hour on this activity.

---

2    *This pattern is changing, too, as we at Hormel find that more and more consumers are substituting turkey for ham as the central ingredient in that sandwich.*

- "Gas stations are more likely to prepare a meal than to repair a car. You have better odds of getting a burrito or a hot dog than bay service."

- "Americans are carrying their food with them more often. This is particularly so for lunches. Most restaurant meals are actually take-out meals."

- The best index of true consumer dedication to preparing food is how often we entertain people in our own homes. In 2004, that number was 16 times a year. In 2008, it had dropped to 11. Over the last 18 years this number has been tracked, it has risen only once and that was in 2001 right after 9-11. Because people are far less likely to have company, they want a meal to be a memorable event for their guests when they *do* cook dinner.

- The increase in number of women working was the driving force behind the growth in in-home and away-from-home value-added food sales. But the long-standing trend of more women entering the workforce has plateaued in the last five years, and it has actually shown a decline from its high in the last two years. While the restaurant business reached its maximum share of meals in 2000, the anticipated effect of more meals being prepared at home has not materialized. "The consumer today also expects more value from meals prepared away from home."

- Ethnic foods tend to trend in popularity. For example the long-standing growth in the Asian food category may now have peaked. Mexican food, including new flavors and recipes, is the foremost ethnic category that continues to experience a steady rise in popularity.

These data imply that consumers are withdrawing themselves from preparing a formal dinner while serving convenient and really good tasting food. But, they aren't. In those scarcer moments that fresh food is served to guests, the governing measure is: It better be good!

Further, while these findings are fascinating, they are indeed already history. Consumer studies are most valuable in what they suggest about the future. What do these provocative facts indicate consumers want going forward? A statement that I coined some years ago sums up the new realities: "Consumers are only limited by *our* inability to anticipate what they need and want." A points-of-difference-driven company should be ahead of consumer demand, and it's certain that being ahead will lead to further value-added products. From a world that knew no change for decades, the meat sector of the food industry has become a streamlined and competitive business, and the nature and rate of increase are bound to accelerate. Only companies with the capacity to continually redefine their points of difference have any hope for a growing, profitable future. Hormel has made this major advance, but no business can be complacent and let this priority slide.

Of all the trends affecting consumer eating and cooking behavior in the last two decades, there are probably eight with the greatest impact:

- Declining basic cooking skills generally, while the interest in cooking as a recreational activity is very evident.
- Women in the workforce, even if many of these women work out of their homes and even though this trend has leveled off  …and then declined in the last five years.[3]

---

3      *It's important to note that this trend has plateaued in the last five years, and it has actually shown a decline in the last two years from its high. We are tracking this change as it may represent a shift of some of our business from eating out (foodservice) to eating at home.*

- Consumers who are highly time-conscious, many of whom have lived time-poor and time-stressed lives for decades.

- A sustained interest in health, although not necessarily a constant and clear understanding of what constitutes healthy eating.

- An increase in the Hispanic population with Hispanic foods becoming a more important part of the mainstream American diet.

- A desire for authentic taste, especially in ethnic foods but always built on a base of both comfort and familiarity with new experiences.

- An aging population more inclined to eat at home and more likely to adopt healthy eating habits.

- And, a growing number of single and dual person households – both young and old – with a significant impact on issues like convenience and portion size.

Then comes the influence of *fashion*. We are accustomed to thinking of fashion in apparel. But, fashions in food are every bit as subject to change – some of them novel, some of them cyclical, and an increasing number of them driven by steadily improving cooking and packaging technology. Further facts help paint the picture:

- Is healthy eating a priority? Absolutely. And a wise one, to be sure. But consumers find it to be *less* of a priority than it was twenty years ago. When new products emerged under the health banner, but failed the taste test, consumers quickly rejected them. Our objective now is to offer healthful foods that provide consumers with flavorful experiences.

- The USDA reports per capita consumption of beef, pork and poultry climbed with reasonable steadiness from 152.3 lbs in 1962 to 222 lbs in 2001. In 2007, that number was 219 lbs as well with somewhat more chicken and less beef being consumed. Overall the food formats in which proteins are eaten may be quite different today than was once the case.

- The effort to avoid fat and cholesterol peaked in 1991 when 48% made a strong effort to avoid it, and 90% made some effort to avoid. By 1999, this was down to 29% making a strong effort and 80% making just *some* attempt.

Actions do indeed speak louder than words. People want more meat proteins. They are also unwilling to sacrifice flavor in their eating experience. And, they want diversity.

Despite this, health considerations remain a genuine concern for consumers. Consequently, it is important for food companies to seek validation from acknowledged authorities in nutrition. Good examples are those JENNIE-O TURKEY STORE® products which carry the American Heart Association endorsement and contain:

- Total fat: 3 grams or less
- Saturated fat: 1 gram or less
- Cholesterol: 20 milligrams or less
- Sodium: 480 milligrams or less

> **FOCUS ON WHAT CONSUMERS *DO*
> VERSUS WHAT THEY *SAY* – AND BE
> A TREND SETTER IN ACTIONS, NOT WORDS.**

The change in proteins has been underway for some time. When Hormel first marketed very lean, fresh SUPER SELECT® pork in the late 1960s, we applied some of these principles that would eventually bring us to the innovation and success we presently enjoy with consumer branded fresh meat. Dramatically improved livestock breeding was producing leaner pork products. The lean-meat type pork actually improved quality throughout our product lines including the SPAM® family of products, dry sausage, bacon, etc. Superior raw materials were also giving us an important point of difference through leaner products. These new products also changed the way the consumer experienced food. Pork, through its leanness and flavor, became ever more popular and continues to grow in demand providing excellent marketing opportunities for new convenient prepared entrées. Further, points of difference and the change in consumer demand have placed pork and turkey in the limelight as the "leanest alternatives in the broad protein" family.[4]

In 2009, what are some of the food trends being watched closely?

- The American palate is slowly evolving from its historical Northern European roots to a global palate, says Dan Hernandez, Hormel's Director of Innovation. The American comfort zone for bolder and more complex flavors is also slowly expanding.

- Providing kids healthy eating choices is a top priority. The clues are everywhere. Consider this one: Researchers at the Johns Hopkins Safety Center estimate over a quarter-million children under the age of six weigh too much for their car seats. Many children are simply too large to fit in standard safety-seats.

- Convenience stores like 7-Eleven are expanding their assortments of iced coffees and upscale snacks.

- The Associated Press reports that "artisanal cheese – handcrafted in small batches using local ingredients – is one of the fastest growing segments of the $59 billion gourmet food industry, with cheese and

---

4      *Our strategic decision to rely on Quality Pork Processors to provide pork product for our operations further strengthened the quality of our raw materials supply.*

dairy expected to see double digit growth through 2012, according to consumer research firm Packaged Facts."

- Laurie Demeritt of The Hartmann Group, a consumer researcher, says "consumers are definitely making conscious decisions to seek out higher quality brands/products and more distinctive flavors." They are also alert to cues for "freshness and minimal processing."

- Forty-five million strong and growing, the Hispanic market is increasingly demanding food products which offer genuine "authenticity."

- According to the journal *Food Processing*, "As foods become more complex, so does flavor. Flavors overlay each other, introducing more and more flavor notes. These foods are so interesting that overeating occurs less often, accomplishing (eventually) the real #1 food industry objective of holding obesity at bay."

- Even in 2006, research firms such as ACNielsen noted an increasing trend toward eating at home.[5] As oil prices skyrocketed in 2008, that preference became even more pronounced. Rising or falling, energy prices influence consumer eating behavior patterns.

- In the summer of 2008, two large restaurant chains – Bennigans and Steak & Ale announced they would be going out of business. Their closings were partly a result of massive energy price increases. Even more so, they were business fatalities caused by a lack of meaningful points of difference within the "casual dining" restaurant category. "'All these bar and grill concepts are very, very similar,' said Bob Goldin, executive vice president of Technomic, a restaurant industry consulting group [quoted in the *New York Times*.] 'They have the same kind of menu, décor, appeal,' which makes it more difficult to establish brand loyalty among customers."

---

5    *As noted earlier, eating at home and preparing at home are two very different things.*

We have experienced huge life-style changes and seismic alterations in how we spend our time and money. No more dramatic change has happened in American life, than the restructuring of the American family. And, no effect of that restructuring has been more pronounced than the way we eat. Lifestyle changes and technology have provided a myriad of options for food that were unimaginable just decades ago. In ***Points of Difference,*** we intend to describe how Hormel actually shaped some of the key changes taking place. Through marketing prowess and operating ingenuity, Hormel moved to leadership with new packaging, new fully prepared and fully cooked entrées.

## THE MORPHING OF THE MEAT INDUSTRY

If people wanted more meat proteins, this trend should have been a real boost for the meat industry and should have headed it toward excellent growth. Contrary to those expectations, the traditional meat industry no longer exists! People talk about the steel industry being devastated. What happened in the meat industry makes steel's plight look like a Sunday school picnic. By the early 1980s, the meat processing industry was in ever-deeper chaos, drowning in either decimated profits or outright losses. First, the mainstream companies were disadvantaged by higher wages and benefits against new competitors – we were among them. Secondly, the traditional meat processors were selling to a consumer who no longer existed.

In 1979, right about the time of my two-pound pork roast revelation, I attended an American Meat Institute meeting for the industry's top executives. McKinsey consultant Tom Wilson presented an incisive study of our industry. "My prediction," Tom said as he stared around the room, "is this: If you don't fundamentally change the way you do business, none of you people will be here in five years." I remember some of the CEOs guffawing and chiding Tom at the time. Not me. How startlingly prophetic his words proved to be! By 1983 major companies were going down like dominos. Swift would be dismantled and others followed quickly. The Wilson Company filed for bankruptcy and Armour failed completely in that period, along with hundreds of other large meat companies.

Consider the giant meat processors of yore: Swift, Armour, Wilson, Rath, Cudahy, Oscar Mayer (long owned by Phillip Morris), and – in a much smaller way at that time – Hormel. Of these, only Hormel survives to be an independent, growing business. Tom Wilson of McKinsey was right on! Indeed Hormel has thrived, but only after trimming away unprofitable commodity revenues while changing its sales mix so that new value-added products account for 93% of revenue growth.

How did Hormel transform itself to identify and market new products? Why are we able to be the technological leader while all of the other meat processors have either gone out of business or have been taken over? At the foundation, I think it was Hormel's realization that the survival of a business is not a matter of chance. Only purposeful companies survive – ones with the determination to change and the elasticity to accommodate it.

Opting to crossover and transform itself into becoming a consumer-branded food company was a first step. That change was gradual but decisive and required both listening and acting. This steady transition enabled us to develop both the competence and the ability to define this new purpose for itself. More importantly, we analyzed the total food industry for new product opportunities. We developed products to go against big companies – some of them traditional food companies. We built a reliable research-and-development process for each of our major groups.

- Our line managers were part of an organized team who identified new product niches throughout the food industry.
- We looked for products that were popular but not being aggressively marketed. They were owned by giants of the food industry with strong market share, but some had fallen asleep and neglected change.

The central issue I'm describing can be termed **the survival of the purposeful** through offering points of difference. A comparison between two firms – Hormel and Rath – is particularly telling as to what was happening in the industry. (Indeed, the two company CEOs, Jay Hormel and Reuben Rath, were good friends.) Rath moved from Dubuque to Waterloo, Iowa in 1891. Prospering there for decades, it was once every bit as fine a company as Hormel, measured by sales, profits, and quality. In those days, Rath was not only as good as Hormel – some say Rath was even a bit better. If you compared the two companies month by month or week by week, you couldn't detect much of a difference in operations or financial performance. But, over time, year by year, you could see the key traits that caused one company to go out of business and the other to thrive. It was Hormel's new products and our other points of difference, especially in technology, that ultimately made our advantage enormous. Step-by-step change is really an additive process that yields decisive results, over time.

Rath was content to be a traditional old-line meat packer with all of its pitfalls. To the very end, it was still canning hams and presenting bacon slices in conventional one-pound packages. Commodity producers of bacon and canned or traditional smoked hams were a part of a vulnerable, indeed a dying market. They found competitors displacing their core assortment replaced by products with high value-added points of difference. "Rath shipped trainloads of commodity product," says Hy-Vee Chairman Emeritus Ron Pearson.[6] "They didn't reinvest."

Here were the essentials:

- Rath, for example, had no grocery products division[7] to serve as a basis for innovative packaging.

- It didn't recognize that it was selling to a consumer who no longer existed.

- It didn't focus on developing important points of difference or value-added products.

- Rath didn't constantly update its plant technology. (Indeed, it didn't need to because there were no new products in its pipeline!)

- And, it didn't monitor and anticipate – let alone respond to – important changes in consumer behavior.

In 1985, saddled with an out-of-date four-story plant, Rath halted operations.

> **NEW PRODUCTS WITH VALUE-ADDED POINTS OF DIFFERENCE DISTINGUISH COMPANIES THAT SURVIVE AND THRIVE FROM THOSE THAT PERISH.**

Later on you will read about the internal revolution that was taking place in the processes of the meat industry both from the standpoint of labor costs as well as technology. These were every bit as dramatic as what was happening to trends in consumer behavior. By the late 1970s and early 80s, the meat industry had developed a cost structure that was

---

6    *Ron Pearson joined Hormel's board in 2007. With more than 225 stores and sales exceeding $6.2 billion, West Des Moines-headquartered Hy-Vee is one of the nation's leading supermarket chains.*

7    *At Hormel Foods, grocery products are those items in the assortment not requiring refrigeration.*

driven by high wages and a history of little or no technology change along with inefficient labor practices. Inflation and massive "cost of living (wage) adjustments" (COLAs) overwhelmed traditional cost-profit formulas in the meat industry in the early 80s. The traditional industry failed to develop new technologies to deal with the labor cost difference. The industry lacked a vision as to how it would escape its identity as a commodity business. But the lethal difference was the appearance of low labor cost entrants who quickly took the business from the old traditionals bound by expensive contracts. (It was equivalent to the national tragedy of the American auto industry which we have since watched destroy itself.)

As it did in a number of other industries, the inevitable backlash also happened in meat processing as vacuum-packing of dressed beef became more popular. Beef imports also flooded into the market from South America. Domestically, so-called 'low-cost' producers – like Iowa Beef Processors (IBP), Cargill's Excel, and others – emerged to reduce the labor cost norms for meat processing to as low as $5.80 an hour starting wage. These non-union packers exploited the 'boxed beef' concepts that had actually been introduced by the majors. 'Boxed beef' reduced the dressed beef carcass to easily-handled and distributed boxed cuts that replaced the traditional side of beef bought by grocery stores and foodservice[8] providers.

Typical of what happened to traditional beef processors, our failing beef operations at the Austin plant had indeed gone one step further than 'boxed beef'. We offered new and revolutionary U.S. Choice boneless beef

---

8        Foodservice operators include all businesses involved in away-from-home eating and food preparation – notably restaurants, take-out and delivery services, hotels, and vending machines.

— vacuum-packed.[9] This was one of numerous production technologies conceived and developed at our old Austin, Minnesota plant. The product was intended for both retail and foodservice customers in an effort to save Hormel's beef business. It did . . . for a couple of years. While we were ahead of the market, the price of this leadership was hardly inexpensive. After we established the concept, new low-cost producers, which offered products devoid of points of difference, copied us and took the market away from us with a labor processing cost of $24.50 a head, versus the hefty $63 we paid to have the same work done! Even though we initially possessed a fundamental value-added difference, ultimately our new vacuum-packed boneless beef could be replicated by lower cost operators. After a couple of years, our innovative point of difference became nothing more than a well-designed concept for an unprofitable commodity.

This massive gap was caused by flawed labor-incentive costs and a lack of new technology in beef processing. Without product branding, beef processing was an easily duplicated process. The ironic result of our having further streamlined a non-branded, processed product was to ***accentuate*** the new, low labor-cost difference between the new entrants and ourselves. In this case, we had innovated ourselves into a trap.

In less than a decade, we would exit beef and parts of our own pork slaughter operation and transform others. Hormel's advantage in pork lay in developing and owning patented technologies and processes. These technological advances allowed us to offset the labor factor to some degree and to match low-cost competitors. However, implementing the technology also consumed considerable cash at a time when interest rates

---

9  *At one time, people thought of Hormel exclusively as a pork processor. In fact, we had beef operations at our Austin and Fremont plants until 1977. Beef processing had been a significant money-loser in our Austin plant for some time. While we continued to be in that business, we were compelled to find ways to make it more efficient. However, high fixed labor costs and the lack of new technology, doomed us. We would never be able to make beef processing competitive given the new playing field.*

were moving upward sharply. Hormel's experience with boxed beef in the late 70s contains an important lesson we have never forgotten, and I'll elaborate on it in a moment.

You can innovate by offering new concepts and still be driven out of the marketplace if you are strangled with an outmoded operating cost structure and lack new technologies even though you have value-added consumer brands. You must either have major or multiple points of difference and added value.

> ## REALIZING INNOVATION
> ## IS NO SURVIVAL GUARANTEE IN ITSELF.

In those days of the late 1970s- early 1980s, the 'Big Three' of the meat industry (Swift, Wilson and Armour) sold their facilities – when they could – to competitors who would reopen them at the new low wage rates. They dropped wages from $10.69 to $8.00-8.25 an hour to the new $5.80 starting wage at IBP and other firms. These once proud names have vanished altogether or remain only as brands owned by new entrants. Swift alone shut down more than 200 plants in a single year![10] Swift was recently sold to a Brazilian company after having been owned by ConAgra and then to a financial consortium which also struggled. The business that remains is primarily commodity.

The fate of the meat industry 'Big Three' told the story. The CEO of Wilson came to me and offered the company for an extremely cheap price. The price might have looked like a bargain, but buying Wilson would have

---

10      *Early in 2007, Swift, which was then owned by private equity and management firms was sold to JBS S.A., a South American meat processor. ConAgra had sold its beef and pork operations in 2002.*

meant assuming pensions that had been unfunded for quite a number of years. Those pensions and health-and-welfare obligations totaled hundreds of millions of dollars, Wilson filed for bankruptcy even after slashing its base pay. During the 1950s, 60s and 70s, when Swift, Armour or Wilson settled its wage package, the union would negotiate one contract and then move the spotlight on to the next major processor who would then fall in line. Swift – #5 on the Fortune 500 list in 1955 and later the core of the conglomerate Esmark – sliced its base pay. Armour followed suit, and virtually every meat packer demanded and gained similar wage relief from its workforce. This included Oscar Mayer, then a premium independent processor of consumer products.

Iowa Beef Processors (IBP) offered boxed beef and commodity pork produced with dramatically lower labor costs and – as I pointed out earlier – was the first major exception.[11] I don't intend to discuss the finer intricacies of labor relations in the meat industry, but – as you will read – Hormel withstood this turbulent time by developing many innovative technologies as well as new products. Hormel's new labor-saving equipment advantages enabled us to pay somewhat higher wages and fringe benefits in our sector, but we could still not afford the necessary changes to ultimately excel as a business. We also had to exit product lines where we lacked those advantages and points of difference.

We were no longer a primary producer of commodity meat products. By design, we were becoming a diversified, consumer-branded food company – a processor utilizing commodity raw materials in manufacturing our

---

11      *Iowa Beef had a reputation as a tough, low-cost operator. Once owned by Occidental Petroleum, IBP was acquired by Tyson in 2001 for more than $3 billion. Iowa Beef's bottom-line was, nonetheless, not as hard-nosed as the imagery might lead you to believe. Hormel was later given the opportunity to buy the company's pork operations. We declined. It turned out our technology made us the lower-cost operator, even with their far lower labor expenses.*

consumer-branded products with considerable value-added points of difference. It was our challenge to take these primals – acquired under rigorous quality standards – and to add the value to them.[12] That recognition changed the fabric of Hormel and mandated a whole series of initiatives in marketing and processing technology that has been built into a strongly based points-of-difference company.

As if there weren't enough vexing problems hitting the industry, a devastating shock came to pork producers and processors in the early 80s. Nitrosamines were assailed by a major national study as being potentially carcinogenic. Nitrosamines are produced in the human body as a result of ingesting the nitrite cures used to preserve many food and meat products. The science of these accusations was seriously flawed; but, beyond that, the required peer review was not conducted until long after the damage had been done. Even so, this unfortunate and unwarranted publicity nearly destroyed the industry's bacon business. When the peer review was finally completed three years later, it was discovered that researchers in the initial study had worked as independent units on three different phases of the project, and the findings were based on flawed information and incomplete science. A person would need to consume enormous quantities of bacon a day for it to be a health concern.

Even when the initial findings were ultimately corrected, many bacon marketers had been irreparably damaged. It has taken the last quarter century to rebuild the bacon business. This was a fiasco that affected the entire pork industry. Happily, Hormel had designed a number of marketing niches for bacon supported by new bacon products with unique points of difference which aided our surviving the nitrosamine scare. Later, I will

---

12    *The pork yield is separated into four basic cuts called primals: shoulder, side, loin, and ham. Each hog yields eight primals.*

describe these various packaging and product options in greater detail. They are symbolic of the dramatic changes altering our *foodscape* – which demand new thinking and new marketing – a process that ultimately translated into market leadership.

In this era of great industry change, Hormel survived because it chose the course of innovation – a course which it has continued to navigate ever since.

Innovation remains a central puzzle in business. How do companies really innovate? In recent years, "Think outside the box!" has become commonplace advice in business. But, is that how creativity really works? Hormel's R&D people are more inclined toward the view offered in a December 2007 *Harvard Business Review* article titled "Breakthrough Thinking from Inside the Box." The article's authors maintain that "most people are not very good at unstructured, abstract brainstorming." Instead of thinking totally outside the box, the authors suggest working with a *new* box and thinking *inside* of that. Their conclusion about managers and professionals: "We have found that if you systematically constrain the scope of their thinking (but not too much) . . . they can regularly generate lots of good ideas – and occasionally some great ones."

The article also points to some research done at the University of Chicago showing how Nobel laureates achieved "breakthroughs. . . Once they asked themselves the right question, their ideas flowed rapidly."

> **THE BEST YIELD FOR INNOVATIVE THINKING MAY COME FROM CAREFULLY CHANGING THE PARAMETERS, RATHER THAN ABANDONING THE PARAMETERS ALTOGETHER.**

Recently I asked Hormel's specialists charged with managing innovation how they stay in touch with consumer habits and trends. Their advice was straightforward and commonsensical. It included the following:

- Identify consumer problems worth solving. Always ask: What products are currently available to address that particular challenge and specifically how do they stack up?

- Have dinner with targeted consumers. It can be a wonderful and highly informative experience. Our Marketing people try to do this at least once a month.

- Live your consumers' lives. See movies, listen to music they enjoy, and 'hang out' at their favorite restaurants and clubs.

- Regularly eat your competitor's products at home. This may sound disloyal, but it's very hard to compete with or excel against what you don't know, especially since your rivals are constantly attempting to improve just as you are.

There is no underestimating the dramatic changes that have redefined the food industry. That said, the consequences of this upheaval have not been without their positive consequences for the consumer. While food costs as a share of the family budget remain remarkably modest, both the quality and the variety of food options have increased in ways unimaginable just a decade ago. Of all the industries, food – although rarely recognized for this innovation and efficiency – has done its job better than any other sector of the economy.

# Energizing the Organization

I grew up in a Hormel family. My father worked in the old Austin, Minnesota, plant. He scaled and weighed the livestock as it came in by rail. Along with six brothers and sisters, I was born and raised in a four-room house, which my father personally expanded as the family grew. Our home was in the Crane Addition neighborhood on the sidings by the railroad tracks, several blocks from the packinghouse, so my father could walk to work.

Getting a job in the plant looked like a secure future, and it was the goal of most young men in Austin at the time. The town was a blue-collar mecca for the nation. Austin was perhaps the most prosperous blue-collar community in America in the 1950s – home to what was termed a 'working-class elite.' "In 1951 [after World War II,] three out of four Austin workers owned their own homes."[1]

When I turned 16 in June 1948, I was a high school sophomore search-

---

1      *Those houses were full of kids too. After World War II, Austin had the highest birthrate in the United States.*

ing for a summer job. In those years, if you were a sixteen-year-old with a big build, you could legally work on the line if you could keep up. Nonetheless, very few young fellows were hired. At the time, a college scholarship seemed a dream beyond my reach. Throughout that June month, I showed up at 5 AM at the employment office for three weeks hoping to land an opening. After a while, I became discouraged. Then, one morning, I was the last person in the waiting room. The employment manager Oscar Neutzman came out and said, "Knowlton, I'm sick and tired of looking at you." I was sure he was going to tell me to stop pestering him. Instead, he said gruffly, "Go out and go to work." He knew I was overjoyed. It was my start, and the relationship still continues 60 years later as chair of the Hormel Foundation.

People often ask me if I ever met Jay Hormel, son of the founder George A. Hormel. Indeed that meeting took place. After working at Hormel for several weeks, I was rushing through the side door of the plant trying to get an early punch on the time clock for the afternoon shift. Jay Hormel was coming out. I didn't see him and knocked him back into a corner of the entry way.[2] I quickly brushed off his clothes. When I realized who he was, I was sure I would be fired. He said, "Why don't you lift up your head and watch where you're going, kid?" I've been trying hard to do that ever since. Little did I have the idea back then that I might follow Jay Hormel as the only other Hormel CEO to have been born in Austin.

In the summer of 1948, after stints in areas wherever they needed me, I ended up working in the gelatin department.[3] I liked the job and was

---

2    *Just for context, I went on to play guard and tackle on both the Austin High School and University of Colorado football teams, and in some games, was on the gridiron for the full 60 minutes.*

3    *Gelatin is a by-product of meat processing. Hormel has been one of the largest suppliers of gelatin basics to the food industry.*

earning gains[4] and incentives. Most importantly, I was taking in $90 a week and never expected to make more money than that.[5] I wanted to quit school and work at Hormel full-time. My dad and my football coach were both adamant about my sticking with school. So were several of my teachers, and I credit their encouragement and confidence with helping me to be recognized as a National Honor Society student in my senior year. Fortunately, the resolve of these caring adults helped establish a totally different future course for my life.

## PRODUCTIVITY:
## THE LEGACY AND THE CHALLENGES

There is an element of Fate in my running into Jay Hormel. Jay was undoubtedly the premier marketer in Hormel history. He also had a tremendous influence in shaping the labor policies and management practices of the company. Before 1985, only a single strike marred Hormel's labor history. It happened in 1933 when three employees were allegedly 'told' by a foreman to sign up for a retirement plan. The strike also spotlighted tensions that had been brewing in the background for some time. The stoppage was short but hardly friendly. Club-wielding strikers smashed plant windows, a foreman was beaten up, and Jay Hormel himself nearly took a drubbing and was allegedly carried out of his office. The strike lasted less than four days, and the strikers got the four-cent per hour

---

4    *"Gains" were a complicated system of supplementing wages which I'll describe in somewhat more detail later.*

5    *By comparison, three years later, as a college freshman, I was offered a summer sales job with Hormel – a very special opportunity – relieving regular sales people during their vacations at $47.50 per week. This was competitive with other sales positions in the industry, but it's further evidence why even college graduates were striving to find jobs on the line at Hormel where one made $90 to $100 a week.*

pay hike they wanted. Governor Floyd Olson visited Austin, but did not call out the militia. Olson was criticized in some circles for not breaking the strike with force. In time, things returned to normal.

In the post-1933 strike era, Jay Hormel came to be regarded as a labor-relations visionary. If anything, the company was considered a 'paternalistic' employer. Employees were protected by one year's advance notice before they could be laid off. Installed by Jay in the 1940s, this practice was called "guaranteed annual wage." We were one of the first companies in the U.S. to offer this benefit to production workers.[6] The plant could have burned down or blown up – and we might have gone bankrupt in the process – but the employees would have been paid. Section 2.b of the U.S. Wage and Hour Law still exists today and is the direct result of Jay Hormel's initiative. By agreement, you could work up to 53 hours in any given week without the hours over forty being treated as overtime. The employee could accrue time off in lieu of overtime.

The business was highly seasonal back then with heavy product availability in the fall-winter months[7]. Some of our people would take as much as six weeks of extended vacation during the summer months when business was slow. Employees willing to adjust their work calendars to peak seasons could create so-called flexible time. Over 1,872 hours in any year, taking into account vacation and holiday time, we paid overtime on those hours that were not used in alternate time off at year's end. In our old Austin plant, if an employee became ill, that person could be off work for a year and never miss his base paycheck.[8] At the end of the year, if you were over

---

6    *As another indication of his innovative labor-relations mindset, Jay Hormel also instituted profit-sharing (which continues to the present day) in an amount equal to several weeks' pay.*

7    *This is no longer true.*

8    *That's not to say they wouldn't miss the considerable incentives they would only be eligible for if they were actually working on the line.*

1,872 hours, Hormel would pay you overtime for those hours. If you were under, the company 'ate' the hours. Eventually the flow of livestock became more balanced, and the guaranteed annual wage developed into less of an advantage to line employees. As this pattern established itself, the union requested a move away from the annual hour system in favor of being paid for overtime weekly as it might be incurred.

The economic stability enjoyed by workers in the community was unheard of anywhere else. Local merchants could and did sell people big-ticket items 'on time' because the retailers knew their customers would get a year's paycheck no matter what happened! Why did Jay Hormel support these programs? He believed that the company didn't need a strong line management team, particularly at the foreman level. He was convinced that well-designed incentive systems – especially generous ones – would minimize the need for direct supervision and motivation. As unusual as Jay Hormel's idea may have seemed, esteemed pro-business forces praised his forward-looking vision. In 1937, *Fortune* magazine commented:

> *'The [Hormel employee annual wage] plan has worked out well on both sides. The company has gained greatly by a stabilized supply of skilled labor [at peak business periods]. The employees have absolute security.'*

In the 1940s and 50s, the union had negotiated several very burdensome provisions. During World War II, Hormel operated as a national security defense plant – supplying crucial Armed Forces rations. The business load was demanding, and it was profitable as well. Many labor concessions were made, especially since there was a large draft-exempted or semi-disabled contingent of employees in the plant workforce at the time. These newly added agreements may have been sensible concessions for the company to make back then, but they were never adjusted later when they lost relevance. The plant, for example, ran two shifts – not one – during the Second World War and that too contributed to an entirely different work-place environment.

*As this Hormel photo from the 1930s illustrates, meat processing was one of the most labor-intensive manufacturing industries*

Accelerating inflation drove starting wages from forty cents an hour in 1935 to the $10.69 base in the early 80s. (As a benchmark, the feder-al minimum wage in 1938 was twenty-five cents per hour.) And, the impact rippled through to the retirement benefits because many Hormel employees stayed for forty- or some for fifty-year careers. Meanwhile, emerging low-cost competitors kept employees for short periods without the requirement of reserving for pension and health-and-welfare benefits.

Jay Hormel had no way of knowing that we would be going through a period of dramatic cost-of-living adjustments through COLA contracts which ultimately were four times the negotiated basic salary increase.[9] This was a major factor in the rapid wage rise for that ten year period when inflation went through the "roof!"[10]

*Minneapolis Star Tribune* writers Dave Hage and Paul Klauda, who wrote the book *No Retreat, No Surrender*, have pointed to a peculiarity in how labor agreements were made at Hormel: "...the contract never expired, as most labor agreements do today, but instead perpetually renewed itself." Each time an issue was tweaked between management and the union, it was documented in a supplementary memo. This constituted a continuous unbroken 'contract' that agreed to practices which had been in effect for almost fifty years. "By 1959... fifteen years worth of memorandums of agreements filled a set of ring binder notebooks that covered a bookshelf nine feet long." The many practices and precedents covered in this way became impossible to manage. Often documented only in handwritten notes, this colossal rulebook proved a constant irritant to achieving positive labor relations, and issues were endlessly negotiated. Most revolved around the work standards that were the basis for our incentive program. But, other major contributors to the productivity-wage problem were the COLA adjustments mentioned above and the flawed incentive program. These incentives had been negotiated and termed, 'guaranteed gains opportunities.' They said that if you put in a machine that produced more efficiently than the previous manual procedure, the

---

9    *Paying a beginning wage of forty cents an hour is a totally different universe than paying $10.69 in base wages with COLA increases, a generous incentive plan, and a benefit-included all-in cost of $24.50 per hour in the Austin plant.*

10    *Another impact of inflation was rising interest rates. Hormel was feeling the dramatic cost of inflation both in wages as well as in financing.*

gain was to be reflected in increased compensation. This provision drove our labor costs even higher.

Dave Larson, our retired Vice President of Human Resources, describes the situation through making this comparison:

> *Over the course of time, employees were able to do their jobs so much faster than before because of new machinery and technology. I once explained it to a union representative this way: 'I hire you to mow my lawn at $10 an hour and give you a push mower. It takes you 8 hours, and I pay you $80. I go out and spend $500 on a rider lawn mower so you can do my whole lawn in 2 hours. Why should I pay you $80 every time you mow my lawn?' The union rep would argue that his productivity gain was still there. I would counter that his productivity was there because of the immense investment we've made. Recovering that investment now requires the mower to do four lawns in eight hours. That economic argument didn't even take into account the health, safety and leisure-time human benefits that employees also experienced by easing the back-breaking work burdens, and we were pleased with the win-win nature of that outcome.*

Such matters as health and safety were primary issues, not secondary ones for us as we improved our technology. One should also mention that our competitors had the same opportunities to invest in advanced technology. Most did not and went out of business. If we overpaid for inefficient use of labor, then we wouldn't have the funds to invest in further new technology as well as to market our new products. With those consequences, we would also be certain to bankrupt ourselves. Given these circumstances we couldn't afford to move in any other direction than to become the technological leader. And, we had to change our product lines at the same time or the business could simply not move forward.

Jay Hormel died of a heart attack in 1954 at the relatively young age of 61 – the same year that I graduated from the University of Colorado. Hormel's labor practices continued pretty much as he established them for the next fifteen years after his death. What Jay Hormel couldn't foresee, well before the rapid advance of inflation – no one could at the time – was that technology would also be a major factor to change the meat sector and the entire food sector just as it has the automotive industry. Even more importantly, Jay Hormel and the CEOs who followed him could not possibly envision the economic impact of rapidly rising inflation that would skyrocket labor costs 2,700% over 45 years, nor the skyrocketing COLAs that were mounting four times faster than union-negotiated hourly increases! The new competitors were also not offering these COLA increases – the highest in the history of inflation-indexed labor agreements. To our knowledge, we were the only company paying wages with an incentive program on such poorly established standards. Nonetheless, we still had the highest quality workforce in the industry.

The combination of industry productivity improvements from new technology and the continued deterioration of the incentive program caused our total labor cost per hour to rise to more than double the basic wage. With added incentives, health and welfare benefits included; Hormel's labor cost per hour at Austin exceeded – as noted – $24.50 at that time! With new products, we were also competing with the total food industry, which had substantially lower wage levels than were to be found in the meat sector. That made our labor-cost position all the more challenging and strained our ability to compete in the general grocery business.

## OVERHAULING ATTITUDES

During my summers while at the University of Colorado and later after graduation when I became a full-time Hormel employee in 1954, my assignments had been in marketing and sales. That included managing all of the sales divisions for the Austin plant between 1959 and 1967, while also occupying the position of Assistant Plant Manager. In October 1969, the position of General Manager of the Austin plant was offered to me. As I have said, the Austin plant then was considered the world's largest. Confusion reigned as to the plant's long-term destiny. The fate of the company relied on this "monster" being brought under control, but would this be possible?

When Jim Holton succeeded Tommy Thompson as president of Hormel in 1969, Jim realized the Austin plant required major surgery; but, no one knew all the particulars and some executives didn't care to see the problems addressed. At the time, the Austin plant manager also had direct responsibility for the plant's sales, with a dotted-line accountability to corporate Marketing. The Austin plant, which accounted for 50% of the company's volume, had been unprofitable for a number of years. That included its sales operations. I knew the plant was in need of dramatic changes that extended far beyond increasing sales and eliminating losses. Antiquation was everywhere. Massive improvements were necessary in the technology and processes used in the plant, especially those affecting the flow of materials and products. In addition to being sales manager, my role as assistant plant manager included responsibility for coordinating all of our production requirements. Taking on responsibility for total operations was an exciting career shift for me. During that period, our team was able to make the plant profitable. To undertake the further changes needed in the plant, it became crucial that plant operations have an open and direct reporting relationship to Jim Holton.

> **WHEN CHARGED WITH INSTITUTING SIGNIFICANT STRATEGIC CHANGE IN A BUSINESS, THERE IS NO REPLACEMENT FOR THE STRONG AND DIRECT SUPPORT OF THE CEO.**

Fortunately, as CEO, Jim was highly supportive of the important changes that were so necessary. We were given the independence to make the decisions to save the company short and long term. Those changes were to take us to the very brink of what we could manage both physically and financially. The major problem beyond antiquation was that 80% of the plant's work schedules were being paid against outmoded standards. We were also paying 'guaranteed gain incentives' in most departments whenever agreed upon standards were not in place. Even elevator operators received these pay supplements!

My predecessor was Harold Butler as plant manager – a wonderful man in so many ways. Harold had decades of experience. His self-restraint was epic. When he got hopping mad at someone – blowing his stack right through the plant's 9-story roof – Harold would let loose with the surliest language he could muster: He'd call the offender a "hay shaker!"

The woes of the Austin plant could hardly be laid at Harold Butler's feet. He inherited some very complex labor relations challenges and had to deal with a perplexing overall organizational structure. This stemmed from a long established pattern of the Hormel corporate organization centering their activities and authority around the Austin plant. Hormel corporate management was hopelessly entangled in running this plant through dotted-line involvements. It complicated decision making in many ways. Since a number of corporate executives wanted to close Austin and move its operations to one of two alternate sites, they were disinterested in solving the problems of the Austin plant. However, since Austin plant management was part of their responsibility, their lack of involvement was an obstacle to implementing solutions to the plant's problems.[11]

When I accepted the position of Austin plant manager, I had the good fortune to know a significant number of the people working there. My earlier plant sales management experiences gave me an edge in managing the Sales staff, since they reported directly to the plant manager, as well as in coordinating the production requirements. Many of the plant employees were fellow townspeople in Austin. Some were high-school classmates. Others had been colleagues when I worked the line as a summer stand-in. Even though I had advanced on the marketing side of the business (starting with positions in the Fremont plant organization during summers and after college and a stint in the Armed Forces), my management jobs with Hormel had all been Austin-based since 1959.

Despite having lived in Austin for so much of my life, something inside me said I really had to know the operations of the old Austin plant even *more* thoroughly. In accepting the managership of the plant, I made an important request: I wanted four months to work on the line and to reacquaint myself with all the people, operations, and the

---

11      *Fortunately, a restructuring ultimately separated corporate management from the Austin plant, as I shall describe.*

problems we were facing. I felt this would be the best way to identify opportunities for change. This is a step I'd recommend to any manager who is charged with overhauling an operation from the ground up. Becoming familiar with all these details first-hand strengthened my ability to participate in the planning for the manufacturing facility to make it as cost-competitive as possible. Advances on this measure were essential to our future. Our labor costs amounted to 18% of our average selling price. The norm for the rest of the industry was 11%, and the industry itself was failing! Ultimately, effective cost management through superior technology also gave us the courage to plan for a new plant to replace the old one.

Every morning during my requested four-month "reacquaintance" period it meant hitting the line at the early morning whistle. The people on the line knew my background. A layman could keep up with most of the lines, and my colleagues tolerated me when I couldn't. These weren't easy jobs, even with productivity standards lower than were appropriate. This was challenging, taxing work. Your hands and wrists had to be in condition to do some of the work since we hadn't developed all the new technologies we would incorporate in those important years following. My most important goal was to have a good understanding of each job involved and to try to determine how we could modernize the processes.

What was my most memorable lesson working the line? One surely was removing small carpal bones and connective tissue out of the picnic hams that go into making Spam. That required intricate knife handwork and motivated us to develop a machine that would extract both the major and the small bones automatically in a single process. You'll learn more about this particular piece of equipment in Chapter 3.

> **DIRECT EXPERIENCE ON THE FLOOR IDENTIFIES WHERE KEY OPERATING POINTS OF DIFFERENCE ARE TO BE HAD AND CAN ADD URGENCY TO MAKING FURTHER IMPROVEMENTS, ESPECIALLY IN TECHNOLOGY.**

Some of the fellows on the line had been at their jobs thirty or forty years and were very skilled at what they did. More than once, I was impressed with their dexterity, their craftsmanship, and their common sense. This was an extraordinarily disciplined and dedicated team. In hindsight, the union was tolerant to let me do what I did: By our contract with the union, management employees were strictly forbidden from performing actual tasks on the line. I pled the case that more of our management should have the same experience so they could have a better understanding of their operation. While this was never really permitted by the then-existing union agreements, these restrictions were fortunately not always strictly enforced.[12]

Down deep, I think that our line employees realized the Austin plant was mired in an economically unworkable system that couldn't go on. They hoped we might be a fair-minded source of reform which could help the team straighten things out and achieve a turnaround that would give Hormel a new future in Austin. Streamlining and updating would be inevitable. We knew it . . . and so did the people on the line, but they also naturally wanted to prolong the pay scales and old practices as long as possible. The magnitude of change needed was so enormous, it was doubtless the reason hundreds of plants in the industry had been abandoned. The work

---

12    *The most extensive exposure for managers to direct line experience came during the 1985-1986 strike described in Chapter 5.*

was simply moved to sites where labor was abundant and no onerous labor practices were in place. To change practices in an existing plant would be a monumental feat, but a necessary one if we were to remain in Austin.

## COST-CUTTING: A SYSTEMATIC PLAN

Our first objective was to make the old Austin plant profitable again. We had to survive until we could afford to make major investments in new technologies. Fortunately we were given a great deal of autonomy. As I have said, this plant had lost money for a number of years.

At the time, corporate management had no overall plan to renovate or replace the old plant. No one at corporate even talked about a new plant in Austin. Several executives didn't want the Austin plant replaced – at least not in Austin. Our management team's mission was to try and correct the shortcomings in the facility we had. At the time, the plant had 3,331 employees. Labor is almost always assumed to be a variable in production operations. Because of the flawed incentive program, which had so many guarantees, our investment in labor had become far more like a fixed cost.

Soon after my four months of fact-finding on the line began, we determined that we needed to run the existing plant wide open. If we operated it at full steam, we could help overcome the flaws caused by the costly incentive system. Only if we maximized volume could we get the biggest return for our payroll dollar. We increased our processing from 7,500 to 10,000 hogs per day in one shift – five days a week and quite often a half day on Saturday – a bold but necessary move. This was Austin's highest output since World War II, when we were considered a defense plant and ran two shifts, and the real challenge became to profitably market this increased volume.

In the 1950s and 60s, our absenteeism at Austin ran as high as 12% which added to our already exorbitant labor costs. The extra workforce needed to cover manning all the work stations was just one of the compounding factors. This situation was intolerable, and it had been going on for a long time. A major dispute also arose. Employees in the pork division staged a 20-week slowdown over the installation of new labor standards. This was a major test of our ability to at least partially address our costly labor agreement. The work slowdown was so frustrating that many of the people on the line didn't know ***how*** to step on the brakes and work at such a reduced pace!

Even though the Austin plant, the company's largest, had an incentive system that produced the highest wages, this antiquated plant remained in some instances the standard against which productivity throughout the rest of the company was measured. Employees in one of our newer, more specialized facilities who 'beat Austin' in their output because of better flow and equipment were considered to be satisfactory performers. In one of these plants, when employees 'beat Austin' they routinely spent extra time in the locker room. This was another symptom of management failing to deal with the long-standing incentive problem. And, we were paying an ever greater price when inflation and COLAs skyrocketed. These complex issues had to be resolved before a new Austin plant could be contemplated.

Realizing that there would be no quick solution to the incentive problem, we decided to tackle costs systematically. We channeled our initial energies along three critical but slightly different fronts:

- What key areas of inefficiency could most readily be improved? What investment would give us the greatest return?

- Given the advances in technology and processes we were developing, what would be legitimate standards for measuring productivity?
- How could we sharpen our systems to increase both volume and productivity?

In 1969, my first year as manager, Hormel had only five industrial engineers in the old Austin plant, and most of them spent their time answering union challenges about attempts to establish better work standards. Past labor agreements and practices hovered over us like a death hold. The union was much better staffed with union stewards – who were, by the way, on the company payroll – to challenge new standards, than management was to analyze and update those standards. Our deteriorating profit situation made solving the problem even more pressing. We spent much of the next two years trying to establish realistic standards. Negotiating these issues demanded a great deal of management time, but that had to be our priority. As general manager, I spent many hours in the so-called "Bullpen" – that space set aside near the offices, where these highly complex agreements were discussed and straightened out.

> ## TO *IMPROVE* PRODUCTIVITY,
> ## ACCURATELY *MEASURING* PRODUCTIVITY IS
> ## THE INESCAPABLE FIRST STEP.

Gradually we increased the number of industrial engineers to 26 and started gathering data on work standards to measure our productivity. Then we asked the question: How could we change what we were doing to make Austin profitable? For any significant project's approval, we established a minimum 100% return-on-investment standard in a single year for all key projects. Even with that hurdle, stacks of projects delivering a return that good or better overwhelmed my office! The entire plant was alive with ideas that led to new processes, layouts and state-of-the-art equipment. (Having had such a favorable arrangement for so long, the union naturally resisted changes.)

To get an immediate return with a minimal financial investment, we sometimes focused on short-term answers which were not always the best long-term solutions. Nonetheless – with returns of 100% in one year – they were certainly attractive, since there was no established long-term alternative to replacing the Austin or Fort Dodge plants. Those projects improving quality and operating efficiency got top priority.

Simultaneously, the management team strove to achieve points of difference in every phase of our operation. One evening, Al Zehner, Superintendent of Pork, planted a tongue-in-cheek renovation proposal in the middle of the gigantic pile of legitimate project requests. It promised a 1,000% return on investment over one month. How? Convert the huge open space behind my office into a beer garden! We all had a laugh – a needed one. These were energizing but demanding times.

## PIECEMEAL COST-CUTTING: LEARNING THE LIMITATIONS

Great attention was paid to total work flow. The input of the industrial engineers and an increasingly strengthened management team allowed us to improve efficiency step-by-step. They also helped us prioritize the significant process changes needed in the business. This cadre of smart, talented operational leaders went on to become the forerunners of the strong management team we have today – a career-oriented group that evolved during this important period of change.

The plant's multi-story structure relied on elevators and battery-operated forklifts to transport goods internally. The 85 elevators were actually an **obstacle** in moving product from one floor to the other and through various stages of manufacturing. We constantly pulled product-in-process in and out of the nine-story refrigeration unit. For example, all freezer product moved from any of nine floors. Waiting for elevators caused delays of all types. The buildup of inventory for holiday hams required extensive freezer storage and resulted in another bottleneck. The production system became so complicated that meaningful time-and-motion studies couldn't analyze it. Expensive? We paid 85 people (and sometimes more, with overlapping shifts) a guaranteed incentive and benefits to operate these elevators. For example, we would move hams to different floors to perform the various stages of ham processing, from initial freezing through curing. And, this practice – as I have said – was at a time when wages and COLAs were skyrocketing.

> ### POOR PRODUCTIVITY CAN BE A FACILITY-DRIVEN PROBLEM AS EASILY AS A HUMAN RESOURCE CHALLENGE.

Over time, the company had also added 101 unnecessary jobs to address elevator-related problems and to deal with the bottlenecks – perpetuating the challenges . . . not solving them. Worst of all, these additional employees received the automatic incentive pay of 41% gains – a guaranteed premium actually driven by machine output.

✿

Was our overall attempt to reduce costs sensible? It surely seemed to be our only avenue. But it wasn't. This path was sensible only if you looked at it short-term. We saw each of the problems in the old plant in isolation, rather than as a series of components in the overall, long-term plan for the future. . . But, make no mistake about it, we still had an ***old plant***. This truth surfaced after we redesigned the Market-Ship department. If there was any one area that could be considered 'low-hanging fruit' in revamping the old Austin plant, Market-Ship was it. Market-Ship was where products left the plant – mostly on trucks – to be delivered to our retail customers. If you consider all the different items that had to be shipped on any one truck, we needed a well-designed system to combine all the shipping items for each truckload. Those individual products could be minor in size and/ or small in number. On the shipping docks, four or five missing secondary items might hold up an entire truck, and this would prevent loading the next truck.

We installed a new Market-Ship system that took 85 positions directly out of this work group and eliminated 16 in related departments, all of which were on incentives. The new Market-Ship system overhauling our product distribution realized a 100% return on investment in 9 months. Wow! We were considered whizzes at the time. But we were kidding ourselves if we thought we had created an enduring modern shipping concept that could answer our long-term distribution needs, particularly since it could not be relocated and integrated into a new plant design. The decision merely bandaged over a far more serious problem. Later, these investments – which made great sense short-term and paid off handsomely in less than a year – were incompatible with the new plant as it would be designed and built.

> **ELIMINATING OR STREAMLINING AN INEFFICIENT OR OBSOLETE PROCESS CAN CREATE A POINT OF DIFFERENCE. THE GOAL SHOULD BE TO BALANCE THE IMMEDIATE NEED TO SURVIVE WITH THE LONG-TERM GOAL TO THRIVE.**

While Market-Ship made us look golden at the time, it lacked long-term validity. Still these decisions created the foundation for the technology our team ultimately developed in the design and building of the new plant. Had the new plant been built within three years, we would also have missed the invaluable opportunity for substantial savings. Indeed, another kind of investment was being made simultaneously in management development. The new technologies and streamlined operations were vital. Even more important was how our career-committed managers were being energized and coalescing as a team.

> **THE MOST DECISIVE POINTS OF DIFFERENCE ARE OFTEN NOT NEW PRODUCTS OR TECHNOLOGIES IN THEMSELVES, BUT MANAGEMENT'S COMMITMENT TO CHANGE.**

Designing a truly advanced new plant is a journey. If approached with the right attitude, it can enliven a management team's outlook toward revolutionary change to secure and sustain a company's leadership position within an industry.

# INFUSING MEANINGFUL INDUSTRIAL ENGINEERING

Through industrial engineering, we were able to install valid standards for 80% of the operations in the old plant. Even some of the employee representatives came to question the validity of a few of the provisions that were being eliminated. One day, I remember a very experienced union agent saying to me, "We don't have anything you didn't give us." His comment was perceptive and shockingly relevant. For the previous forty years, that had certainly been the case. The quality of our people, the quality of work and the quality of our product were all very high.

Our workforce was made up of fine, skilled individuals who were naturally trying to make as much money as they could, and they weren't going to concede necessary adjustments easily. Keeping our people the best paid in the industry was a goal. While the real question nonetheless was: "What is fair and what is the best wage we can afford to pay?" The wages we were paying in the plant were so high that college graduates, as I have said, were anxious to be hired on our production lines!

Early in my tenure as Austin plant manager, it became clear to me that revitalizing the plant meant overhauling our concept of first-line supervision. We had to return to a view of the foreman that founder George A. Hormel embraced. For George A.[13], qualified and motivated first-level supervision was indispensable. "Every day I made the rounds of every department," he once wrote. "Management, for the worker, isn't the front office, it's the foremen. I met with them daily. Since the foremen are the hub . . . They were always the best I could find."

---

13    *In this book, I will sometimes refer to founder George A. Hormel simply as George A.*

> **EMPOWERED, MOTIVATED FIRST-LEVEL
> SUPERVISORS ARE A KEY POINT OF DIFFERENCE.
> FOR EMPLOYEES TO RESPECT SUPERVISORS,
> MANAGEMENT HAS TO RESPECT THEM FIRST.**

While the industrial engineers were important in creating meaningful standards, they were also a critical talent source for us as we upgraded our management team. They gave a new generation of foremen both new authority and credibility. Industrial engineers provided a staffing source for a team of supervisors who were more analytical, better able to measure work, and more qualified to design and develop new layouts and technologies.

This new level of performance brought constructive competition and caused many incumbents to rise to the occasion and perform superbly. This combination of new and seasoned resources – the cadre of industrial engineers along with our quality-control and well-trained production managers – proved to be a terrific competitive edge. Our goal was to create optimum blend with the team already in place, increase our prospects of retaining the best people, and motivate the experienced people to new heights. In the opinion of industry observers, our organization evolved into the best management team in any industry anywhere.

> **IF YOU NEED PEOPLE WITH NEW SKILL SETS,
> BRING THEM IN STEADILY, *NOT ABRUPTLY*,
> WHILE YOU *CONTINUE TO* SURFACE
> LEADERS INTERNALLY.**

# ATTITUDE AND COMMUNICATIONS: PIVOTAL BUILDING BLOCKS

Another facet of management performance sorely in need of improvement was communication. Dick Schaefer, P-9's union agent, was a bright person who could have been in Hormel's management. The union's internal communication program was frankly superior to management's back in 1969. Union leadership used its network of five company-paid union stewards in the Austin plant to develop its own instant communication network. When changes were to be implemented or issues arose, as I indicated, the union seemed better and faster at informing employees on the line than management was in updating its first-level supervisors.

We needed to make radical modifications and brought the supervisors into the plant manager's conference room to keep them informed first and up to the minute on any of the rapidly developing changes. This altered information flow was central to restoring direction and credibility. We knew we had turned an important corner when some of the best and most respected line employees stepped forward and asked to be considered for line management openings and performed well when given the opportunity.

> **MANAGEMENT ONLY STAYS ON TOP OF THE BUSINESS IF IT DEMONSTRATES LEADERSHIP INTERNALLY *THROUGH* CLEAR COMMUNICATIONS.**

Just as we needed to communicate better with our first-level supervisors, they in turn needed to communicate more effectively with their departments. We developed a much clearer profile of what made our supervisors successful. Some of those key characteristics were interpersonal skills. One of the most important traits we sought to develop was consistency in maintaining standards day after day; first with the expectation that new methods would be designed and implemented. We realized line employees needed to expect a certain reliable rhythm. We also put a strong new emphasis on a manager's training skills.

Colleagues had warned me about taking on managing the old Austin plant since I was already advancing rapidly on the marketing side of the business. Many of our people said the old plant was a loser, and the people who ran it had become losers. What could you expect after years of association with what most everyone contended was a dying operation? Remember the context: During the 1980s the majors – Swift, Armour and Wilson – and hundreds of smaller operators were all going down. Those who said the Austin plant management were losers were wrong. I had been associated with these people before and had confidence in them. In reality, the managers in the old Austin plant wanted nothing more than the opportunity to be part of a winning team and to demonstrate their abilities.[14]

After my four month 'tour of duty' learning operations, the challenge as general manager was to help re-establish key cultural values. I was determined I'd be there first in the morning. Instead of showing up at 6:30, I'd set a new tempo and arrive at six. They were all there! Then I backed up my arrival time to 5:45. They matched it! These managers were so motivated and ready for change, I knew immediately we could handle anything.

---

14    *If only Ken Dahlgren, John Halvorson, Oscar Lindstrom, Al Zehner, Sam House and many others too numerous to mention were still alive to know how much their groundbreaking contributions to the old Austin plant are valued today.*

Of all the experiences in my management career, my days heading that management team and all the problems at the Austin plant were among the most challenging and rewarding. Because of the team's efforts, we turned the Austin plant from a loss into a profit maker surpassing all of our other operations. After two years, we beat the Fremont, Nebraska, plant – which had been, and still is, a shining star in our total operations.

The foremost objectives imprinted in the back of my mind were:

- What manual work could be mechanized?
- What work processes could be altered to prevent debilitating injuries?
- Which departments might we have to close or overhaul?

We only had a limited amount of capital, and we wanted to make sure we invested in projects which would deliver the maximum return. But, we also wanted our people to know that we weren't spending a dime on anything that didn't have good return. The improvements couldn't be arbitrarily mandated. Change required contractual commitment of the entire team. From his new post at corporate, Harold Butler gave strong support for that brief period before he retired, and Jim Holton was stellar. That said, it was often very difficult to correct the underlying issue: Until plausible benchmarks existed to measure the work levels that were in place, and compensated with full incentive pay, the plant would be doomed to run 'off standard.' Paying substantial guaranteed incentives for unmeasured work would continue to be a massive economic challenge for us.

## OPERATIONAL POINTS OF DIFFERENCE: AN INTEGRATED PACKAGE

In a variety of ways, we were able to create a mix of different strengths. As I said, we recruited industrial engineers, quality control and production management. The greatly expanded base of industrial engineers infused analytical, college-educated talent. But, a number of our new promotions were seasoned veterans. Some may have lacked college-degree backgrounds, but they had enormous reservoirs of practical experience and were bright, dedicated employees.

The ingenuity of Hormel's people was impressive. During World War II, when mechanical parts were nowhere to be found, Hormel engineers and employees designed, developed, and built machines that were revolutionary, fashioning parts and equipment that would have been unavailable during war time. This demanded design genius! The solutions went on to become company legends.

Another point of difference in the evolution of the management team was our willingness to rotate people through different disciplines. We were fortunate to retain these talented people for a full career – unusual in today's world. We were able to attract top quality talent because we could offer assurances that these individuals could build a well-rounded career. With the exception of one key person, we were able to retain all of the talent that we wanted.

My assignment as Austin plant general manager taught me some indelible and valuable lessons. One of the most important: It is more constructive to redirect people than to discard them. I am proud to say this has become a cornerstone of the Hormel culture. In one highly visible way, we have differed with a management practice that has come into vogue in recent years: dismissing the bottom ten percent of management staff each year. We refuse to set an arbitrary percentage of people whom we define as unwanted. Artificially removing a set number of people is an unnecessary waste of talent, especially if a company has done a good job of screening candidates in the first place.

Companies maintaining such a narrow slant on people pay another costly price. Because of an undue emphasis on specialization, companies underestimate the value of managers who have a broad familiarity with the business. Tightly specialized units with highly insulated staffing also spawn political factions and can make for a very parochial company in deciding who stays and who leaves. In truth, managers often fit better in certain jobs than in others. The arbitrary ten percent cut makes it unlikely that a manager will be transferred to another sector where that person could make a greater contribution. Raising the hurdle ten percent each year is less of a motivator to excel and can create a highly political environment. Additionally, it certainly doesn't foster either employee loyalty or sound career development, and my conviction is based on a lot of experience at every level in a growing company.

> **REGULARLY PURGING AN ARBITRARY PERCENTAGE OF YOUR STAFF IS AN UNPRODUCTIVE WASTE OF TRAINED TALENT.**

Systematically review the base of internal talent. Identify the expertise you need. Find the best fits for your people. In a growing company, the emphasis should be on finding opportunities for people, not on discarding talent mismatched for particular jobs. This practice doesn't condone poor performance. Quite to the contrary. We are anxious to match people to those jobs in which they can excel and to do so in a timely way.

Staffing wasn't the only breakthrough in reviving the Austin plant. Surely there were also important breakthroughs in product quality and marketing such as the CURE 81® ham that had great significance for the Austin plant's profitability. You will read about these in the fourth chapter – dedicated to our marketing program.

# POINTS OF DIFFERENCE
## *Energizing an Organization*

- Are your first-level supervisors empowered? Do employees believe that top management respects them? Are they motivated to identify and pursue those new points of difference a company needs to attain exceptional performance . . . and to sustain it?

- Is your company creating the best promotional opportunities that motivate people? Is your company providing growth avenues?

- What behaviors are you rewarding or incenting that may undercut the very big-picture goals you want to achieve?

- Are you giving talented young people the opportunity to *manage* early in their careers?

- Are people focused on new opportunities for success, improvement and change, or are they hesitant and willing to settle for the status quo?

- Are line managers truly encouraging employees to look for changes that could improve how jobs are done? Is corporate management collaborating with line managers as a team?

- Is safety given top priority in each and every operation and in every new technology and process?

- Is top management willing to confront and resolve lingering complex problems?
- Do you regularly check important practices and procedures to see if they may have outlived their usefulness?
- Most importantly, are your people energized and motivated to seek and accomplish constructive change?

# CHAPTER 3

# *Re-Casting Hormel's Technology*

**T**he first structure in Hormel's old Austin plant was a modified creamery acquired by the company in 1891. Over decades of constant additions and remodeling, the plant grew to be 54 acres under one roof, 9 floors high. During much of its existence, the plant

57

was considered to be the largest in the world. It was the size of a respectable farm . . . but not nearly as manageable.

Operating practices were constantly rethought and updated. In 1922, one of the first innovations was the design and installation of a 100-ton ice-making machine. It rendered chopping blocks of storage ice from the Cedar River in the dead of winter a thing of the past. George A. Hormel himself appreciated the power of technology as a point of difference, even to the extent of designing a patented meat-washing machine in 1928. The company was given a national award for pioneering humane slaughtering techniques in 1951. The plant offered a host of other advances on many fronts. Hormel had steam cookers, smoke rooms, and even its own canning plant. New operations were added over time, and the result was an often chaotic array of exceptional technology – highly differentiated, but not necessarily planned for flow and optimum efficiency. The lesson: If you continually add operations, adjoining one building after another, the resulting facility is bound to be inefficient.

The old Austin plant was the site of continual innovation, but the constant renovation this caused led to a facility that became consummately difficult to operate. This facility was a logistic challenge for many reasons. For one, you could never squeeze new equipment in easily. Unfortunately the plant wasn't always tall enough in the right places! We had the restriction of ten-foot ceilings in much of the processing space. For example, our automatic picnic ham de-boner – a crucial piece of equipment – required a 15-16-foot ceiling to operate in the old Austin plant. We were forever adjusting parts of the ceiling or the widths of aisles and floors. It was difficult to get our arms around the internal flow of material and product because of the numerous interior walls that obstructed the logical and efficient movement of goods.

In fact, we discovered entire sections of the plant had been walled off – creating vaults. One could still find liquor bottles drained dry by outside construction crews from generations earlier when these sections were sealed off! Most packinghouses in our industry were plagued with similar structural handicaps, but not on such a colossal scale. In addition, as I have said, elevators everywhere – 85 of them – obstructed the smooth flow of products in process.

One subtle but debilitating force in the plant's operation was the organizational backdrop. The plants in our structure at that time (the old Austin plant especially) were regarded as "sales centers" as much as they were seen as production and shipping facilities. That prevented each plant from realizing its potential as a highly efficient production facility, optimizing economies of scale. Independent retail stores required a full line of products, and plants made sense as regional sales centers during this bygone era. With national chain stores and warehouses beginning to emerge, sales-centered plants were doomed to obsolescence.

In 1927, Jay Hormel developed a revolutionary idea called the 'sausage truck,' which a salesman drove to sell and deliver fresh plant products to the retailers in his territory. It was the most important advance in transporting meat products since Gustavus Swift's breakthrough of the refrigerated rail car. It didn't take long before Hormel had 250 such trucks, chiefly in the Midwest. (In my first summer from college, I drove several sausage truck routes.) Why so many trucks? As noted, back then, independent retailers thrived. Most of these accounts required replenishment and service twice or even three times a week. A meat supplier sold *and* delivered because this was the most economical solution at the time.

By 1945, distribution of the products made by a plant was handled by salesmen in what were known as route cars, which were the replacement for sausage trucks. Salesmen in the route cars negotiated the sales. Delivery was later made by larger delivery trucks, some of them from our own fleet. Separating sales and deliveries made economic sense. For a long time, the cost efficiency of the route car distribution system had merit. The selling process, however, still revolved around the individual plants. In 1969, the Austin plant was as much a sales and distribution hub for its region as it was a manufacturing facility.

As the retail industry streamlined itself with new warehouses, the logic of a food manufacturer operating a series of general-purpose plants to service retail warehouses diminished. The new thrust would be to focus plants to specific products. Today much of our distribution is done by such major retail accounts as Walmart, Kroger, Safeway, SUPERVALU, and its Albert-sons component as well as a number of sizable regional chains usually through their own warehouses. Their distribution has made the manufac-turer's all-purpose selling approaches outmoded.

## THE OLD AUSTIN PLANT GOES ON THE TECHNOLOGICAL OPERATING TABLE

The Austin plant's role changed, but its technology lagged far behind what the facility needed to achieve. We literally had to put this old plant on a technological operating table. Our mindset was paradoxical: While we may have wanted a technologically advanced plant, the only way to afford it was to create a base of profitability through solving the inefficiencies of the old plant. As I have described, often we would need to do so with hundreds of interim systems and processes that unfortunately had no long-term viability.

Some of the changes incorporated as much new technology as was economically affordable. Ken Dahlgren and Oscar Lindstrom, dedicated managers of the Mechanical Division, did their best to accommodate the changes and to adapt new technology from an engineering standpoint. These were massive challenges. As with many others on the Hormel team in this era of change, the mechanical engineers worked long hours, but the results in new technologies were revolutionary and far-reaching. While dramatically updated technology would be a costly investment, it soon became apparent that superior technology would yield the best return in expense savings while maintaining product quality. Only then would we have funds to upgrade and expand our marketing thrust.

Our people were highly motivated to constantly develop new technologies. Their success in designing and building a new piece of equipment revolutionized pork processing for us. Leather sourcing is an intricate business and one of the most labor-intensive aspects of the pork processing operation. The leather sourcing device, designed and built by our engineers in Austin, was a monumental breakthrough. This was installed first in our Fremont plant, which was smaller with a better flow of tasks. We had problems perfecting our first trials even on this smaller scale. I visited the Fremont test because the device had come to be known as my 'pet project.' No one wanted to tell me it would fail . . . but almost everyone was sure it would. I saw this test as a bellwether for our people who were seeking new technologies in everything we were doing. Had we failed at this project, it would have crippled our momentum as we sought new technologies. Ultimately we succeeded with this breakthrough and much, much more.

In the meat processing industry, early attempts at leather sourcing were marginal because the foremost goal was to increase meat yield, and each individual hide had to be removed manually. The labor investment was substantial, resulting in a bottom-line sixty-cent per unit charge for labor and 'rendering,' but this manufacturing step was necessary before further processing was possible.

The patented Hormel leather sourcing device was developed principally by Lyndon Leining – one of our brightest mechanical engineering geniuses – and his associates. Bill Swanson, one of our top Operations managers was our on-site coordinator and leader in charge of this project. After making its own incision, the device removes the hide, untouched by human hands. The resulting material is large, full, and uniformly thick. As opposed to incurring a normal 60-cent labor and rendering expenditure to remove this first-stage leather, we chalked up a net *gain* of an average of $3.00 for each piece of leather and produced more than a thousand quality hides per hour! The value of the resulting leather rose over time because the size dimensions – the length and girth – of the hog continually increased. The number of hides was substantial. (In 2008, Hormel processed 19,000 hogs per day.)

The above is a nice return, but the labor-saving technology was a big point of difference compared with our competitors. What happens to these quality leather pieces? They were and are used for car upholstery, jackets, shoes, and other applications. We have exported much of our product to foreign manufacturers. A domestic customer – Wolverine – is another big user of these hides.

The return on this unduplicated process remains a major advantage. The skinning machine was symbolic of our search for innovation that would lead to further streamlining. It spurred everyone to look for new processes, new technology, and new equipment to provide greater efficiency and cost savings throughout all operations. The revolutionary leather sourcing device was especially important because it was equipment we built ourselves. It started a flood of new ideas and results.

A concern for leather may seem secondary if you're in the pork business, but I've often reflected on George A. Hormel's career. As he went on to become a legend in the meatpacking industry, he spent four years on the road buying beef hides from farmers for the Chicago merchant Oberne, Hosick. When you are in this business in a serious way, you try to think of the best destination for every component. Pork processors meant it when they said they used everything but the squeal.

> **YOU CREATE A WINNING POINT-OF-DIFFERENCE IF *YOUR* BYPRODUCT EFFICIENTLY BECOMES A PERFECT RAW MATERIAL FOR ANOTHER INDUSTRY.**

## PORK PROCESSING TECHNOLOGY: EARLY SUCCESSES

In important ways, Hormel was far ahead of its competition in designing a program to purchase select premium lean hogs. This created a decisive point of difference. Our edge wasn't restricted to our ability to select and buy superior pork. For decades, we also had a commitment to be at the forefront of pork processing as well.

Picnic ham (taken from the pork shoulder) mixed with standard ham form the total ingredients in Spam – save the seasonings. The flavor and consistency of picnics are perfect for Spam, but this cut has three bone structures in it. In pork-shoulder boning, the challenge is to remove the carpal bones out of the shoulder meat in one process. This problem needed a technological solution. Manual ham-boning is highly labor intensive and can be wrist-injury prone. Effectively mechanizing the deboning of picnic hams would be a real breakthrough for us.

Our predecessors at Hormel had also tried to build a deboner, but those early prototypes were huge and ungainly. They had many short-comings. One concept coupled the extraction mechanism with high-pressure water. Because the water diluted and purged the proteins out of the product, the process wasn't workable. Our research graveyard was full of prototypes and models, but the quest for a picnic deboner remained unanswered.

After doing a search and trying to resurrect some old concepts, Frank Brown, our Vice President of Engineering, and I attended an American Meat Institute convention in Chicago. At this convention, we met a wonderful man named Peter Kobussen, whose business was based in the Netherlands. Kobussen said his firm Protecon could build a machine to address this hefty manufacturing expense. It would cost $125,000 – a terrific bargain given our previous investments and expectations and the magnitude of the problem. Based on this projection, I gave Peter and Frank the go-ahead to move forward.

Conceptually Kobussen was right. Six months later he arrived from Holland with his machine. He asked if the deal was still on. We said absolutely *if* we retained the North American rights. Protecon came up with a massive hydraulic piston. It exerted about 25,000 pounds of pressure per square inch. The first time we tested this machine, it shattered! The supporting struts couldn't withstand the stress exerted, and the upper frame failed.

A powerful ram like this could never work in a building with a ceiling just 9-10 feet high. Another reason the deboner collapsed was that the European version was not designed to deliver the volume at the production rate we needed to maintain. But, we could see the principle was right. Our engineers rebuilt the machine. The whole fine-tuning process took about one-and-a-half years, and the apparatus that emerged was very nearly what we use today. The resulting bone-free pork shoulder along with boneless ham made a nice can of Spam, with substantial labor savings.

This machine remains one of the technological points of difference giving us a competitive edge. As with so many of the technological improvements that allowed us to manufacture better products for the consumer, the impetus for developing the deboner was initially driven by the goal of cutting costs. The picnic de-boner experience makes another important point about innovation generally. Outside innovations sparked improvements in our own workshops… as well as in those operations we contracted.

> **ALL POINTS OF DIFFERENCE ARE NOT INTERNALLY DEVELOPED. TRUSTED OUTSIDE EXPERTISE CAN HELP OVERCOME KEY IMPASSES.**

Today one of the centerpieces of the Austin plant is the production of Spam. On a sizable scale, the ham de-boning machine has impacted our efficiency in manufacturing Spam since 1982. Today, this entire section operates two shifts and there are fewer than twenty people overseeing the whole process at any given time. All the picnic shoulders are boned automatically. The raw materials and finished product are moved entirely with robotized systems. The fully automated cooking chamber is almost seven stories high, and 45,000 cans are in it at all times the plant is in operation. This equipment turns out as many as 440 finished cans a minute. That technology was all developed by us and is unique to Hormel – as with the Spam cooker that was custom built for us by Stork Brothers in Amsterdam.

Nobody else has such automated manufacturing. No one else in the world would have a use for it! Today we have processing plants in China, and we have looked at the economics of producing Spam there. The truth is that we wouldn't be able to match the cost efficiency of the Austin and Fremont operations where Spam is made today.

Another factor is worth mentioning: Automation is still not that widespread, even in rapidly industrializing locations such as China. Since we use such a small number of people to produce such a large amount of product in the case of Spam, it would not be economical to re-create the machinery even in countries where labor is relatively inexpensive. In my opinion, the quest for comparable technology should be a goal throughout U.S. industry whenever we have the opportunity to establish and grow strong product franchises. We underestimate the technological advantages we already enjoy, often making short-sighted comparisons with seemingly inexpensive labor that grows more costly daily and may not be nearly as reliable in its output.

> **CUTTING-EDGE TECHNOLOGY MUST LEAD TO PROFITABLE ADVANTAGES, CONTROLLED WHERE POSSIBLE THROUGH PATENTS SO THAT THE COMPETITIVE EDGE IS SUSTAINED.**

You might expect the words 'technology' or 'technological' to appear often in a book about a robotics firm. One would not expect to find them 187 times in a discussion of Hormel's transition – although that is indeed how frequently they are mentioned in this book. I can't say enough about the importance of technology. But that emphasis can't stand without a counterbalance. Let me cite an example from a totally different industry. James Surowiecki wrote an astute analysis of Toyota's success in a May 2008 issue of the *New Yorker* in which he maintains:

> *... Toyota has long been the auto industry's most profitable and innovative firm... [I]f Toyota doesn't look like an innovative company it's only because our definition of innovation... is far too narrow. Toyota's innovation... [has] focused on process rather than on product, on the factory floor rather than on the showroom.*

Surowiecki goes on to describe Toyota's "incremental process" of innovation driven by "a million new ideas a year" – the majority "from ordinary workers." This disciplined approach to performance and improvement – this "sheer relentlessness" – is "phenomenally difficult to duplicate." A comparable step-at-a-time philosophy was essential to the culture that redefined Hormel as a points-of-difference company. Such a mentality was especially important in innovating and testing technology in the crucial transition from Hormel's old Austin plant to the new facility.

A company can have the best technology in the world – and it should – but don't expect technology alone to put you across the goal line. Technology has to work hand-in-hand with attitude and mindset for the advantage to pay off. This includes a human determination to get every little thing right on a daily basis.

Traditional summer sausage was George A. Hormel's lead product, ultimately sharing top billing with his Canadian bacon. It was the front-running item for the sausage trucks Jay Hormel devised in 1927. And, it became the cornerstone for Hormel's steadily growing dry meats business that today includes Genoa, salami, pepperoni and especially prosciutto. This was an old-fashioned form of sausage processing, some of which required dry-cure smoking and aging. To use many of these products in prepared foods, the casings must be removed. We had to be able to strip the casings off such products as sausages of various lengths automatically without damaging the contents.

Our engineers came up with an automated 'smart' rack system that carried the sausage through all the processing stages. When the sausage exited the oven for the chill room, it would be refrigerated and stripped of its casings on the same rack. This continuous process handled the product just one time. We built specialized plants dedicated solely to dry sausage. When the pepperoni business for pizza exploded, we were ready for it. The late John Furman, then VP of our dry sausage department, and Frank Brown and his engineering staff were largely responsible for originating and developing this concept; but its realization required a close collaboration of engineers with line managers, and it was one of hundreds of technological enhancements our team introduced.

> **IS YOUR BUSINESS ABOUT TO HAVE GREAT GROWTH IN A PARTICULAR CATEGORY? A KEY POINT OF DIFFERENCE WILL BE YOUR ABILITY TO DEVELOP A COST-EFFICIENT OPERATION TO MATCH A SURGE IN DEMAND.**

Specialized processing racks, built by our own engineering department, were also important for keeping hams uniformly shaped. We invented a rack that exerted a downward force on a boned ham. Frank Brown led this initiative with Ken Tribbett doing the design, and Frank recalls: "The meat stayed securely in the rack and the rack shaped the Cure 81 ham. A different rack was designed for the prosciutto ham. Those same racks that shaped the meat were moved into the processing ovens and then into the chillers. We learned the more you minimized handling, the more perfect the product looked at the end of the production process."

> **POINTS OF DIFFERENCE ARE NOT JUST IMPORTANT TO *LAUNCHING* A NEW PRODUCT. THEY ALSO APPLY TO PRODUCING YOUR *BEST* ITEMS BETTER AND MORE EFFICIENTLY.**

# THE QUEST TO BE
# A TECHNOLOGICAL LEADER

In 1988, we received plaudits from *Forbes* Magazine for emerging as the leading *marketing innovator* in the entire food industry. While we're delighted with that recognition, our real point of difference was in becoming the ***technological leader*** through our extensive automated operations. After completing our overhaul of Austin, Ottumwa and several smaller plants; we trimmed $46 million annually in operating expenses large and small – most attributable to cutting-edge technologies and an especially effective workforce. During this important period, our contribution to earnings from productivity improvements actually exceeded the effect of increased sales!

And, you can never stop innovating. During this period, we also developed an unending list of advances solving safety challenges. You can never be satisfied with the plateau you reach. This self-critical step-by-step process has since become a daily regimen and operational creed at Hormel. In manufacturing, technological innovation and new processes define an exciting journey that has to be constantly pursued. As the old adage has it, "The solution to any one problem simply redefines the problem."

My own experience as a football lineman for both Austin High and at the University of Colorado prompts me to echo an observation made countless times about college National Championship and NFL Superbowl victories: Superior competitive points-of-difference are more often anchored in reliable blocking-and-tackling and impeccable discipline than in flamboyant offense. I believe the very same is true for successful businesses . . . and perhaps even more so.

Many of the machines we developed and invented for the new Austin plant emerged between 1969 and 1974 in the old Austin plant. Through tackling one problem after another, the Austin team was making headway against the antiquated facility. In project after project, we realized excellent piecemeal expense savings and trimmed headcount through attrition. The Austin plant booked a profit for four consecutive years – not as much as we would have liked, but a considerable improvement from the past. Hormel's board considered the job our team had done with the old Austin plant to have been exemplary. Yet there was no getting away from the underlying reality of the antiquated facility. While it would have been easy to defer the long-term plant issues because of the numerous short-term improvements with sizable returns, a long-term solution was absolutely imperative.

In 1974, I was named corporate VP of Operations, fortunate to continue my reporting relationship to CEO Jim Holton. Jim gave us endless support to aggressively attack the antiquation and the almost desperate need for change.

Our foremost challenge became: ***What should we do about the Austin plant longer term?*** More and more, the big picture took shape. The industry was handcuffed by outdated plants that were being closed. Were new buildings a certain *miracle cure*? Spanking new plants for firms like Armour weren't profitable either. Why? They failed to address outdated procedures and were ultimately sold. Not only did Hormel need a new flagship facility at Austin, we also required a dramatically different approach to operating it within.

Despite hundreds of corrections, the prognosis for the old Austin plant grew increasingly glum. It suffered from countless cases of clogged arteries. We did a serious study of all the projects we had scheduled or contemplated – the *conservative* cost was projected to be $33-$35 million dollars for basic changes to correct just *some* of the more glaring identified problems, while never dealing with the reality of the central issue.

We agonized over that multi-million-dollar number; but as we sunk our teeth into it, we realized we hadn't yet even fathomed the depth of the bad news. ***What exactly would we get for this investment, knowing that we were certain to exceed the estimate?*** A very iffy payback. I wanted everyone to know we would still have an old plant! The more we studied the problem, the clearer it became: Remodeling would be by far the most *expensive* temporizing measure and a scant long-term solution. Despite the many changes we had made in the old plant, we still had to address the issue of making our product flow more efficient. We had to be relentless in our pursuit of automation. Our long-term future demanded a plant that could support the necessary advanced technologies.

> **IT'S FOOLISH TO INVEST MILLIONS IN MAKING A MANUFACTURING PROCESS MORE EFFICIENT, IF THE OVERALL SYSTEM IS *OBSOLETE*.**

Once we became convinced that a new plant was our only option, we were determined to make it happen. It was time to stop kidding ourselves that a patched-up system would allow us to provide the efficiency and return necessary for the growth of a successful company into the future. It would be a big gamble, but it would be a *bigger* gamble not to invest in an advanced high-tech facility. It would be the turning point for our future. Failure was not an option.

The constant paralysis and substandard performance of the old Austin plant couldn't support the profit formulas for the new products we were developing. A new, technologically advanced plant would address a whole range of cost issues, not just labor, and would also serve a significant psychological and motivational purpose. As a worthy flagship, it would create new benchmarks for an entire plant system. The emphasis on a *system* would increasingly characterize our manufacturing operations.[1]

In 1974, I went before the Hormel board and presented our case for a new plant. It was a daunting experience. Factions among our directors and officers opposed rebuilding in Austin. We had reached a watershed. While we had now improved operations and were slightly profitable, the old plant would never deliver the necessary returns. Relying on it, Hormel, as a company, in my opinion, would fail as the vast majority of our competitors did. The board's challenges were tough; but the directors Jim Holton, former Minnesota Governor Elmer Anderson, Geri Joseph, Woody Berg and Don Grangaard helped the other board members see that a new plant was our only option.[2] Its price tag ultimately exceeded $100 million when we incorporated new technologies that would give us the necessary point-of-difference boost for the future.

From the mid-1970s through mid-1980s, the United States was wrenched by economic turbulence. To appreciate the magnitude of a new

1     *At that time we had 27 plants, but 15 of these were essentially distribution points and were closed in the early 1980s. Today Hormel Foods has 14 manufacturing plants, not including those plants operated within Hormel subsidiaries.*

2     *I recall with pride an incident that happened some years later. The Anti-Defamation League had bestowed its Man of Achievement Award on me, and Minnesota Governor Elmer Anderson appeared in a video for that event. He praised the quality of the recommendation to build the new plant in Austin. At the time of my board presentation, what I remember most was the board's challenges as much as their partnership in the new plant proposal. Their initial skepticism kept me on my toes to prove that the decision to build a new plant was the right one. Fifteen years later on the occasion of the Award, I was flattered when Governor Anderson "praised the boldness of this young man's decision."*

plant's price tag, it's useful to step back for a moment and to examine the economic backdrop surrounding Hormel's transition:

- There were two oil crises, and they had profound economic significance. The first, in 1973, moved the price per barrel from roughly $3 to over $12. The second, in 1979, skyrocketed oil from $14 to nearly $40.

- During the 1980s and 1990s, a thousand savings-and-loan institutions went out of business leading to a $125 billion government bailout. The S&L crisis was largely caused by poor loan policies. S&L's often engaged in high-risk – better said, reckless – lending, and often promoted their loans with premiums like kitchen appliances. When the S&L's went sour, one famous bumper sticker read: "Buy a savings & loan . . . and, get a toaster free!" Sound familiar? In 2008, hapless Fannie Mae and Freddie Mac drifted into the conservatorship of the Federal Housing Finance Agency. Soon afterwards, the overall precariousness of other financial giants was exposed.

- The Federal Funds Rate climbed to its high between 1979 and 1983, reaching a peak of nearly 20% in 1981.

- During the 1970s and 1980s. In addition to the Hormel strike, which will be described later, some other notable stoppages included:
    - 1970    U.S. postal workers
    - 1970    General Motors
    - 1972    Farrah Clothing
    - 1972    Major League Baseball
    - 1975    *Washington Post*
    - 1977    Coors Beer
    - 1977    J.P. Stevens

> – 1981  Air Traffic Controllers
>
> – 1986  TWA Flight Attendants

- Between 1978 and 1982, the Consumer Price Index shot up... at times 7 to 10% per year.

- No single event caused this combination of factors. However, William McChesney Martin left his post as Federal Reserve Chairman in 1970, after serving 5 presidents during 29 years. Martin was famed for his prudence in reining in the economy, knowing when "to take away the punch bowl just as the party gets going." After Martin's departure and for years following, the Fed and several other leadership authorities lacked a similar dedication to restraint.

That $100-million initial price tag for the new plant had awesome implications. If we were to stay in the food business, we needed to invest in product development, in new technology, and in marketing on a massive scale. That meant investment and it meant risk. However, it was not without precedent in Hormel's history. In 1892, when George A. Hormel built his first two-story packinghouse, the business was submerged with debt. After the Panic of 1893 struck, George A. nearly turned over the keys to the business to his banker because the downturn made it impossible for him to meet loan repayments. Fortunately for all of us the banker turned down the offer.

A new plant would commit us to a minimum of $100 million in debt. This was more than three times our net profits between the years 1981 and 1983. In fact, the $100 million estimate proved conservative and our actual debt level at times exceeded $130 million. Our high-risk financial situation and the huge 17% interest rates made it clear we needed to pay off this money as soon as we could. We had borrowed to build the new facilities, replete with advanced technology. If we were to stay in the food business, we needed to invest in product development, in new technology, and in marketing on a massive scale. That meant investment and risk. We had to fund promotion of 134 new products that demanded strong marketing support. We were on our way if we could get the facility built. Without new product successes, the plant investment would have been meaningless.

Every nickel invested in the new plant had to exceed a 40% investment return hurdle rate – a demanding standard in any industry – but particularly so for ours. However, this investment also gave us an imposing edge as other competitors were content simply to remain passive in the face of changing industry dynamics. For us, massive interest rates coincided with huge costs to retire approximately 1,850 employees at generous contract-guaranteed pensions – 1.5 times the normal retirement rate – and other transition expenses. And, we were simultaneously operating both the old and the new plants. During the subsequent years, there were more things to worry about than we wanted to be known. Financial realities such as these were the reason no one in the industry wanted to replace a plant in the same location.

Al Alsaker, who had such sound insights and was a brilliant financial vice president on our management team, came up with a highly innovative investment strategy that helped us significantly in meeting part of the pension obligations and transition costs. It was a true hedge as we invested the first fruits of lower production costs stemming from improved technology. These funds were placed in 10-year Treasury bills at 13.75 to 14.25%, anticipating interest rates would decline, as they indeed did. These tough decisions were central to making our huge transition, and how I wish Al Alsaker – who made these thoughtful contributions while suffering from intensely painful arthritis – was still alive so I could thank him for his insight.

## THE NEW AUSTIN PLANT: CRAFTING A DECISIVE POINT OF DIFFERENCE

The Hormel board's tentative approval to build a new plant brought with it inevitable but sensitive labor relations impacts. It took three years to finalize an agreement with the union in 1978 which offset the severely outdated incentive program, in force for 41 years. The new plant itself didn't open until September 1982, more than three years after the decision was made to build it. The labor relations issues involved were complex and deserve comment.

By the late 1970s and early 1980s, inflation had run rampant. Cost of living adjustments (COLAs) veered out of control as I described in Chapter 2. *In the early 1980s, our Austin plant employees benefited from totally unforeseen COLA increases than from the negotiated annual raises, to the relative tune of approximately one dollar versus 25 cents!*

COLAs were the final blow to many of the old leaders such as Swift, Armour, Wilson, etc. Many of our new competitors – such as Iowa Beef – had no COLA provisions in their labor agreements. We couldn't begin to be competitive with the wage levels we were obliged to pay and live with the results. The work of Hormel's employees was always of high quality, but the productivity level of our payroll investment was increasingly sub-standard when incentive pay was included.

Fortunately our new plant would allow us to counteract some of this slippage. Wages, which, as I have said, were 18% of expenses versus the standard of 11% for our competitors and among the most costly in all industry, were now a far larger part of our production costs. That was one reason why we acquired or built some mid-sized plants in other places. However, what we produced in remote locations still totaled less than half of the output of Austin.

We then went to the Austin workforce and said: 'We'll either have to change these practices and contracts, or we'll need to close much of this plant and invest in facilities elsewhere.' In the *Citizen Hormel* chapter, I elaborate on Hormel's integral relationship with the city of Austin. However, if we had been unable to change labor practices in Austin, it could have meant relocating much of the old Austin plant to another site.[3] Seeking an alternative location for these key labor-intensive aspects of the business was absolutely contrary to our overriding objectives, and we were determined to exhaust every option before that might take place.

In 1978 we negotiated a transition contract agreement that allowed us to isolate COLAs on incentive payments and establish individual employee escrow funds with these monies. These were agreements designed to replace the incentive payments to our employees as we transitioned into the new plant. While the new wages would be higher than the industry's, the question was how would our employees deal with these downward adjustments in their take-home pay? As Dave Larson, retired Vice President of Human Resources, explains it:

> *When the new plant opened, all the employees who transferred from the old plant to the new plant were paid for a straight 40-hour week.*

---

3    *A strategic cornerstone of BMW's and Honda's manufacturing in the United States was building plants outside of Detroit, the traditional American automotive center.*

*As long as the money lasted, funds were taken out of their individual escrow accounts to supplement their wages and to make sure they were earning no less than they had in the old plant. A large number of older people just took their escrow money as a lump sum and opted to retire along with 1.5 times pension benefits.*

The average age of employees in the old Austin plant was 53 years with a norm of 30 years seniority, requiring huge pension accruals that made up most of the nearly $83 million in costs that we had projected if we closed the old plant. We faced this pension liability whether we rebuilt in Austin or moved to a new location. In providing for these pensions, we contributed nearly as much to the pension fund as we made in profits.

We were on a very steep and slippery slope indeed – right on the very edge of the ravine. Our financial performance improved but was relatively flat while running the old plant. Simultaneously investing in the new facility, funding expensive employee exit programs, and incurring the costs of record-breaking interest levels was an awesome task. We were able to modestly exceed our previous years' profit which was miraculous considering all of the one time transaction costs. While our profits were substandard, they were impressive, when compared with the huge and critical transition costs we were experiencing. In retrospect, it was financially one of the most important and critical times in Hormel's history.

## MULTIPLE CHALLENGES BESET
## HORMEL MANAGEMENT IN THE 1980'S

- The traditional meat-packing industry, operating with expensive labor contracts, reels from the impact of new, low-cost competitors.

- The antiquated Austin plant – by far Hormel's largest and most inefficient despite major productivity advances – is crippled by severe logistic inefficiencies and has become perilously uncompetitive.

- An unwarranted nitrosamine health scare severely damages public attitude toward bacon products.

- Labor contracts require the company to pay wage incentives to employees even when productivity gains are realized solely through technological advances.

- Cost of Living Allowance increases mount at a rate 4 times faster than union-negotiated hourly advances.

- Once a decision is made to build a new plant, Hormel is saddled with a debt load varying between $100 and $130 million, often borrowing money at an unprecedented 17% interest rate.

- As part of the transition to the new Austin plant, 1,850 employees retire at 1.5 times the contract-guaranteed pension rate.

- In 1985-1986, a 16-month-long landmark strike at the new Austin plant compels management to operate the plant, threatening to divert both energy and focus.

- Competitive survival necessitates the innovation and aggressive marketing of 134 new products.

One particular impediment in designing the new plant exposed the difficulties of the dotted-line reporting relationship between corporate Marketing and the in-plant Sales departments.

The sales function was needlessly duplicated, and Marketing and Operations were organizationally entangled in a crippling way. We needed to streamline our organizational structure to correct the resulting paralysis. Instead of Marketing focusing on developing new products with plans and promotions to build market share, it was spending time rethinking production design and operational processes. Operations was distracted from its main mission. This had been going on for decades, and many would say our marketing growth was somewhat dormant during this time. This traditional organizational structure – with its seemingly conflicting internal missions – threatened the efficient engineering design of the new plant. While our structure may have been typical for the old meat-processing industry, it also prevented both Marketing and Operations from being properly specialized professional divisions and hindered each from performing optimally.

Dynamic marketing leadership demanded we offer new, well-designed, unique, value-added products that would win national market share. Having separate sales operations in individual plants, reporting to the plants themselves, resulted in an added handicap. Regional thinking impeded the development of a genuine national sales strategy. If such a national plan existed, Operations could dedicate itself to the goal of technological leadership within the industry. Meaningful cooperation between Marketing and Operations would help realize our overall profitability, market share and growth objectives.

Nowhere was Marketing's counterproductive involvement in Operations more evident than in early sketches for the new plant. Bill Hunter explains:

> *In early plans, both raw material sourcing and final production were to become independent operations within Hormel and move to the perimeter of the plant. Their work would no longer flow through the large internal processing rooms. This would have defeated operating efficiency and undercut flexibility to respond to changes in future demand. Streamlining the flow of raw materials and finished products would be impossible. One management group wanted to source raw materials separately, even to the point of boning their own hams from sources outside the company. Another product group also wanted the same independence. Only when the organizational structure was clarified and the team concept prevailed was this design issue straightened out.*

In any company-wide project, look for the organizational impasses which block major improvements to efficiency.

> **ORGANIZATION STRUCTURE CAN CREATE UNANTICIPATED BUT CRIPPLING BOTTLENECKS, ESPECIALLY IN PLANT AND FACILITIES DESIGN.**

During this important period, we reorganized and redefined the functions and structure of our Marketing and Operations Divisions. Underlying these changes was a need for clarity of performance and function. Unified under a single command, a welcomed spirit of teamwork emerged quickly – one that allowed us to focus on achieving genuine, integrated points of difference.

# THE NEW AUSTIN PLANT'S LABOR IMPACT

As we planned the transition to the new plant, it would have been natural to abandon the old plant and invest totally in the operation of the new facility. Sounds simple, but we had to operate both locations to cover our business so our customers experienced a seamless change. It was costly, though necessary. We couldn't afford a lapse. In fact, we needed solid evidence that we were making progress in providing better products and better services. Knowing a unifying figure was needed, we placed Jim Hall, an exemplary team leader, as Executive Vice President in charge of Meat Products and Grocery Products Marketing.

We exploited the transition from old to new plant to best advantage. We used the remaining time we had in the old Austin plant to test many of the new innovations we were including in the new plant. As we transferred operations, plenty of space was freed up for experimentation in the old location. These abandoned sections became an excellent proving ground and incubation chamber. This included the revolutionary flow-through to Market-Ship advances I described in the last chapter. The skinning operation and the picnic ham boners were just two other examples, and there were many more.

# AUTOMATION:
# THE TICKET TO PRODUCTIVITY AND SAFETY

Our Fremont plant was an important influence on the design of the new Austin facility. Jay Hormel had bought an existing beef processing plant in Fremont, Nebraska. Between 1948 and 1950, he then proceeded to build a brand new pork plant adjoining it with flow-through linkage to the older facility. This new plant was a first for us and the first of its kind in the packing industry.

At Fremont, a single-level, open-layout design with 24-26 foot high ceilings resulted in a story-and-a-half of very adaptable operating space. In the pork processing section; there were few columns, creating a large, maximum-flexibility work space – easily adapting to change. The higher ceilings at Fremont allowed us to put product containers and shipping boxes or utilities such as refrigeration, on a mezzanine tier above the floor, and to bring these elements down when needed. Structural steel was out of the question because our constant clean-up and sanitizing would have condemned us to perpetual maintenance and repainting. That entailed a workable pre-stressed concrete construction – not an easy matter in those days.

As its initial and guiding manager, Tommy Thompson, who later became CEO of Hormel, did much to establish the efficiency of the Fremont plant. He was determined to make Fremont a top producer and did so to such an extent that Fremont's performance norms became the company's new productivity standard.

> **YOU CAN DESIGN THE MOST TECHNOLOGICALLY ADVANCED MANUFACTURING PLANT IN THE WORLD, BUT ARCHAIC OPERATING PRACTICES EASILY UNDERMINE TECHNOLOGY.**

Every state-of-the-art technology – including some conceptual innovations first addressed in Fremont – would be employed in the new Austin plant. This facility was to be absolutely unique – the ultimate in the food industry. The new plant incorporated every key consideration in technological design: quality, production flow, processing efficiency, and – most importantly – safety. We involved our people on the line to identify which jobs caused the greatest injuries and disabilities. That input prioritized the equipment design changes we went on to incorporate. The new plant drastically reduced lost-time injuries especially those disabilities related to carpal tunnel syndrome and back.

The result: Today, we have the best safety program on record in our industry, along with being one of the most cost-efficient producers – a combination of two winning points of difference. But these achievements required investments that were risky because such an extensive reliance on advanced technology was untried in the food industry.

A key design consideration: No one was to do heavy lifting in the new plant, and that required increased reliance on bins and pallets – portable platforms used for moving and storing. These pallets carry raw materials and finished products throughout the plant. They are transported using robots or 'bots as our people call them. This equipment transfers products to automatic palletizers throughout the entire day, and pneumatic equipment air-lifts all bags of spices and similar ingredients. 'Bots palletize the finished products and send them to storage and shipping areas automatically. Ultimately the entire grocery and most of the meat product shipping areas in the new plant were robotized. The automation achieved many things. Among them, it allowed us to provide reliable inventory for a far broader range of products with both enhanced safety and great economies.

The new Austin plant was envisioned to be totally computerized: almost one-million-one-hundred-thousand square feet – the size of 23 football fields (and expanded even further to today's size of 1.3 million square feet). We created a huge, first-in-first-out automatic storage and retrieval system, designed to manage 25 million pounds of refrigerated product. A complex information technology system runs the cooler. Huge quantities of fresh, frozen and even fully cooked ingredients are routed semi-automatically to production departments. Finished products are transferred automatically to a shipping complex with a capacity to handle an additional 20 million pounds. There is an equivalent amount in dry storage, and this area is totally **dark**. In other words, no one needs to be there to move and manage the inventory and bring it to the trucks.

Wherever possible, new equipment and systems were first tested in the old Austin plant or in other plants such as Fremont. But, there were also large, unique elements that couldn't be refined in the older facilities. For example, we couldn't test the extensive programs running the new plant's refrigerated storage area in the old plant. Nor could we try the inventory retrieval system out in the old plant, since it relied on a vast network of robotics. As to the new, tailor-made computer system; the consensus was to test each component of it in the new plant one piece at a time. Take it slow, people advised. In addition to testing each system element separately, there was a hesitancy to simulate how it would function at maximum output. Some of us felt differently. We were employing an IBM program that had never performed at the large scale we were to operate. We had to identify potential problems that would only emerge when the system was running at full capacity. Ultimately we decided against the consensus. We were determined to have a dry run in the new plant before we were totally on line. Often it's not until you run a system at its peak that flaws show up.

Sure enough, when fully loaded on a test basis, the IBM program crashed and stopped us in our tracks. The problem would never have emerged if we hadn't run it to full capacity on a trial basis. The breakdown stalled operations in the whole plant for three days. Gary Ray, retired President of Protein Products, recalls:

> *All of our products like bacon and Cure 81 hams were just stuck there. You couldn't override the system and handle the product manually. Until we fixed the programming error, we wouldn't be able to ship the product to our customers. At the time, we had no backup system to prevent this from happening again. For a while, we thought we had made a huge mistake with the design of this very important part of the plant.*

Looking back, it was just an unusual startup situation with very advanced technology. The normal rules didn't apply.

> **TO ENSURE CRIPPLING FLAWS WON'T DISRUPT OPERATIONS AT PEAK PERIODS, INSIST ON TRIAL TESTING AUTOMATED SYSTEMS AT MAXIMUM CAPACITY.**

IBM's top people descended on Austin to solve the problem. Had we not straightened out the system failure in advance, the plant would have *seemed* totally operational. Then, at full capacity, a breakdown could have crippled us for weeks. Whenever I think back of how the retrieval system malfunctioned in our first tests, I am reminded of what happened in 1995 when the new Denver International Airport began operation. Its highly sophisticated, though untested, baggage handling technology experienced a 'nervous breakdown' over its 26 miles of tracks and belts. That systems failure paralyzed early operation of the entire airport and was a graphic further example of how crucial pre-testing is for large-scale automation. This Denver Airport glitch ultimately cost hundreds of millions of dollars. In 2005, ten years after its unveiling, United Airlines – the only carrier to persevere with the system – decided to abandon it.

Ironically, history repeated itself with a simlar malfunction of the baggage handling system in the opening of British Airways Terminal 5 in London's Heathrow Airport in 2008.

Automation is important of course, but I can't stress the human asset enough. Our line people were constantly involved to make sure the technology worked soundly, especially – as I have said – regarding safety improvements.

What's the scale of automated shipping activity in the automatic storage and retrieval system of the Austin plant today? The distribution center component sends out roughly 500 outbound trailers a week – a powerful point of difference in distribution efficiency. And, the shipping is s-m-o-o-t-h!

## AN ENGINEERING CULTURE TAKES SHAPE

One could sense that an identifiable engineering culture was taking shape at Hormel. The specification documents for the new plant rivaled the size of the New York telephone directory. We became the industry standard for specification bidding. If we hadn't, suppliers would have skinned us alive in charging for the demanding quality standards we set for equipment! The precision of our specifications had directly related our ability to control the price of equipment and facilities. Without exact, comparative specifications, we were liable to pay a high price for average or even substandard performance. Also, our technology was becoming a powerful proprietary edge that had to be guarded. We had to be more vigilant about protecting it: Unless tightly controlled, vendors have the habit of talking with their other customers... meaning, of course, our competitors.

Designing the new Austin plant was a gigantic undertaking – both structurally and strategically. Its success would determine the future for both Hormel and the city of Austin, so the stakes were the very highest. Counterparts in the industry chuckled and then quickly predicted that we would fail. "Hormel is making the largest commitment ever to a highly-automated plant, essentially putting the survival of the company on the line," they contended. *Knowlton's Folly* some termed it. Then again, some had called it *Hormel's Folly* when George A. had invested in building his first plant in 1892. Despite the criticism, we were determined our company could not and **would** not fail.

We retrained the people who were still operating the old plant while we brought the new one on line. Certain functions were started in the new plant as others remained in the old. Interim logistics were hair-raising. There were problems we couldn't foresee and model beforehand in a cost-effective way. However, everywhere we could, we tried to avoid system-crippling breakdowns by having component processes up and running beforehand. This caution may have been intuitive. One thing is certain: The added investment proved cost-effective, especially as we were later able to apply these core technologies in other new plants such as our Osceola facility, and our rebuilt pork processing plant in Fremont. This technology also influenced manufacturing sites for completely different categories such as turkey with Jennie-O Turkey Store and DAN'S PRIZE® beef and pork products.

Under the leadership of Frank Brown, then Ken Regner, Larry Pfeil and now under Jim Schroeder; a definite company culture for expertise in engineering has evolved. It remains both efficient and creative today. That culture has demanded as much precision in *using* the equipment as in designing and buying it. For example, the engineer who developed our smokehouse ovens was responsible for going out to make sure they were operated correctly as modified for different locations. He would make monthly inspections in such plants as Austin, Fremont, Beloit, Dallas, and Atlanta. If the local managers weren't operating the equipment properly, he'd be on top of them. If the equipment wasn't working right, local managers would challenge corporate engineering.

When equipment breaks down, often either the proper procedures aren't clearly spelled out or the disciplines to use them aren't enforced. If engineering operates in a way that is isolated from the business, things are more prone to break down in general. Even worse, isolation prevents you from readying the next innovations the business needs. Cross-disciplinary teams – consisting of Research and Development, Marketing, and Accounting – were crucial when we considered anticipating and making these changes. Experience strengthened the credibility and professionalism of our teams, and the team effort ensured our finest results.

> **ENGINEERING INVOLVEMENT WITH DAY-TO-DAY OPERATION OF EQUIPMENT CREATES A KEY POINT OF DIFFERENCE. DISCIPLINED USE OF EQUIPMENT REDUCES DOWN TIME AND PREVENTS COSTLY REPAIRS LATER.**

All of our major plants were contracted, designed, and built by our own Engineering Group. Our Engineering staff designed most of the advanced technological equipment, as I have said, and much of it was patented. Under strict confidentiality controls, we also employed engineering contractors to build new pieces of equipment, most of which were unduplicated in the world. Hormel contracted for Lou Rich, and we even acquired engineering firms such as Algona Engineering. We purchased (and recently sold) the AFECO subsidiary – a top-of-the-line outfit in working with stainless steel and anodized aluminum – to produce much of our proprietary equipment for our new plants. Being in the technology engineering business demanded that we design unique machinery and processes that would make a genuine technological difference.

The Hormel team was encouraged to improvise collaborative arrangements with construction and engineering suppliers. We did so confidently because we were demanding in selecting vendors and spent a lot of time evaluating their quality and skills. And, we learned to **over-spec** machinery – especially the most revolutionary innovations – to guarantee the needed reliability. We would start at the top and then ease off a little bit to get the cost down, consistent with our evaluations.

> **SAVINGS FROM BEING A TECHNOLOGICAL LEADER CAN ENABLE YOU TO INVEST IN MARKETING AND ADDITIONAL NEW TECHNOLOGY.**

Engineering and architecture have always fascinated me. We built a series of new plants, so it's an interest that gave us plenty of opportunity to cultivate innovative ideas. Since the new Austin plant came on line, its impact was great – as I have emphasized – on influencing the design of other facilities.

## THE TECHNOLOGICAL REDO AND HORMEL'S PROFITABILITY

As Hormel's manufacturing operations became more efficient in throughput and flow, our marketing opportunities multiplied. Improved manufacturing technology enabled us to be more innovative at marketing and brand development. We could manufacture derivative products and alternative versions so much more easily.

Technology has revolutionized our profit formula today. The savings that technology enabled us to realize in operations were re-invested in marketing at a scale of millions and allow us to enter ventures into new food categories. In 1980, our marketing budget was $17 million. Starting in the 1980s, we sharply raised our annual marketing investment. Now we spend about $120 million on marketing, especially advertising and promotion to build the continuing array of new products. Because we are so streamlined, today our profit formula is more sensitive to ingredients such as the price of pepper than it is to basic operating expenses.

**TO ESTABLISH YOURSELF AS A MARKETING INNOVATOR, STRIVE FOR TECHNOLOGICAL LEADERSHIP WITH THE MOST COST-EFFICIENT PROCESSES.**

*The Hormel foods Austin plant today –*
*from a technology standpoint, unrivalled as a food processing center*

# POINTS OF DIFFERENCE
## *Creating an Engineering Culture*

- Do you have a clear understanding of how improving your manufacturing technology can benefit your bottom-line?

- Does your organization value technology for what it can enable you to do in other areas of the business?

- When you look at technological solutions, do you see them in isolation . . . or, as part of a total system? Do you measure them for the value they may add to overall manufacturing efficiency, product quality or consumer value?

- Do you look to specialized outside organizations to help provide you with breakthrough solutions? Is your organization crippled by "not-invented-here" thinking?

- Do you test systems to see how they will perform at maximum capacity?

- When a new piece of manufacturing equipment fails, do you examine it to see what you have learned from the time, money and effort invested?

- Is your program of technological investment randomly planned or carefully prioritized to match your fundamental operating needs?

- Do you safeguard the competitive edge of your proprietary manufacturing technologies with patents and security controls?

# Marketing

## THE MICROWAVE AND MORE

Hormel was an aggressive marketing-oriented company almost from the start of its 118 years, but that marketing thrust underwent an important resurgence in the early 1980s. As with many firms, Hormel has had a *multiple* marketing profile. For more than fifty of the early years, the company's business was divided into two principal categories: meat products and shelf-stable goods. Meat products include commodity meats – pork and beef – and such processed items as ham, bacon and sausage. Shelf-stable grocery products include SPAM®, DINTY MOORE® Beef Stew and HORMEL® Chili.

Today, Hormel divides its consumer-product categories into two major product divisions: Grocery Products and Meat Products. "Ethnic" is a sub-area of Grocery Products, and "Deli" is a sub-area of Meat Products. In addition, Hormel offers a broad assortment of items to fast-growing food-service markets such as fast food, restaurants and hotels. Of all these businesses, none grew and changed more radically in the 1980s than products:

- for the consumer's microwave,

- for the rapidly expanding foodservice industry, and

- to satisfy the rapidly increased demand for turkey products.

George A. Hormel – Hormel's founder – lived by the motto, "Originate, don't imitate." He was simultaneously driven by another force. He wanted to add value to the products he sold to improve his profitability. His first great success was in making a top-quality summer sausage. George A. also knew that the most valuable fresh pork cut was the loin. He went on to remove the backbone from this primal and cured the remaining meat. The resulting item had a bacon flavor, but it was much leaner. The product was an instant success when it was introduced in 1895. George A. sold it as "Hormel's Sugar-Cured Pig Back Bacon." Today we know it as Canadian bacon. This product was perhaps the first true illustration of a combined Hormel processing and marketing innovation.

George A.'s son Jay Hormel, more than any other figure in Hormel's past, set the standard for innovative marketing. In 1926, Jay's first management challenge was to develop a process to can a ham which lengthened its preservability. He brought in a European expert to help create the first canned ham in America. The company then targeted the introduction of a 12-ounce canned luncheon meat. Jay guided the development of Spam, which emerged as a product in 1937. That even included overseeing its naming. Spam is an acronym for SPiced hAM.[1]

---

1      *Hormel takes the matter of Spam and its identification with junk e-mail very seriously. Using the word as a description for unsolicited commercial e-mail grew out of a skit on* Monty Python's Flying Circus. *The company accepts that use of the term. (The trade name has also gotten fresh notoriety with the hit Broadway show* Spamalot.*) However, Hormel has a valuable franchise to protect. When someone uses the term in a derogatory way and accompanies it with a picture of the product, that crosses over the line. As does using it in the name of another product not owned by Hormel. Guidelines were arrived at after careful deliberation and can be found at the Spam website: www.spam.com.*

During World War II, comedian Bob Hope used to joke that "Spam was the ham that didn't pass its physical." In 1959, "The popularity of Spam luncheon meat was obvious in the burglary of a store in Monte Vista, Colorado. Thieves who broke into the store 'took only three things – money, tobacco and all the Spam luncheon meat in the store.'"

Spam has played an interesting supporting role in U.S. relations with Russia and the Soviet Union. During World War II, we shipped millions of pounds of a product called *Tushonka* to our Soviet allies. Packed in a 28-oz. Pullman tin, this seasoned Boston butt pork dish had a high tallow content. The Soviets scooped out the tallow and used it as ersatz butter.[2] On their visits to the United States, I personally presented cans of Spam to first Mikhail Gorbachev and later to Boris Yeltsin.

*In World War II, Russians needed dictionaries to reveal what Spam meant.*
*Decades later Boris Yeltsin and his economic leadership*
*marveled at our preservation technology*

2    *A cartoon of the time depicted Soviet soldiers standing next to cartons of Spam, puzzling over a dictionary because they couldn't find the term.*

The Yeltsin exchange was particularly memorable because we also gave him a pigskin jacket. When I presented it to him on the podium, he insisted on reciprocating with his suitcoat. "But, you can't have my pants!" he said slyly. He wouldn't hear of our exchanging coats back at the end of the day. His suitcoat was a rather baggy fit for me, and my sense of diplomacy later compelled me to return it. Before I did, I found the dogtags of two American soldiers who had been missing in Vietnam[3] in a side pocket. Yeltsin had received identifications from two mothers of missing American soldiers while he was in Washington in the hopes that he could help locate further information about their whereabouts.

Yeltsin was excited by the thought of building a meat-processing factory with visions of Spam production in Russia. He asked me what the preservability of our refrigerated grocery-store products was, and I said it ranged from 60 to120 days. He held up three fingers. "Three **days**…" he marveled shaking his head in disbelief, "Our average perishability is three days."

Is Spam a tired brand… a vestige of a bygone era? Rumors of Spam's imminent demise surface with regularity. With the best of intentions, American Can, the chief supplier of Spam metal cans did a study in the early 1980s. They concluded that Spam was not a contemporary product and that it didn't match emerging dietary preferences. Spam would be extinct in ten years, they predicted. I muttered, "Like heck it will," but the study roused us to respond.

Today more than 7 billion cans of Spam of an ever-increasing spectrum of types have been sold. Although Spam is now the subject of

---

3    *Denied until 1991 (the year in which the Soviet Union was dissolved), the admission ultimately came that 3,000 Soviet troops fought against the Americans during the Vietnam War.*

its own museum in Austin, it is hardly extinct! The threat, however, motivated us to update our marketing concepts with such innovations as SPAMBURGER® hamburgers. Spam has even been immortalized on stage in the recent Broadway smash – *Spamalot.*

The economic woes of 2008-2009 have once again galvanized press attention to the perennial appeal of Spam as a popular alternative during downturns. As of mid-2009... and for some time, our Spam operations in Austin and Fremont have been running two shifts, seven days a week to keep up with demand.

Jay Hormel applied similar marketing magic to building such brands as Dinty Moore beef stew and Hormel chili con carne. Jay was also an aggressive promoter using national entertainment celebrities to spotlight Hormel products. He himself characterized the stew and chili as 'poor man's dishes' – aimed straight for the psyche of generations who came of age during the Great Depression and the shortages of World War II. Today these products are more associated with traditional tastes, preferred by people who are tighter on time than they are on money. They are part of our Grocery Products Division and are available in convenient microwaveable versions that are table-ready, often in just 75 seconds.

In the chili area, we acquired the STAGG® brand which increased our presence in the growing West and Southwest-style chili segments of the business. For maturing categories, we have found that improving the packaging is also necessary to keep the product updated, and we are committed to our continued pursuit of superior packaging. For both Stagg and Hormel chili, as examples, we recently experimented with a microwaveable Tetra Recart package. Unfortunately, the package was "prematurely right." Management expert Peter Drucker penned some now famous words when he wrote: "The greatest mistake a trend-spotter can make — and one, alas, almost impossible to prevent or correct — is to be prematurely right."

> **WITH ANY TECHNOLOGICAL MILESTONE, FACTOR ITS ADVANTAGES INTO EXISTING PRODUCTS AS WELL AS THOSE NEW PRODUCTS FOR WHICH THE TECHNOLOGY MAY HAVE BEEN INNOVATED.**

## HORMEL'S MARKETING RESURGENCE

After Jay Hormel's death in 1954, Hormel lapsed into a quiet period of innovation dormancy — with a couple of notable exceptions. As I have mentioned, the company had built a strong repertory of branded items (especially in Grocery Products), and it maintained its enviable quality standards. It would be easy to rest on its laurels and coast, some felt.

Hormel's most notable innovation advance by far was the breakthrough Cure 81 ham in 1962. At the time, the 'whole ham' market was dominated by bone-in hams and canned hams. In the latter case, manufacturers added water to "bulk out" the weight of the ham which was sold on a price-per-pound basis. In 1961, Hormel surveyed a thousand homemakers nation-wide and found that they saw through the practice of adding water to hams and were fed up with it.

Given breakthroughs in pork breeding and in technology, Hormel found it possible to offer the consumer a new and revolutionary type of ham that was far leaner than the market norm. The advertising agency BBD&O was the real innovator on our behalf in developing both the name and the marketing concept of our new Cure 81 ham. As a result, Hormel was able to reap the benefits of offering a superior product concept that remains successful today.

Cure 81 was a milestone in establishing marketing points of difference at Hormel. First, the ham was – as I said – leaner. We took all of the gristle and fat out and eliminated the shank meat. The three major muscles left were pure ham. The product was also boneless, non-water-added, unique in flavor, and registered with its own serial number, so that a ham could be traced if there was any quality issue.

These differentiators were extraordinary at that time. Cure 81 was perhaps the first time we consciously thought about combining multiple *points of difference* in designing and marketing a product. There was nothing like Cure 81 in the marketplace, and the company was desperate for a success story. We had a sales force hungering for any semblance of a winner. Clearly we had one in Cure 81.

In theory, the Cure 81 concept was flawless. The Cure 81 ham's launch proved to be anything but!

In charge of sales in the Hormel Austin plant, it was my job to introduce the Cure 81 to grocery retailers such as Jewel Tea and National Tea in Chicago. These were major customers whom I knew personally. When we cut into the ham at the first product demonstration/presentation, an event attended by this chain's top executives, water ran out all over the CEO's desk.

What an embarrassment! We called Austin immediately and talked first with the plant management explaining the disastrous unveiling of the Cure 81. The word then traveled fast to Hormel's Chairman and CEO Tommy Thompson. He and others were deeply upset as well and literally 'camped out' in the Austin plant for about a week until the quality problem was remedied. The message was clear! Day after day, executives reviewed and cut product, until it met every quality attribute and claim we had established.

Quality standards for new products at Hormel were reborn through this milestone. (Hopefully these standards will never waver again.) From that event forward, Cure 81 and its successors as breakthrough products have distinguished Hormel as a benchmark of highest quality. The incident in Chicago became a quality guidepost governing our new product launches. It was and has proved a valuable reminder for every new product launch since.

> **SHORTCOMINGS IN QUALITY CONTROL ARE NEVER MORE PAINFUL, NOR MORE VISIBLE THAN IN LAUNCHING NEW PRODUCTS. LOG THESE EPISODES IN THE FIRM'S MEMORY.**

My advice to firms generally: When things don't go exactly right at a launch, use the experience as a lesson and reminder throughout the organization of the importance of stringent quality control. Out of adversity comes strength, especially when the setback is vividly remembered.

In launching Cure 81, we didn't have money for institutional advertising to reach consumers, but we were able to get 4-color cooperative advertising support. This backing came from such leading retail chains as Safeway and Giant in Washington D.C., SUPERVALU-Cub and many others. The product and marketing points of difference were so strong that regional chains and large independents backed the Cure 81 program as well. Such retail support for a new product was unprecedented. We ran full-page ads featuring these grocers and were able to purchase those ads at the retailers' advertising rate. This was exactly half of that we would have had to pay if we had bought the identical advertising independently. At the same time, we sold carloads of Cure 81 hams to those same customers. The Cure 81 experience led to a realization: We didn't need an overwhelming advertising budget to launch a product, if the product's points of difference were truly unique and strong enough.

> **VIEW PROMOTIONAL ALLOWANCES AS A FLEXIBLE BUDGET NOT A TRADITION-BOUND GIVEN AS TO HOW THEY MUST BE SPENT.**

Our strides with Cure 81 were not realized overnight. Step by step, we learned how to utilize our marketing leverage and promotional allowances received from retailers more creatively. The Cure 81 experience proved to us that we could get grocery-chain cooperation by offering a product which gave the retail partner a true competitive edge. Cure 81 emerged just about the time retailers began to charge 'slotting fees' for prime product placement within stores. This was a watershed that marked a more adversarial stance between many manufacturers and retailers. However, Hormel has long embraced the view that nothing beats being a creative, anticipatory partner on the retailer's behalf. That attitude will earn a host of tangible benefits as in advertising leverage and powerful intangibles in terms of informal product support by retail management.

As to Cure 81's launch, we maximized the value of every dollar spent to sell product. In the early years of Cure 81, the individual plants, not a centralized Marketing department, were responsible for product sales. None of the plants, including Austin Plant Sales, had much of a formal advertising budget at that time, yet the Austin sales organization was able to sell Cure 81's 20 million of the total company's 30 million pounds through the retail partnerships I've described.

Coupled with the expense reductions, Cure 81 was a crucial factor in the old Austin plant's profit comeback in the mid-1980s. As indicated, this product also renewed Hormel's commitment to finding and exploiting creative, multiple points of marketing difference.

Another memorable lesson came out of the early days of Cure 81. Other competitors tried to duplicate the success of our ham, including a West Coast firm named Bar-S. Pork demand-and-supply pressured the price of premium quality ham to a price above 99 cents a pound in the 1970s. When this happened, our rivals believed that consumers wouldn't accept a price greater than a dollar-a-pound. One by one, competitors chose to add water to their hams and left a little more fat to keep the retail price below a dollar-a-pound. On the other hand, we kept stringent quality standards intact. We let the retail price rise as high as $1.19 and $1.29 and found that the customer was willing to pay for premium quality. Additionally, Cure 81 also represented a breakthrough in disciplining the uniformity of our pricing to retailers, and this too contributed to elevating the regard in which retailers held us. Indeed, our business continued to grow because consumers were responding to the product's multiple points of difference – differences we rigorously and consistently maintained. Sales response was enormous.

In the opinion of retailers, the staying power of Cure 81 to withstand price competition was a landmark and has become a cornerstone of what Hormel stands for today. That sentiment is well captured by Hy-Vee Chairman Emeritus Ron Pearson:

> *Hormel was the first to invent and perfect a quality ham in Cure 81. It gave consumers a high-quality choice for this item versus some very average competition. Hormel has continued to lead the market in value-added products, especially on the quality measure. Because so many products are introduced, price soon becomes the only issue because the quality is absent. Hormel stands out because its product quality supports pricing that's profitable both for itself and the retailer. Hormel's only close competitors in value-added quality are General Mills and Kraft, and these are much larger companies.*

As I have described in Chapter 1, when we first marketed Super Select pork through the old Austin plant in the late 1960s, we applied some of these same marketing principles. Development of superior raw materials gave us points-of-difference advantages in an array of products, including consumer-branded wieners. This sort of differentiation demands close attention to an entire chain of factors, beginning with the raw materials themselves.

Super Select required that we purchase outstanding leaner pork confident that the consumer would willingly pay for the value-added. Even more than having a positive impact on the profitability of the old Austin plant – which it did – introducing this line also had a profound effect on how we were to market fresh meat.

To build brand identification for Super Select pork at retail, we provided Hormel packaging labels to stores using our program. It was yet another way Super Select pork established an innovative point of difference for the new concept of branded consumer-packaging for fresh meat. This attention to detail also delivered us an 8-cents-per-pound premium. The end consumer responded well, but it took years for us to extend labeling to other fresh meat lines. The consumer may have recognized the quality advantages of Super Select faster than we ourselves did. Branded fresh meat seems like such a simple concept today, but the road to this milestone was a long-term evolution.

Following Cure 81's success, the company had a slower period of new product development. It wasn't until the early 1980s that we truly grasped innovation would be essential to our survival. True to our founder's wisdom, the choice was simple: innovate or disappear. Driven by our fight for survival, Hormel's management team members – conservative by nature – were becoming gutsier, entrepreneurial risk-takers in every aspect of our business, especially in manufacturing and new product development. The search for new points of difference in marketing and product development was underway.

High quality, cutting-edge consumer products like Hormel's pre-cooked bacon were hitting the grocer's shelf, the microwave products section was launched, and the Foodservice Group was growing rapidly and gaining acclaim in the marketplace. The Spam brand was returning to a solid growth pattern, and our dry sausage business and our Grocery Product Division were both highly successful.

In an eighteen-month period during 1985-87, we would go on to introduce a total of 134 new products – the highest rate of introduction in the total food industry! Beginning in 1987, we were ranked in the top three major food companies for new product introductions in the industry every year, and that became our reputation. We have earned that distinction from 1986 through the turn of the century and on to today.

> **EVERY COMPANY MUST REALIZE THAT CONTINUOUS INNOVATION ISN'T A CHOICE. IT'S AN INESCAPABLE REQUIREMENT FOR SURVIVAL AND GROWTH.**

Commodity fresh meat typically carries a margin of 1 to 2%. Such margins were simply unsatisfactory for our targeted profit formula. We were determined to move ourselves higher up the 'value ladder.' If you add value and reduce costs, the overall margins can rise to 5% and more. Also, the more you add value, the more you limit your exposure to fluctuations in commodity prices. We wanted to shake ourselves free from being a commodity supplier. Our constant goal was to transform Hormel from being a traditional meatpacker into a diversified, branded food company, offering a broad range of value-added products. In fact, most large grocery product manufacturers today have evolved toward integrated lines of food items.

One of Hormel's most important advantages was developing its Grocery Division early on.[4] At times, we faced tough competition on price, but Jay Hormel had put Hormel into the lead. Our edge was in delivering the taste and quality consumers wanted. This created our present leading market share in such categories as shelf-stable Spam, hash, chili, and

---

4    *Oscar Mayer was once the undisputed king of the sausage makers. Back in the heyday of intra-industry competition, Tommy Thompson, Hormel's CEO at the time, was once quoted to say that he wouldn't trade Hormel's canned goods business for Oscar Mayer's sausage business.*

stew. In recent years, we've taken commanding control of this market and most of our original competitors are now gone. Not only did these items provide earnings stability for the company, they were also a key anchor for our employees' job security. They still make important contributions to profit growth at Hormel. A thoughtful look at our annual reports in recent years will show that Grocery Products continues to be an excellent profit generator especially in a whole new group of fully prepared microwaveable versions.

In 1977, as a reference point, commodity pork amounted to sixty percent of our fresh meat sales, but its contribution to profit was far less… and is even less today. For a hundred years, people incorrectly assumed that the Meat Products Division generated the majority of our profits because it had the largest volume.

For decades, union contracts in retail stores insisted on the right to continue packaging fresh meat at the store level. The arrival of new packaging technology coupled with the quality of our fresh pork have now gained acceptance at the retail customer and consumer level. Fresh meat is making a resurgence, but not as a commodity product. Our mix of products is different today with branded consumer-packaged fresh meat and fully cooked refrigerated meat being significant new category trends.

## LEARNING TO TALK TURKEY

In recent years, we have seen significant breakthroughs in our turkey business, and we are now the largest manufacturer of branded and consumerized turkey products. In many respects, our entry into the turkey business provided us with the opportunity to duplicate the enormous successes we had achieved with Cure 81 hams and other items.

Retailers have come a long way from regarding turkey as a seasonal commodity to recognizing this business as a legitimate continuous category with multiple value-added offerings.

Ron Pearson, Chairman Emeritus of Hy-Vee, remarks:

> *Turkey was once a seasonal product that sold only at Thanksgiving and during the holiday season. Retailers were pretty much out of the turkey business between January and October. Hormel brought the consumer multiple turkey choices in a clearly definable category, emphasizing the health appeals inherent in turkey as well as other pluses. Turkey is now a permanent part of the store – a year-round business just like chicken.*

In turkey products, we now provide the consumer with a range of products and multiple points of difference, including an exceptional degree of ease, convenience, and reliability – all critical value-added traits.

Let me recount some insightful findings about attitudes toward fresh turkey we learned in 2003. When young couples were preparing to host their first Thanksgiving Dinner, we asked them about their foremost expectations and apprehensions, and we learned:

- They were worried that many things could go wrong, and preparation of the turkey was the centerpiece of their fears.
- Thawing a frozen turkey posed problems. If thawed in the fridge, valuable space for other holiday foods was sacrificed. Consumers asked: If thawed in the sink or on the counter, would the kitchen be kept safe and sanitary? When can you be certain that the bird is fully thawed?
- Which recipe is right and how do you guarantee proper seasoning?

- Handling the raw bird, especially the giblets and the neck, was seen as disagreeable.

- If a fresh turkey was opted for over a frozen one, that would mean fighting the crowds in the grocery store during the Tuesday or Wednesday before Thanksgiving.

- With all the disadvantages of starting with a frozen or a fresh turkey, consumers were nonetheless acutely aware of the price differential with between preparing their own turkey and buying a prepared turkey at the deli – 69 cents a pound versus $4 or $5 a pound.

- Relent and buy the pre-cooked turkey at a deli? Even more than the cost was a pervasive feeling of guilt over not having prepared the turkey themselves should a table-ready turkey be bought.

We found these same sentiments repeated time and again. So in the fall of 2004, under the tutelage of Jeff Etttinger, then president of Jennie-O and now the CEO of the company, we came out with a new product: the JENNIE-O TURKEY STORE® OVEN READY™ turkey in a pre-sealed cooking bag. This turkey is cleaned, seasoned, and frozen. All the consumer has to do is to take it out of the freezer, cut six slits in the bag, set the bag in a roasting pan, and cook the turkey for three and a half hours. No handling of the turkey is involved until it is table-ready.

This new turkey product is foolproof and completely self-contained. The retail price: about $2-a-pound. Who gets the credit? Didn't the consumer cook the bird from start to finish?

*The Jennie-O Turkey Store Oven Ready turkey in a pre-sealed cooking bag offers a point of difference that has redefined turkey preparation for many consumers.*

The product's first years have been promising. The reasons why? Excellent quality, convenience and a guarantee of satisfaction are multiple points of difference which are relevant and important to the consumer.

> **CONSUMERS TODAY WANT PRODUCTS WITH *MULTIPLE* POINTS OF DIFFERENCE. THAT INCLUDES RELIABLE QUALITY, FLAVOR, PACKAGING, CONVENIENCE, AND RELATIVE VALUE.**

## VALUE-ADDED BRANDING

By 1990, up to 70% of our products were sold with brand identification. Branding and value-added attributes are ever-growing components of Hormel's product offering today. According to Hormel CEO Jeff Ettinger:

*In 2007, Hormel sold over a billion dollars worth of products that had not been invented or developed prior to the year 2000. The company has come a long way from being a high-quality commodity meat processor. That quality standard has remained intact. Hormel is all about being a branded, value-added food company. **As of year-end 2007, 78% of the products we sold were value-added.** We have been characterized in the financial community as a 'nimble niche player.' We have thrived in niches, in certain platform areas where we are as competitive as anyone. Although we may be $6 billion in size, we more than hold our own against a number of entities which are $10 to $20 billion in size.*

## RESULTS-ORIENTED RESEARCH

In the early 1980s we asked ourselves: How could we best revitalize our innovation program? What were the barriers to developing new products? Naturally, we looked to our Research area. What *were* we researching?

We had three major product groups charged with developing new products, but we were just starting the new product development thrust.

Before 1981, the mission of Research and Development was ninety-percent dedicated to quality-assaying product. Quality control is important. In fact, quality control is extremely important. Food processing is – along with pharmaceuticals, air transportation, and nuclear power – at the forefront of tightly regulated industries in the world. Food quality should be rigorously monitored. . . and our own internal standards are stronger than the government's in many instances. Consumer safety and quality control are crucial when you offer such products as fresh consumer-packaged meat, dry sausage, and shelf-stable items. Assaying quality, however, has little to do with new product development.

I don't believe that researchers should be 'mad scientists' dreaming up new product ideas in an ivory tower laboratory. Instead, they must be a key stimulus and resource promoting innovation in line organizations. In the 1980s, we needed to totally revamp our research and development commitment and concept so that research was truly in the business of new product innovation that adds a genuine value feature.

> **MAKE SURE THAT YOUR 'RESEARCH DEPARTMENT' IS REALLY DOING FORWARD-LOOKING RESEARCH... AND NOT ONLY ROUTINE TESTING AND QUALITY CONTROL.**

## HORMEL'S MISSION: PRODUCT FOCUSED

Recognizing that we wanted to become a cutting edge diversified food company, how would we approach this challenge? For Research and Development's work to be accepted and actionable, line managers in Marketing and Operations had to be the prime initiators. Research needed to be a facilitator, a service for hire. Everyone in the organization has the opportunity to contribute new ideas and ways of looking at the marketplace. For some line people, that required both the willingness and the active desire to take more risks. This demanded a big cultural change. We were asking people, used to being conservative, to think entrepreneurially and to look for multiple points of difference.

It was amazing how quickly our people became actively involved, first under Dr. Forrest Dryden, our recently retired Vice President of Research and Development, who provided leadership for this function from the early 1980s, through the 1990s, and beyond. Forrest was at the helm of this department as we more than doubled the size of our research facilities. Under Dr. Phillip Minerich, the department's head, the size of our initial research operations has continued to grow. Research became the action-oriented innovator of new processes, new products, and marketing-based value-added factors. We also paid special attention to those competitors whom we saw as under-performing with appealing items that were not properly positioned.

> **WELCOME NEW PRODUCT CONCEPTS FROM *ALL* PARTS OF THE COMPANY, BUT ASSIGN PRODUCT MANAGEMENT GROUPS KEY RESPONSIBILITY FOR NEW PRODUCT DEVELOPMENT.**

During our quest to become the leading market innovator in the early 1980s, we established three top priorities:

1) We wanted to create consumer-branded products for our Fresh Meat Division, emphasizing points of difference.
2) We set out to evolve a host of products for the grocery shelf.
3) And we sought to establish a major division dedicated to foodservice.

Meeting those objectives, we had to break down what had become three different 'silos' within the company – the Shelf-Stable Division with its packaged products like Spam, the Meat Products Group which handled the fresh commodity goods, and the processed meats unit responsible for dry sausage and Cure 81. Back then, we included all of our foodservice products sold to restaurant and hotels as a part of the Meat Products Division.[5]

---

5    *When Foodservice celebrated its first year as a billion-dollar business, it  clearly became a major division in its own right, and its recognition as such is strategically warranted.*

# NEW PRODUCT DEVELOPMENT

Eliminating the barriers to achieve these ambitious goals required the use of interdisciplinary teams. The work of the teams was (and is) continually monitored by our top officer group. We established a team for every project. We learned product concept development teams should generally be led by Marketing managers, and ours were. Each team was made up of a marketing leader and included members from Research, Engineering, Production, Quality Control, and Finance. Once the experience of successful team projects is established, people welcome the process. These teams should not be rigidly defined but driven by the special needs of the project. Our top managers would meet regularly with the teams to review products and assess their potential in the marketplace. Research was a central topic at our senior management meetings. At these sessions, I'm proud to say we never looked back at those things that didn't work out – we either corrected them or moved on. We never pointed fingers if a product failed or was prematurely launched into a market that was not ready for it. We concentrated instead on making adjustments and redirecting efforts that the experience taught us.

The process of new product development grew to be commonplace, and the discipline of new-product introduction became smoother, more efficient, and highly successful as a model of step-by-step team coordination. With HORMEL® TOP SHELF™ and a host of other revolutionary products, we learned again and again those Peter Drucker words about being "prematurely right." We accepted that as inevitable.

> **USE CROSS-DISCIPLINARY TEAMS TO REDUCE OVERALL RISK AND TO GIVE THE TEMPO OF CHANGE A COMPELLING RHYTHM.**

If you make research an internal service organization, be prepared for some pretty tough customers. For decades, the 'bacon bits' which many people loved to sprinkle on salads and soups weren't made by us . . .and they weren't made from bacon. They were a soy product flavored to taste like bacon. Sort of.

Bob Patterson, our now retired Marketing vice president of Grocery Products, wouldn't give up. "Why can't we have a shelf-stable bacon topping made out of real bacon?" he kept demanding. The product development staff took on the challenge. Hormel not only has one HORMEL® bacon toppings product today, we have several. And, Nielsen rates us as the leader in the niche – having nudged the once dominant soy imitations to the side. In 2005 we came out with a stand-up resealable pouch for the bacon bits and pieces that replaces the jar altogether. It's shelf-stable until opened. The package has an oxygen-absorbing packet in it which allows the product to be stored in the fridge for six months after opening. Consumers have given this new format's convenience rave reviews.

> **YOUR RANGE OF SUCCESSFUL PRODUCTS IS ONLY LIMITED BY YOUR INABILITY TO ANTICIPATE WHAT CUSTOMERS WANT AND NEED... AND, MOST IMPORTANTLY, BY HOW EFFECTIVELY INNOVATION IS PRESENTED TO THEM IN THE MARKETPLACE.**

Over time, a constant flow of new products established a fresh leadership reputation for us among both retailers and foodservice customers. You enjoy an important psychological edge in the industry when you are recognized as an innovator. As Mike Wright, retired CEO of the huge grocery distribution and retail chain SUPERVALU, put it: "Retailers just love new products. They're the lifeblood of any growing retailer." If you have a reputation for constantly developing successful new entrants, that gives you both a special status and important operating leverage with supermarkets. As I said earlier, Hormel unveiled 134 new products in the eighteen months prior to April 1987. The drumbeat of new products rolling out of Austin captivated industry attention.

In 1987, *Prepared Foods* magazine named Hormel the New Products Company of the Year. This distinction was well earned and was just one of many accolades the company was receiving. The most important recognition happened at the cash register with a sharp growth in profitable sales… and in the new and more respectful way the industry saw us. All of our efforts to transform ourselves into a food company registered excellent results.

We were generating an annual 18% compounded growth rate. That performance gave us further credibility with our retail and foodservice customers that we were rapidly transforming ourselves. Providing retailers new products in every sector was a cornerstone of that transformation and in realizing a genuine points-of-difference advantage.

We took our focus on product so seriously, it shaped every aspect of our mission statement. After grappling with creating a mission statement for many months, we were confident enough to publish it in our 1984 annual report to shareholders. That statement reads: "To be a leader in the food field with highly differentiated quality products that attain optimum share of market while meeting established profit objectives." This statement was intentionally simple, but its three fundamental concepts were also tightly linked:

- ***Highly differentiated*** is the first term, and it is built on unique and meaningful points of difference, and 'value-added.' It forced — and forces — us to examine every process, every package, every marketing concept and every new product idea for meaningful points of difference.

- ***Quality*** is the heritage that George A. Hormel gave us.

- ***Optimum*** does not necessarily mean maximum or #1, but it ***does*** mean being the best in a niche — that is what matters for us.[6] The result: We achieved that mission and surpassed the profitability hurdle in the 1980s and continue to do so today.

That mission statement was a clear, straightforward guide at a time when we had no articulated purpose. The mission was a framework waiting for further evolutionary definition and development. I'm proud to say it served as an effective guiding beacon to both Hormel's growth and to the consistency of its performance. Only recently has Hormel updated its mission statement to build on those principles articulated back in 1984. The key avenues to product innovation remain combining point of difference and value-added. It's easy to dream about points of difference in marketing.

The gap between *wishing* for a difference and *getting* it can be vast. In Beaverton, Oregon, Nike has its fabled "Innovation Kitchen." So do we, and our tasting operation is exactly that. We upgraded our test facilities in important ways during the 1980s, and we have continued to do so.

---

6 *The late John Furman, Vice President of Dry Sausage, contributed the word 'optimum' to our mission statement. I'll elaborate on its significance in a moment.*

In our product development workshops, Hormel can quickly cook up trial batches and experiment with individual containers, explore new processes or other packaging, one at a time. Recently, and for the third time, we have more than doubled the size of our Research and Development building. We also created a display room structured like a supermarket in this facility to help our visiting retail customers visualize the extent of our line. And, we continually expand our kitchen and simulate new supermarket presentations to reflect our growing product assortment.[7]

On any given morning in today's Hormel, we may have six 'cutting sessions' underway. During the development life of any product, these sessions take place relentlessly week after week. They usually last about an hour, sometimes less. Marketing, Production, Engineering, and Research team members all meet. They also examine new packaging and other containers in which the product will be sold. If the product or the label doesn't match design expectations, production is challenged to explain why.

At these sessions, the team may open the container, heat the contents, and taste the product or explore the impact of a packaging change or a flavor attribute.[8] The team leader logs any problem or opportunity that's identified. Then each point is systematically addressed, and a strong emphasis is put on sharply defining points of difference. We put great stock in maintaining a brisk development pace. At any given point in time, a problem must be advanced in a week at most. It doesn't sit there and fester.

Another use of the cutting session is to advance only prudent changes in existing products. As one simple example, in 2005, our quality control

---

7    *I will discuss this display facility – which is called* The Marketplace *– in more detail in Chapter 6.*

8    *As products reach market place potential, company officers frequently attend these cuttings. No food organization will steadfastly resist when the chairman hints a product needs a "tad more salt," but our people steel themselves against 'executive suggestion' better than I have seen elsewhere in the industry!*

people saw a way to reduce the manufacturing costs for one of our dry sausage products. The savings involved were less than a hundred-thousand dollars. Nonetheless, before the modification was made; representatives of the Meat Products, Grocery Products, and Foodservice Divisions met for three consecutive cuttings before a go-ahead was given to make the change.

## OPTIMUM SHARE BEATS BEING #1

Market share is a critical measure of business success, but the concept is fraught with peril. *It is all too easy to emphasize maximum market share as a business target rather than optimum share of market.* As I have said, I contend consumers are only limited by what we offer them; and, if we can envision what consumers will respond to, then the broader marketplace is ours. We use the word optimum rather than #1 because we believe there are niches within a market that are more important than being the overall leader in a mass-market category. We first identify the niche we want to address before pursuing any potential opportunity.

We almost never establish a goal of being #1 in a mass market. That's a meaningless target. For example, our boneless Cure 81 hams are #1 in the niche of non-water-added hams, rather than the massive and less demanding total boneless-ham market which includes all of the water-added products. We want to dominate *selected* niches in the mass market with varying attributes.

What does 'optimum' mean to Hormel? An illustration may help. We have often debated whether we should be in the restaurant business. Other Minnesota food manufacturers like General Mills and Pillsbury (now a part of General Mills) entered, at one time or another, the restaurant business with varying success. We don't own a single restaurant. However, we *are* the #1 producer of pepperoni. We're not the first in pizza, but we're the first in pepperoni. We bring the pepperoni to the party, regardless who's making the pizza. That's a mouthful.

Pepperoni has paid lots of Hormel's bills over the years. What has made HORMEL® pepperoni so desirable? Certainly one factor is that many pepperonis 'cup' when cooked on a pizza, turning each pepperoni slice into a small receptacle filled with melted fat. Because of its leanness and composition, our sliced pepperoni essentially lies appetizingly flat.

> ### STRIVE TO BE OPTIMUM. FOCUS ON BEING #1 IN NICHES RATHER THAN #1 IN A MASS MARKET.

We are the leader in bacon thanks to the determined efforts of a series of fine managers. That we are generally considered #1 in bacon overall today – if you combine our bacon volume in retail and foodservice – is really coincidental. In bacon, 20 years ago, we ranked as #4 or #5, depending on who was doing the rating. So we shifted our focus and asked, how many different niches for bacon are there? Shelf-stable, non-refrigerated, pre-fried, microwaveable and foodservice LAYOUT PACK® bacon are just five . . . and the list is much longer. We also created new niche concepts such as developing technology that would allow bacon to be prepared at home more easily. For example, we even devised a pad in our microwave packaging that reduced cleanup time for the bacon preparer at home.

Once we identified key niches, we aimed at being the leading brand in those where we could excel profitably. Collectively, if the niches add up, then you're #1 in the category. That's even more golden![9]

As I have mentioned, today we rank nationally as being #1 or #2 in 34 different product categories! As a result, fully 79% of Hormel's sales come from

---

9    *I'll have more to say about bacon in the context of foodservice later.*

higher margin, name-brand products. Niche management enabled those achievements. We have found this tightly focused targeting consistently superior to a shotgun approach. Being #1 across the board carries huge business and psychological baggage, and you have to pay for it. You end up defending a status symbol rather than preserving a meaningful opportunity to be profitable.

Being #1 can prove costly. For years, Sears was #1 in the general-merchandise retail industry. Then Walmart came along. The byways of competition are loaded with #1s which have been transformed or ousted by competition: General Motors, Ford, Montgomery Ward, A&P, and Bell Labs . . . to name just a few more of a long list in business history.

## THE MICROWAVE:
## A HORIZON GREATER THAN THE FREEZER

No doubt, the home freezer had a substantial impact on how people stocked up on food, especially fresh meat. Another technology – the microwave – was to have an even greater impact on how consumers prepared food. More than any other innovation, it helped craft our marketing philosophies on risk, innovation, and differentiation.

In 1947, Percy Lebaron Spencer, a Raytheon engineer in defense technology, was simplifying the magnetron – an essential microwave element used to transmit radar signals. One day, Spencer noticed that his magnetron melted a chocolate bar sitting in his pocket. Raytheon saw the possibilities and acquired Amana – the refrigerator manufacturer – to use it as a launching pad for manufacturing microwave ovens. Raytheon's consumer version was unveiled in 1967 and was called the *Radarange*. For nearly two decades, the microwave oven remained space-age technology. Then, within years, these new ovens created a cultural explosion.

When we first looked at microwaves in 1981, fewer than 25% of households had them, and their primary purpose was to boil water. Now, well over 90% have a microwave, if not two or more. You can buy a standard-priced unit today for $50, and this technological journey isn't over yet. Geri Joseph, a retired director of Hormel Foods and a keen observer of consumer trends, gives us high marks for spotting the significance of the microwave. "Early on, Hormel saw the importance of many more women being in the working world outside the home…" she says, "and the impact this would have on food preparation." The microwave has provided an excellent opportunity to build niches which were apparent fairly early.

*The demanding marketing challenge is managing identified niches to the point of sustained profitability and optimum market share.* Sustained niche dominance goes well beyond niche identification and requires vigilant refinement of points of difference as the niches mature. The development of products that are truly flavorful, economical and superior in quality has required intense effort and dedication. *Dogged persistence is a hallmark of Hormel's competitive style.*

Some say that the microwave will influence merchandising food products as much as the freezer did. In fact, I think the influence of the microwave will be far *more* profound. It's quite possible that the heyday of the freezer has peaked, while the full potential of the microwave is unrealized.

Looking back, General Foods experimented with frozen dinners in the 1930s, and Swanson and Stouffer's launched frozen dinner lines after World War II. We created our own Frozen Foods Division in 1987 and were proud of the frozen products we offered. Frozen food is, nonetheless, a competitive battleground that has been tainted by a past of many sub-standard quality offerings. Some manufacturers offer products that are frankly short on value. You can't short-change the consumer for long. That's not all. You can easily and even fatally damage the category. That makes it difficult to re-attract a wary consumer when shortcomings are corrected.

Operating expense is another pivotal issue. As energy costs continue to climb, retailers will become more and more excited about shelf stable options: Using room temperature shelf-space to merchandise product is a whole lot cheaper than operating a freezer cabinet. If the retailer tries to reflect those freezer costs in his margins, he may well encounter price resistance from consumers. In the home, energy is saved again since the room-temperature product only takes a couple of minutes or less to heat. Many microwaveable products of all sorts still don't measure up to the quality of either the homemade or foodservice level you find in hotels or restaurants, but our new microwaveable entrées are now quickly matching those standards.

In 1988, *Forbes* magazine dubbed me 'Mister Microwave.' It's a flattering distinction and much grander than justified, but the magazine surely knew where my head was, and it was our whole team that got us to our formidable position in microwaveable products. I told *Forbes* in 1988, "I swallowed hard for a company this size and spent $1.1 million for two pieces of equipment to do the research [on microwave applications.] We were betting. Strategically, we wanted to tap the microwave market, and we knew we had to be bold." Since you can't heat a metal can in the microwave, it was the microwave that spurred us to develop new shelf-stable products that could be packaged and prepared in non-metal containers. Selfishly we were protecting our brands like Hormel Chili, Dinty Moore Beef Stew and guaranteeing the opportunity to add many others.

When we first explored bacon for the microwave, the chief challenge was to develop a packaging container that could simulate broiling. In 1984, Broiled & Browned sausage, Hormel's first microwave-modified product was introduced. In 1987, Top Shelf microwaveable shelf-stable entrées emerged. As Jim Hall, our now retired Executive Vice President for Meat Products and Prepared Foods, likes to put it, "We've been interested in packaging technology since Jay Hormel came out with the first canned ham."

The concept of putting entrées into a microwaveable container was similar to creating an '*unfrozen* frozen' entrée. When we introduced Top Shelf technology, we developed the first commercial plastic retortable[10] container sold in the country. Top Shelf was the first unfrozen, shelf-stable entrée designed for the microwave. I want to focus on Top Shelf because that line is no longer around while the concept has gone on to flourish. Our experience with this brand offers a series of lessons about: Hormel, incremental change, the management of risk, and perseverance.

# POINTS-OF-DIFFERENCE
## *Innovation and Risk Management*

We spent a lot of money on research and advertising in launching this product. We introduced Top Shelf items with products that were higher end and used former talk-show host Dick Cavett as our spokesperson. He was very credible to discerning consumers in assuring them that the product was safe and that the quality was high. The items included lemon fillet of cod and fiesta chicken with rice. We expected white-collar workers would carry these items to work in their briefcases and heat them up

---

10      As the food industry uses the term, **retorted** means fully cooked before it appears on the grocer's shelf. The product inside is sterile – free from harmful organisms.

in the office microwave. Our reasoning: This could be a quick, easy meal for them. The product concept didn't match the consumer's expectation. We learned this targeted market was neither ready nor willing to try shelf-stable meals. This consumer was more likely to take out from a fast-food restaurant or to order in take-out.

Our choice of product name was also flawed. Retailers displayed the product on the top shelf – out of 'eye reach' – which caused customers to miss it entirely. Out of sight, out of mind. Top Shelf also set a level of consumer expectation that was too high. It was good, but not gourmet. Most importantly, consumers were simply not ready for Top Shelf… no matter how much education we would have realistically been prepared to include. Consumers were suspicious of shelf-stable products because of poor quality experiences with box-packaged items marketed by other brands.

We were "prematurely right" again. We've stubbed our toe in this way before, but I'm glad that we did stay with it. While consumers weren't ready for shelf-stable Top Shelf when it appeared, they were fully receptive to our later shelf-stable Hormel product line when it was introduced.[11]

From a technological standpoint, Top Shelf was a considerable challenge. But it was a very important stepping stone for us that ultimately led us to success. With Top Shelf, the consumer was buying packaging that may have seemed simple, but it rivaled the technological ingenuity of our new Austin plant. At one time, homes and restaurants were pretty simply equipped with can openers, refrigerator-freezers, and ranges. Since the emergence

---

11    *We made the same sort of 'mistake' when we came up with* Famous Foods of the World – *a line of different ethnic products introduced in the 1960s. Its price-value relationship needed sharpening, and credibility for the consumer required that ethnic foods be part of separate lines. Now Hormel enjoys an ever-growing share of the burgeoning ethnic food market in a host of classifications.*

of the microwave, we must now provide the consumer with containers that use highly sophisticated technology. The trick is this: to deliver 'child's play' usability often requires very advanced engineering.

KID'S KITCHEN®, the children's version of Top Shelf was a tough challenge in itself because we all know that kids are choosier eaters than adults. Kid's Kitchen has stuck around to this very day, and it's been a durable performer. When we began the Top Shelf line, we were at the forefront of the industry in microwave packaging. Over time, we have gotten better and better. We spent more money researching Top Shelf than we did any other marketing initiative in the company's history. Top Shelf contributed to the speed with which we later developed microwave products. It was expensive and frustrating. That's reality. It takes a lot of time to develop a superior concept, but our experience gave us the conviction that it paid off to persevere.

Is Top Shelf still around? Yes and no. The line was first renamed as DINTY MOORE AMERICAN CLASSICS® and Hormel research showed our chances were better with blue-collar households with two wage earners. In 1991-1992, we moved toward more standard items like beef stew, chili, chicken with rice, and chicken with noodles. Until the beginning of 2004, the product was presented in a sealed paperboard box, like a typical frozen food box, but presented unrefrigerated on the grocer's shelf. As technology advanced further, we were able to change the package from a square tray with a multi-layer aluminum lid to an oval bowl with a plastic lid, eliminating the box altogether.

All the consumer had to do was to poke three holes in the lid. Renaming the product HORMEL® COMPLEATS™, also emphasized that it was ready to heat. Larry Vorpahl, then Vice President of Marketing for

Grocery Products and now Group Vice President for Consumer Products Sales, was instrumental in shepherding many of these cutting-edge changes. He explains:

*When consumers looked at American Classics, they really didn't have confidence or know what was in there: Was it a mix? . . . Or, a dried product to which they needed to add something? We sharpened the cover graphics and — most importantly — developed a paperboard sleeve that slipped over the bowl. That visibility reinforced this was a pre-made product. We also put the item under the Hormel brand directly, which we found had a much stronger, more contemporary position in consumers' minds. At first we didn't change any of the formulas or recipes for the products inside.*

1987          1992          2004

2007          2009

*History of HORMEL® Microwave Trays*

Sales were up 82% in 2005! And, that strength continues in 2009. Responding to the product line's rapid growth, we have announced the construction of an entirely new plant in Dubuque, Iowa dedicated to Compleats. We already have several plants making Compleats today. It will be five once the Dubuque plant opens in late 2009. The line is on its way to becoming the finest food success in a long time. We are expanding the Compleats line with enticing new offerings like Sesame Chicken and Beef Steak & Peppers.

Failure is a necessary investment in learning. Product and packaging 'failures' often prove to be the stepping stones to ultimate success. The key point is that it took nearly twenty years to fine-tune the format until it matched the exact need the consumer wanted filled. It all started with Top Shelf and Peter Drucker's caution about being "prematurely right."

How many products today are successful with similar journeys in their history?

Dr. Forrest Dryden recalls:

> *Without Top Shelf packaging, we wouldn't have begun developing the tray or how to put an easy-open lid on such a product. We wouldn't have been grappling with how to eliminate any trace of spore contamination in this shelf-stable product. These steps led in turn to the micro-cup, which has been so important to products like Kid's Kitchen. Top Shelf was a necessary and immensely valuable 'failure' for us. It's a classic in marketing evolution. We would never own such a substantial share of the kids' microwave entrée market had it not been for the Top Shelf technology as a first step.*

> ### HISTORY MAY SAY A NEW IDEA WAS A FAILURE. BUT THAT 'FAILURE' MIGHT BE THE BREAKTHROUGH THAT ACTUALLY TRIGGERS THE NEXT MAJOR STEP – POTENTIALLY CREATING THE INDUSTRY LEADER.

The Compleats line has proved to be a colossal hit, but such success is not the norm. Hormel CEO Jeff Ettinger says:

> *There is a reason why singles are easier to hit than home runs. The further you push the envelope with innovation, the harder it may be for consumers to accept it, because they don't quite have a frame of reference for it. Top Shelf was once way ahead of its time. The consumers have caught up to it now.*

Jeff continues to challenge the Hormel team to advance the powerful, hard-won marketing advantage enjoyed by Compleats today through a relentless drive for innovative packaging and assortment options.

We paid a price for offering consumers this superior packaging early. However, the downstream gain was far greater because today we enjoy the success of occupying a leadership position in high quality.

As I said, the technology component of what consumers are buying in microwaveable items today is substantially greater than it was twenty years ago. In developing new products, we now look at packaging technology as carefully as we consider product content options. Packaging, as I have commented, is one of the best ways to introduce innovation to mature product categories. And, innovation can mean subtracting unwanted product traits as well as adding desirable ones. Unsuccessful packaging had been the central obstacle to realizing Compleats' great success, and it is quite likely that all of the other potential advances in this product have yet to be realized.

> TODAY CONSUMERS 'READ' THE PACKAGE FAR BEYOND PRINTED MESSAGES. PACKAGE DESIGN HAS TO COMMUNICATE A PRODUCT'S USE AND CONVENIENCE.

In 2006, Hormel once again moved ahead of the curve on a product concept that required us to immerse ourselves in new processes and technology. It is a radically innovative approach to lunchmeat preservation. We now offer a line of all-natural, sliced lunchmeat preserved with what we call high-pressure processing, utilizing 87,000 pounds of water pressure per-square-inch to extend the shelf life of the product by eliminating spoilage bacteria.[12] This creates a very safe product and also allows for a post-package activation process with no preservatives. We market it in our Foodservice Division under the trade name TRUETASTE™. In consumer product applications, this preservative technology first appeared as NATURAL CHOICE® branded lunchmeat. This procedure certainly won't be restricted only to lunchmeat in the future. The names emphasize that the product tastes like its primary ingredients, free of the effects of additives and preservatives. In the grocery store, we market these packaged lunchmeats as both natural and "no preservative" products. By the way, after

---

12    *The attentive reader will have noted in Chapter 3 that Hormel abandoned "high-pressure water extraction" of bones from pork shoulder because it "diluted and purged the proteins out of the product." TrueTaste and Natural Choice products are pasteurized after the product is packaged using high-pressure water. The meat product itself is never in contact with water.*

opening, these lunchmeats will last as long as or longer than their preserva-tive-treated counterparts, because the high-pressure processing creates such a high purity level on initial packaging. This process is creating an entirely new product category in the supermarket. Natural Choice products soared from just over $20 million sales to $55 million in sales in 2007.

Jim Schroeder, our current Vice President of Engineering, has stressed that the new high pressure technology as developed at Hormel has dual design benefits: safety for the consumer in the meat products it creates . . . and safety for our employees in harnessing a technology that is both delicate and highly demanding in the magnitudes of pressure it requires.

The payoff in product innovation has been well worth the investment. During the period of 1982-1991, 93% of Hormel's incremental volume came from value-added products. In 1988, as I have said, *Forbes* – among the most discerning of business publications – recognized us as the lead-ing food innovator, not just in meat, but in all of food. *Forbes* was just one of the leading business publications praising the creative achievements of our management. ***Furthermore, Hormel has focused on maintaining an optimum mix of new and established products.***

When innovation became an industry watchword, too many companies were led astray by developing 'novelty' entries which vanished from the shelves almost as quickly as they appeared. In 2002, Alan Elliott wrote in *Investor's Business Daily*: "Hormel has a long track record of brand survival. Almost 70% of its products were developed more than six years ago. Two-thirds of them hit the shelves in the 1980s or earlier. Its number of new products, those less than five years old, has increased about 5% a year.

They now make up a third of the total mix. 'No one in the food industry has worked harder at getting the product mix improvement than Hormel, [former Prudential Securities analyst John] McMillin said. 'It's the most compelling part of the [Hormel] story.'"

The commitment to new product sales remains a high corporate priority for Hormel. In the year 2000, the company announced its intention to generate $1 billion in sales from new products launched in this decade, beginning fiscal year 2000 and ending fiscal year 2009.

By the end of fiscal year 2007, Hormel Foods reported total sales of $6.19 billion with more than $1 billion generated from new product sales. This goal was achieved two years earlier than anticipated. The most successful new products included HORMEL party trays, HORMEL Natural Choice pre-sliced deli meats, HORMEL Compleats microwave meals, and Jennie-O oven ready items. Reaching this milestone, the company announced an even more aggressive goal of achieving $2 billion in total sales of products created since 2000 by the year 2012.

> **CREATE AN OPTIMUM BALANCE OF NEW AND EXISTING ITEMS AND SEEK OUT WAYS TO OFFER CURRENT PRODUCTS IN MEANINGFUL, INNOVATIVE FORMATS.**

Creative diversity can also be a powerful defensive strategy. A 2007 Credit Suisse investment report on Hormel zeroed in on the turkey business. It called attention to our conviction that offering "value-added" turkey items was one way of insulating our margins from fluctuations in commodity prices. In 2008, the investment firm PiperJaffray praised our "diverse product offering" as an edge in combating "cost inflation."

Successful marketers in our company say: **Look for niches! Look for points-of-difference!** But, don't do it by chance or speculation. It's easy for people to develop big egos and to think of themselves as geniuses dreaming up products. That's not our angle. Instead, we systematically review every grocery and refrigerated category for either strengths or opportunities. Our premise: Teamwork and collaboration create a bigger and sounder pool of ideas. Teamwork also reduces the risk of individuals going forward without the necessary input of their colleagues. The team leader is responsible for creating a workable vision that motivates the team's members. Then, it's his or her job to challenge colleagues: "If you think there is a market for this product, what exactly will make it a winner?" It's this kind of pursuit which helped build our dominant positions in the salsa and microwave product categories and many others.

> ## MARKETING INNOVATION DEMANDS
> ## SUCCESSFUL RISK MANAGEMENT.

Whatever approach you take to marketing, you won't come up with very many homeruns like Spam. And, we understand that we won't be successful with every one of our ventures. You have to be able to afford some failure or to readjust along the way. Nothing gets people in an organization to take intelligent risks more than when the CEO personally signs on to a project. During my first years as CEO, as noted earlier, I signed on to *every* project. As time passed, our management team understood we were personally committed to the "working pattern" that was established. This encouraged everyone to search for new products, processes, new concepts and just as important, new technologies. ***This quest for innovation would become a hallmark of our culture and a sought-after trait in every employee.***

Developing new products should reward intelligent risk-taking. Product development should not be regarded as the occasional goldstrike among a series of kamikaze missions. How do you guard against excessive risk? The total background of the team is an important safeguard. The experience 'safety net' is crucial. When you have only so much capital, you carefully choose those products you launch.

We've had product lines that have failed. Catfish, for example, is an outstanding, lean source of protein, and it's tasty, too. We once tried to introduce farm-cultivated fresh catfish as an attractively packaged item to be used much like tuna. The catfish recipe concepts scored well on market tests, and the nutrition arguments for catfish were convincing. The barrier: Consumers only really like catfish deep-fried. So much for the compelling nutritional argument for catfish in the first place! Additionally, the catfish industry also suffered from serious price-fixing problems, making it difficult to compete in other respects. Catfish was a failed venture for us, and we exited the business.

As I said, we entered turkey in 1986, when this was largely a commodity business. Now it's more than a billion-dollar-a-year product line for us, and we dominate the branded turkey category. Turkey fulfilled every market goal we had in mind, including developing turkey as a consumer-branded product. Still, it has taken two decades of constantly and systematically searching for opportunity that has allowed us to develop a premium turkey breast stuffed with cheese and rice… or, fresh ground turkey with appetizing color and the right consistency. We built the turkey business steadily, and we were able to do so because we had ready and ample management talent to grow it aggressively after we acquired Jennie-O and later The Turkey Store. Turkey is the most efficient feed-to-meat animal protein, and we knew we had great potential if we could convert the commodity business we bought into a true value-added category.

Failure, although abhorred, may be a necessary investment. An unsuccessful product can point you in the right direction to a very big success. A point I have made, but one worth repeating: ***We identify the failure of a concept, but we never identify failure with an individual… provided that person is working with intelligence and commitment.*** Of course, we may find that a team member might fit better elsewhere in the organization. Ask me the name of the person responsible for our last big failure, and I won't recall it. Not if the person who took the risk is diligent and dedicated. I define risk as being on the slippery slope. When you're standing on the edge of one, you don't see it as a risk. Moving ahead is just something you have to do. One thing about being on the edge, it gives you an excellent view of the entire landscape.

It isn't the case that highly successful firms ***don't*** occasionally fail in reaching goals. It ***is*** the case that firms with staying power know ***how*** to fail and then to persevere in a constructive way.

> **DE-STIGMATIZE FAILURE. THINK SUCCESS.**
> **ESTABLISH AN ENVIRONMENT THAT IS BOTH**
> **RISK- AND CHANGE-FRIENDLY, AND REMAIN**
> **POSITIVE WHEN SETBACKS HAPPEN.**

One of the failings of the meatpacking industry – as I pointed out with Rath – was that the firms stayed with a traditional line of products, and almost all of them had the *same* product lines. They offered little points-of-difference – just the same cuts of hams, bacon, sausage, etc. We decided to retain these core products along with our pantry products, but to **CONTEMPORIZE** them. We continue to do so today. And, we'll continue to transform these products with advances in technology, packaging and new concepts.

## SEARCH OUT INNOVATIVE, RELIABLE PARTNERS

The impulse toward making a big innovative splash prompts firms to do things solely on their own. How do you overcome the initial investment hurdle that's usually needed? Reliable partners can accelerate a firm's capacity to innovate. Incurring the total investment for a bold new strategic change isn't just expensive. It's unnecessary and unwise. When possible, we have favored partnering with our suppliers in developing programs such as new packaging. To reach a particular result, the total amount of money spent by us and our suppliers is probably the same, but it's not solely *our* money, and we have containers in the market place to show for it. Some of our competitors have invested fortunes with no clear result. If we think there's a place for a certain sort of tray or cup, we'll approach a supplier. We arrive at terms that give them an attractive opportunity downstream. We pledge to do our best to perfect the product that will go into the container; but, at times, the supplier will have to share in the development costs.

> **INTELLIGENTLY SHARE DEVELOPMENTAL EXPENSES WITH SUPPLIERS LIKELY TO BENEFIT FROM YOUR MARKETING PROWESS AND SCOPE.**

In recent years, one of Hormel's great achievements has been the pre-cooked shelf-stable line – now called Hormel Compleats – I cited earlier in discussing Top Shelf as an example of being "prematurely right." I raise it again, because of the multiple points of difference involved:

1) the significance of packaging technology in adding value and quality for the consumer,
2) the essential role of partnership in working with suppliers,
3) how consumers evaluate quality and price in purchasing value-added products, and
4) consumer readiness to accept packaging innovation.

We're not that brilliant, and – as I noted – the consumer is not always ready for revolutionary change. Product innovation is a stepwise process and relies as much on consumer comfort with the concept as on technological rightness. As you think through the incremental development of a product, you must constantly assess the product from a key vantage point: How will the consumer regard this change? Points of difference – as I have stressed – need to be valuable and relevant to the consumer, or they are not points of difference that are *consequential.*

> **A TRUE INNOVATOR RISKS BEING "PREMATURELY RIGHT." FOR THE BEST ODDS OF HAVING *BOTH* THE RIGHT ANSWER AND THE RIGHT TIMING, TRY TO THINK LIKE A CONSUMER.**

## A BAG FULL OF SURPRISES

Nearly a quarter century ago, we started on the road to Hormel refrigerated entrées. They are today a 17-18 ounce refrigerated, multi-serving line of microwaveable meals. These pre-marinated entrées are table-ready in mere minutes. In an important way, it was one consequence of our Foodservice program which I will describe later in more detail.

At our Dubuque operation in 1985, Hormel launched the highly imaginative concept of pre-marination to achieve superior tenderness in pork products for its Foodservice division. Rather than being a systematic corporate program, this breakthrough was really an instinctive sense on the part of Jim Cole and his colleagues that convinced us we could do something innovative to tenderize pork naturally. It took time to effectively combine this with the feature of precooking and to expand this combined concept out of Foodservice and into the retail realm. The concept enabled consumers to serve highly desirable items like pot roast and meat loaf at home. Hormel's innovation was a major achievement. Prepared products of this sort were tainted by a disappointing reputation in the eyes of consumers, and our new offerings truly met the flavor standard of the best in home cooking.

In the early 1990s, an outside resource, Concept Foods, saw so-called 'comfort foods' like pot roast and meat loaf staging a comeback in restaurants. Then our people engaged Concept Foods to help develop this trend's retail potential.

People wanted to serve such entrées at home, but they didn't want to **prepare** them at home. The analysis was summed up this way: Microwaveable and frozen beef products had a reheated flavor and looked unappetizing. The industry regarded the cooked product as a way to use up poorer quality beef. Manufacturers loaded up the product with soy and grain fillers, and this was clearly not Mom's cooking. The challenge was to create an authentic lean product without a reheated flavor.

This was a case of a foodservice concept for restaurants and hotels that ultimately made its way to the consumer's kitchen. In 1993, Concept Foods set out to make pre-cooked meat in a bag for the home. They had already prepared millions of pounds of roast beef and pot roast in bags and sold their products to restaurants. It was enormously successful, and consumers recognized the quality.

It took considerable effort to perfect a cooking film container for home use. The obstacle was **not** in perfecting the product inside, but in developing the bag in which it would be both sold and cooked. During extensive study of consumer behavior, other important findings emerged. First, consumers didn't want to dirty a pan (or pans) cooking the product. In addition to the cooking pouch, that meant a disposable cooking tray was also a must for the consumer package. Second, while customers wanted 'comfort food' like grandma used to make, they wouldn't tolerate the **perception** of fat.

Then came the pricing component. Initially we expected consumers would compare packages of different weights, and products would be priced by size. For example, customers would expect beef roast to cost more than meat loaf. Not so. Both retailers and customers wanted a range of options including beef, pork, and chicken in uniformly sized servings, comparably priced with each other. This was a stunning sea change.

The end consumer – recognizing the added-value of skilled preparation, rigorous quality control and uniform product options – was now ready to buy refrigerator-case meats as they once purchased canned goods off the shelf![13]

---

13    *I'll have more to say about the impact of 'exact weight' fresh meat in the chapter on working with retail customers. Not only has this been an operational benefit for them, but it has simplified their marketing in offering "two-for-one" bargains and pricing promotions across multiple lines.*

*Hormel fully prepared entrées in microwaveable containers have been a wonderful success story and represent the effective application of a meaningful point of difference in foodservice to meal prepapation at home.*

The Hormel Marketing Group successfully brought the refrigerated entrée line to market under the Hormel brand. Within three weeks of rolling out the product, same store sales doubled! Word-of-mouth customer endorsements were spectacular. We ultimately bought and absorbed Concept Foods. Most recently, our newest line of refrigerator containers of roast beef, pork, turkey, and meat loaf have been achieving great success.

> **EMPHASIZE THOSE VALUES AND ATTRIBUTES IMPORTANT TO YOUR INTERMEDIARY CUSTOMERS (E.G., RETAILERS) AS WELL AS YOUR ULTIMATE CONSUMERS.**

*Ethnic Mexican food is of ever-growing significance to the American market.*
*An important point of difference has been Hormel Foods' ability to address this*
*opportunity market with mainstream product lines such as Chi-Chi's and*
*the more specialized products offered in the Herdez line.*

The list of Hormel's marketing triumphs is enviable. I could discuss how we recognized the importance of salsa back in the 1980s – it now outranks ketchup as America's leading condiment – and how we became one of the top three marketers of branded salsa in the United States.[14] Indeed, we have expanded our entire Mexican line – with brands like HERDEZ® and CHI-CHI'S® – to satisfy both the native ethnic customer as well as the general consumer's taste. And, I could cite how our expansion in other ethnic foods has brought us a new line of Asian products. We have also undertaken a major initiative in meeting the special needs of the aging consumer with products from our Hormel Health Labs line that combine flavor and food satisfaction while meeting strict dietary guidelines.

---

14 *In my opinion, salsa is a business that Heinz should have owned from the start. With their pre-eminence in processing tomatoes for condiments, they could have made salsa in their sleep. Marno McDermott, Jr., the founder of Chi-Chi's, is a 1956 graduate of Austin High School. His mother was the union business manager for the P-9 local union at Hormel. McDermott had the vision to found the Chi-Chi's Mexican restaurant chain in 1975 with former Green Bay Packers football player Max McGee. Along the way, Hormel bought the rights to market salsa under the Chi-Chi's name as a grocery product.*

The specifics are significant, but equally important are the principles behind the marketing initiatives we have undertaken. They have worked for Hormel and may not work for all businesses. Still, try them on for size and see if they might have a place in your company. Let me repeat just a few of the most important ones.

# POINTS-OF-DIFFERENCE MARKETING

- Consumers are only limited by a marketer's inability to envision what customers will respond to positively. If you have the vision, the marketplace is yours.

- If you restrict your marketing input to history as captured by conventional market research, history is likely to be the limit of what you can expect to achieve.

- The challenge is to *anticipate* the consumer of the future without being premature. If you are premature, keep working and looking for changes while the consumer learns and absorbs the points of difference you have incorporated.

- Major market breakthroughs rarely happen overnight. They demand step-by-step perseverance and aggressive work to match exactly what the consumer wants.

- Points of difference leading to added value are what distinguish a strong brand from a run-of-the-mill offering or routine private label products. A forward-looking organization will identify true points of difference to provide 'value-added' in everything it does, and especially in product development and marketing. Points of difference, if correctly managed, translate to profitability.

- Choose to establish optimum market position, rather than being #1. The niches within a market are absolutely essential. Identify the niche or niches you want to command before pursuing a potential opportunity.

- Don't look to the Research department to come up with new marketing ideas. Research should be a service for hire and a catalyst for fresh ideas. There are no restrictions as to where new product ideas come from in a vibrant company. However, product innovations are generally the responsibility of line managers in Marketing and Operations.

- Every product must be highly differentiated from its competitors. If it can't bring a *meaningful* point of difference, then don't waste your time on it.

- A fifth or sixth ranked brand can only be salvaged by injecting a highly revolutionary differentiator. Otherwise, trying to maintain such a low-ranking position will be both frustrating and financially unrewarding.

- Proprietary advanced technology not only improves operating efficiency and impacts costs, it can also enable marketing innovations in products that are beyond the reach of your competitors.

- Don't expect instant success with every venture. The price of development should factor in readjustments along the way. Either correct quickly or move right on by. Remember, a flawed product or concept can be a milestone to a significant innovation.

- If you want to have people take intelligent risks and work hard to make them succeed, the CEO should personally sign on to new projects – especially if change-friendly culture is not firmly seated in the organization. Once this risk-taking mindset is established, the CEO's signature on each project may no longer be necessary; but top management can never stop cultivating this risk-taking attitude.

- Identify the failings of a concept, but never emphasize personal failure.

- Define risk as being on the edge of a slippery slope. When you're standing on the edge of one, you don't see it as a risk. Moving ahead is just something you have to do to survive. And, while you are on the edge, realize it can offer a priceless vantage point to the entire marketplace. Be sure to use it.

# Redefining the Workforce

I n 1985-1986 – now nearly a quarter-century ago – Hormel experienced the worst labor disruption in its history, a strike at the huge new Austin plant. This is a strike Hormel didn't want. . . a strike our employees' own International Union didn't want . . . and, one that should never have happened. We had no choice but to take the strike. We couldn't have met the union local's demands and still be in business today. When it was clear that a strike was inevitable, we were determined that we would be ready to run our business and that we would deploy our management expertise to match the demands of the situation. Technically the strike was mounted by P-9, the Austin Local of the United Food and Commercial Workers (UFCW).

## BUT, WAS IT REALLY?

The Local 9's leadership immediately before and during the strike was elected to office in a low-turnout vote in December 1983. Except for one other location that was quickly sold, the union chapters representing all other Hormel plants announced they would not support the strike and did so months before it began. In fact, they signed agreements for the top wage and benefit contract in the industry, and they remained true to their agreement. The same terms were offered the employees in Austin, but they were rejected. In December 1985, midway through the strike, a federal mediator proposed a compromise contract to the local chapter which was voted down twice.

Finally, after a year of striking, the international union ***ordered*** an end to the strike and the union boycott of Hormel. When the Local ignored the order, the UFCW placed the Local in trusteeship in July 1986 and removed its management. A new four-year contract with the Austin local was signed the following month. I believe the heads of the P-9 Local during the strike figured management would never risk Hormel's newly established leadership status in the food industry by submitting to a strike, especially a long one. However, we also knew the inevitable economic consequences of their demands, and we had no choice. The opinion of Lewie Anderson, Vice President of the UFCW International, was: It was "the wrong target at the wrong time."

## SO, WHY DID THE STRIKE HAPPEN IN THE FIRST PLACE?

In a moment, I'll describe our view of the specifics of the Austin labor dispute. One must first understand what was going on with organized labor in general at the time. In the 1980s, the U.S. labor movement was slowly deteriorating and losing membership. This trend was especially pronounced in the meat processing sector. Iowa Beef Processors (IBP) and others were  operating at levels below the wage-and-benefit programs in effect at such majors as Swift, Armour and Wilson. Hormel was to become a 'test case' for the future.

In the mid-1980s, and in retrospect, Minnesota was hardly the place to launch a counter-attack. The Minnesota mining industry had collapsed, and the state's economy was reeling as many manufacturing firms were exiting the state as well. More and more college grads – as I noted earlier – were attracted by the high wages of jobs on the line at Hormel. Against these odds and despite our ranking and reputation as the top wage-payer in the industry, the leaders of P-9 were intent on winning national acclaim by making an example of Hormel. The local Hormel confrontation was selected to showcase Labor's envisioned turnaround in a major way. Consequently, Austin became a pivotal combat zone.

The strike has been deemed by experts as the foremost labor confrontation of the last half-century. As the healthiest firm *in* and the emerging leader *of* an industry, albeit a dying one, we were the one targeted to bend or break. The Local union's strategy assumed we would never take a strike, and therefore the Local believed it would be able to negotiate a contract that would receive national attention.

Earlier I detailed the 1978 agreement which allowed us to remove incentives from the plant wage agreement. Our resolutions with P-9 that had paved the way for the building of the new plant had eliminated an onerous and outdated incentive compensation system. Jim Holton, my predecessor as CEO, put it succinctly in 1978:

*Our situation had eroded over time to the point where the wages of our people – those not at machine-controlled operations – averaged 87 percent above the top rates in the industry. Unfortunately, the company was not getting anything like 87 percent more production.*

The only way to justify building a new plant was to eliminate the flawed incentive system, which had become a constant focal point of strife and contention.

> **REASSESS INCENTIVE SYSTEMS. DO THEY SERVE THEIR INTENDED PURPOSE TODAY? OFTEN INCENTIVES BECOME DISINCENTIVES, ESPECIALLY WHEN THEY DON'T REFLECT THE IMPACT OF NEW TECHNOLOGIES AND PROCESSES.**

We broke ground for the new Austin facility in June 1979. Our plan was to trim the old Austin facility's in-plant numbers from 2,950 to 1,150 as a starting size for the new plant. This would be a significant reduction, and only the most advanced technology could make it possible to meaningfully increase production volume. Our bold plan called for no layoffs, and one-and-a-half times normal pension for those over fifty years of age and with more than thirty years of service, if they opted for early retirement. This was an aggressive and costly program to say the least but it was necessary to establish an efficient, new cost base. (Simultaneously we incurred the expense of building the new plant and buying our way out of the onerous incentive system at a time when the cost of money was astronomical and while we were ambitiously developing new products. This three-year stretch was to be demanding to say the least, and the fact that the plan was realized without a hitch remains a particular point of pride in Hormel even today!)

Many new firms in the industry had no pension plans whatever. Some old companies just walked away from their pension commitments and closed their doors. The new 'low-cost' processors in the beef and pork industries paid such modest wages that few employees stayed beyond five years. For these firms, therefore, extensive funding for pensions wasn't necessary. Our employees usually stayed with Hormel their entire careers.

Operating without any significant pension burden gave these low-wage competitors the additional cost advantage of modest or non-existent pension programs along with minimum health and welfare benefits. With low labor costs and minimal fringes, the outcome would be obvious. The new competitors would doubtless next target the pork industry after transforming beef. Concessions had reduced the starting hourly wage from $10.69 for Swift, Armour, and Wilson to $8.00 and $8.50 for Oscar Mayer (which had already eliminated its pork slaughter operations). But even those levels were now pricey, vying with the $6.50 per hour base of the new rapidly growing, low cost competitors such as IBP, ConAgra or Cargill. A wholesale retrenchment in hourly wages was now an indisputable fact of life in the meat-processing industry.

After considerable negotiation for a long-term contract, much planning, and other essential groundwork; our new Austin plant – the company's and allegedly the world's largest in food processing – began production in May 1982. The 8-year transition contract that had been signed in 1978 guaranteed the union could not change the contract or stage a strike in our new Austin plant until September 13, 1985, three years after the facility had been opened. During the transition from the old plant to the new one, we combined the two facilities on the same profit-and-loss statement. Running parts of both the old and new plants simultaneously caused excessive but unavoidable costs. In the first three months of joint operations, Austin lost more than $11 million and ran profitably only a single week. Even with careful advance testing and painstaking preparation, new technology was costly to implement, particularly while we had to run the old plant at the same time. The biggest factor though was the one-time costs associated with the very human resource expenses we were attempting to control. If this investment failed, all the things we were trying to do would have fallen like dominos. Such changes are an interrelated series, not isolated events.

I knew if the Austin plant didn't succeed, my career was finished. So was the city of Austin. Keeping these worries out of mind took a firm resolve and determination. Meanwhile the enormous competitive meltdown in meatpacking was taking place. Nonetheless, we continued to focus on becoming a leader in the broader food field.

## AUSTIN: BOLTING FROM SISTER PLANTS AND THE INTERNATIONAL UNION

In 1984, employees at our Austin plant were making a base wage of $10.69 an hour (with skilled rates up to $14.50) with an agreed upon escrow account that brought them to their higher wage levels when they had been paid incentives in the past. This had been an increase from $4.00 in about 1950 which shows how exponentially our labor cost had soared.

Our labor expenses were in the same league as the auto industry, as I have noted. We told our union employees company-wide to expect a wage reduction, although we assured them they would continue to be the best paid workers in the industry. The next step was to align base wages themselves above the new norms that prevailed in meat processing. Our industry was collapsing – the leaders, Swift, Armour, Wilson, etc. – were failing despite receiving wage concessions ranging from a starting wage of $8.00 to $8.25. Oscar Mayer was also challenged, paying an even higher starting wage of $8.50. Hormel's relationship with the Austin union local was beginning to unravel. Local union leadership was determined to gain all of the old wages and benefits back at a time when the rest of the industry was going down.

## A HUMAN PERSPECTIVE

My own family had been involved in the pork industry for some time. Both of my grandfathers were livestock dealers, and one of my dad's brothers was a buyer in this specialty as well. My father was a union member and worked in the livestock scaling (weighing) part of the Hormel business. Especially in the fall of the year, I remember him going back to work after dinner and after having already put in a full day beginning at 6 AM. Every other Sunday, he would also do full-day shifts, and I remember him taking me along to watch him weighing the hogs. He did this to earn $11 to $12 a week. With seven children, my dad was desperate for work and considered himself lucky to have a job. Believe me, at a tender age, I understood the reasoning of unions. It helped fuel my determination to work for a company committed to paying the best wages.

Often as CEO, I would wake up in the middle of the night from an uneasy sleep and ask myself: What are the fairest and the best terms we could afford to offer to our employees? I awoke one morning with my mind settled that a basic wage of $9.00 moving up to $10.00 one year later would satisfy the employees in all of our plants, including Austin. We also stated an intention to return to a base rate of $10.69 as soon as we could. This wage package would be well above the industry norm. Despite its fairness, I also recognized that I would take considerable ridicule and pressure from my industry peer group of CEOs whose firms were trying – unsuccessfully – to survive while paying $8.00-$8.50 in base wages. Hormel was the last company in the industry to address the wage problem by offering what the UFCW international union heralded as the most favorable contract in the industry. Unlike other key firms in the sector, Hormel made only minor cutbacks in its benefit package. Employees in the six other major Hormel plants understood what was happening in the industry and accepted our proposal of $9/$10. The seventh, P-9 – the Austin union Local of the United Food and Commercial Workers – nixed the offer.

According to Hormel's retired Vice President of Human Resources Dave Larson:

> *Many of the younger line employees who moved over to the new plant had been with Hormel for ten or even twenty years. They were still earning supplements that the company had established to assure them an adjustment period which would allow them to keep their old plant salaries until the funds would run out several years later when they ultimately struck. But some of them came to regret that the escrow money would eventually run out, even though they would still have the best contract in the industry. The fact that we were forced to lower the base wage in 1984 added to their concerns. They felt that they would be working for less than they had been earning ten years earlier. They went to the union and said, 'We're going to change this thing back. The company is spending more than $100 million on the new plant. Once the contract is up in 1985, we're going to tell them we want all our old programs back. If you don't give it to us, we'll strike. Your new Taj*

*Mahal will sit there completely idle unless you make the concessions.'*

The Austin Local's rejection of the $9/$10 wage package had an ironic side-effect: The only contract we had in-force at Austin **demanded** Hormel offer the average of the Big Three producers' starting wage. At the time, the Big Three (Swift, Armour and Wilson) along with Oscar Mayer were paying a "reduced" starting wage as low as $8.00 with Oscar Mayer at $8.50. We didn't want to cut back wages below the $9.00 level, but we were contractually **bound** to match the pay scales of our competitors and to reduce the base wage in the Austin plant to $8.25. Had we implemented the $9.00 rate already in place with the new contract in our other plants, P-9 could have paradoxically charged us with an unfair labor practice. We may have been bound, but the reaction was predictable. The leadership of the Austin Local used our tied hands to incite the workforce even more. The P-9 Local voted to strike and delivered its notice of the intention to start the stoppage on August 16, 1985.

Because the Austin plant became the center where dissident Labor was going to stage its turnaround in America, the city was transformed into a mecca attracting Labor forces from across the nation. Austin became an adopted home to splinter Labor factions in other industries. These groups were based in San Francisco, Pittsburgh, Philadelphia, Detroit, St. Paul, and elsewhere.

Who were the key players leading the maverick P-9 Local? Jim Guyette had wrested leadership of the Local from John Anker by a margin of 351-312 in what I characterized earlier as a low-membership voter turnout. Only about a third of those eligible participated in the election. It would prove to be a fateful vote, for it would create the circumstances for the one time in history in which our Austin workforce would reject the contract offered by Hormel. Jim Guyette was a born-and-raised Austin native who had worked at Hormel, but he was part of the new group described earlier by Dave Larson.

To say the least, Jim Guyette was an unconventional bargaining partner. Seasoned negotiators knew you never dealt with more than one issue at a time. In the view of our negotiating team, he tended to throw all of the issues on the table at once – a tangle that would be impossible to resolve. Some analysts said that it was his private agenda to bring us to our knees so he could start a new union movement. Further he was openly defiant of his own international union.

Jim Guyette was not the only adversary we had to face. Guyette had enlisted the services of an outside labor organizer from New York named Ray Rogers, who headed an outfit called Corporate Campaign. Even more than Guyette, Rogers was to influence P-9's strategy and tone. Ray Rogers was a Massachusetts-born union organizer who grew up in a blue-collar family. From 1976 to 1980, he led a campaign against textile giant J.P. Stevens, made legendary in the box-office hit film *Norma Rae*. Over history, many strike campaigns had been waged trying to get people to stop buying products made by strike-targeted firms. These tactics usually fizzled.

The lynchpin of Rogers' strategy was to go after financial firms associated with the company that was the actual strike target. For J.P. Stevens, that meant attacking Manufacturers Hanover Bank and – **especially** – Metropolitan Life Insurance, which was J.P. Stevens' leading lender. Rogers succeeded. Ray Rogers waged his campaigns through hyping national media attention. In our case, he targeted the First Bank System since First

Bank's CEO DeWalt Ankeny sat on the Hormel board. That may have been the strategy, but Hormel was no J. P. Stevens. We were providing the top wages and fringes in our industry; and, as I have said, this standard was especially important for me. I knew the only way we could preserve our ability to be the top wage payer rested on the cost efficiency of our standing as technological leader.

Hormel and its Austin union local had managed to avoid significant union strife for so long partly because the company generally capitulated. An outsider like Ray Rogers was a new variable added to the equation. Rogers had made a name for himself, and he was no stranger to capitalism. His initial analysis of the Hormel situation cost the union local $40,000. If the union won the contemplated strike, Corporate Campaign would get an additional sizeable bonus. Our calculations projected that Rogers' firm would earn $340,000, more than my annual compensation. With Rogers in the picture, we knew that this would be a 'death lock' since both his bonus and his reputation were at stake. At the same time, it appeared Guyette thought he was going to score a victory for a newly defined concept of unionism. Rogers' methods were – others have speculated – going to be Guyette's springboard to defining a new union tactic and concept.

Ray Rogers' organizational slogan proclaimed: ***Tools to confront power with power***. In addition to J.P. Stevens, Rogers had also crossed swords with Browne & Sharpe, International Paper, and New York Air. He was a heady orator and assured people that Hormel wouldn't take a strike, which proved a serious miscalculation. When the vote to strike was cast, he at first predicted there would be no strike . . . and then, if there were a strike, that it would only last two weeks.

Corporate Campaign was a new type of adversary. They knew if they could break the solidarity and confidence of the Hormel management team, they would get their way. They had never lost a battle before. Just after we heard that Rogers was entering the equation, I got an expert view of him from Arne Weber. Arne is a brilliant economist whom Secretary of Labor George Shultz brought into the first Nixon cabinet as his Assistant Secretary. Arne backgrounded me on where Rogers had been and his general approach.[1]

In October 1984, Ray Rogers debuted before his new clientele in Austin in a barn-burner of a two-and-a-half-hour speech.[2] Some observers believed that Rogers and Guyette were out to cripple and even destroy Hormel if it became necessary. This wasn't healthy bargaining in the tradition of a free-market economy. A plan had been crafted to create a new sort of social system, in which the union, as they conceived it, would have a free hand in distributing company assets, no matter whether it was employees or technology which had enhanced the firm's asset pool. Rogers outlined a multi-point program to bring Hormel to its knees. Unquestionably Rogers was presenting a new perspective to our Austin employees. Rogers was also appealing to their emotions. And, he painted what some saw as an enticing vision. To its great credit, the international union tried hard to convince the Austin Local that they were turning down the industry's best contract. Lewie Anderson, VP of the UFCW International, openly debated Guyette; but it was to no avail.

What were the Austin Local P-9's counter-demands?

- A base pay of $12.50 an hour (versus the prevailing industry stan-

---

1        *I had known Arne when he was President of my alma mater, the University of Colorado. Later in his career, he became President of Northwestern University, retiring as Chancellor of that distinguished institution.*

2        *It is an interesting twist of history that Ray Rogers' Austin speech took place in the auditorium of Austin's High School – known today as the Richard L. Knowlton Auditorium.*

dard of $8.00-8.50 with some low-cost operators paying a base as low as $6.50),

- reinstatement of incentives that had been abolished in the new plant agreement,
- a return to an already union-conceded cost-of-living adjustment, and,
- a wellness-pay bonus of 10% a week for all employees who showed up for work.

The reinstatement of a flawed incentive program alone would have destroyed us. In addition, the strategists – Jim Guyette and Ray Rogers – wanted the option to slow down production to 50% of the standard work pace at any time and an absolutely unrestricted right to strike. And, it didn't stop there. They also demanded the right to carry this contract to every Hormel plant anywhere in the world.

The Local's leadership wanted to keep its members in the dark about the inescapable economic realities of its demands as well as the industry. Dave Hage and Paul Klauda, referenced earlier, exposed the glaring flaws in the logic. If the company gave in on all of their demands, calculations were that Hormel would be broke in 1.5 years. The stakes were the very survival of the company.

We had done our own math and determined we had two choices,

1) sell the new Austin plant as we did with the facility at Ottumwa, with the probability that one of the new low labor-cost companies would be a successful bidder, or
2) sell part of the plant, retaining only the consumer-products portion.

Neither of those alternatives were acceptable to me, and they were never seriously entertained. We decided to hold firm, resolved to be ever more committed to our technological leadership in the industry. Step by step, we were learning just how important technological leadership would be to the strategic future of our company.

## HORMEL'S 1985 ANNUAL MEETING IN ATLANTA

My most memorable confrontation with Guyette and Rogers took place during Hormel's annual shareholder meeting in Atlanta, Georgia in January 1985. At the meeting, Ray Rogers himself aimed a question at me and, with typical bite, commented that the employees might be asking for *too little*. I had taken a pay cut in my annual income to $339,000 – considerably less than my position and salary were pegged to merit competitively. (In this era, it was the practice for Hormel CEOs to set their own salary and bonus.) Hormel's board of directors had taken me to task for *refusing* to increase my compensation because of its already low position in the industry. If I implemented this cut, the board contended, I would compress the salaries of those below me. They feared we would start losing key people.[3] An outside study confirmed their view, revealing that our top managers were being compensated in the bottom quartile of the industry at the time, yet we were the only ones achieving growth. Despite performing at the top of the industry, my salary was 67% below the norm and actually below the rumored total package of $340,000 that Rogers and Corporate Campaign stood to be paid from waging a successful strike at Hormel. I intended to maintain that differential.

At the annual meeting, I announced that Hormel would raise its share-

---

3    *In fact, none did leave. Although the outside directors were highly perceptive, they couldn't anticipate the strong loyalty that existed within this team.*

holder dividend for the 26th consecutive year following another record results in sales and profits. Ray Rogers challenged the dividend increase as unconscionable. The dividend was still only about 2.5% of the stock's value. Interest rates were running 10.5%, and we had paid interest as high as 17% in building the new plant. I remember posing a counter-question to them, asking Ray Rogers if he would take the large sum that his firm was being paid out of the Local union treasury and put it in the bank to earn 2.5% in interest?

"Would you be willing to bank the value of all Hormel's assets at 2.5%?" I queried, "If you would, that's what the dividend you find so unacceptable would earn." The point about unconscionable dividends was dropped.

## LABOR STRIFE: MARKETING POINTS-OF-DIFFERENCE JEOPARDIZED

There are important lessons in the sad events of this labor disruption related to a company seeking and displaying points of difference. Despite all the positive consequences for competitiveness and survival, **being different** also singles you out for attention. If you are going to reverse the fortunes of a firm in a dying industry, you have no choice but to rapidly accept changing some of the guidelines for the sake of the firm's survival. Indeed your competitive counterpart firms may already be doing so. If **you** don't – and you may even risk doing so too late – **you** are likely to join them in extinction.

***Being resolute in the pursuit of being stronger can – paradoxically – make you more vulnerable on certain issues.*** At Hormel, for example, we were a party to agreements that presumed we would always operate in prosperous times. It's fair to say that we had continued to make money. However, it was not enough to cover the reinvestment needed to maintain or to increase market share. And, an economic downturn could have easily placed us in jeopardy.

> **THERE IS AN INEVITABLE DOWNSIDE OF INNOVATING POINTS OF DIFFERENCE. IT CAN MAKE YOU THE TARGET FOR COMPETITORS WHO CAN'T OR WON'T KEEP UP WITH THE PACE OF WAGES, FRINGES AND OVERALL COSTS.**

As I have emphasized, Hormel's reenergized management team had become gutsier, entrepreneurial risk-takers in every aspect of our business, especially in manufacturing technology and new product development. Our high-quality, cutting-edge consumer products like pre-cooked bacon were hitting the grocer's shelf, the microwave products section was launched, and the Foodservice Division was gaining powerful momentum. The Spam brand was returning to a solid growth pattern. Hormel's Cure 81 ham program, our dry sausage business, and the Grocery Product Divisions were all highly successful.

We ranked in the top three for new product introductions in the total food industry every year from 1986 on. We were well on our way to winning the game through streamlining every phase of production and marketing of these new products while fast becoming the recognized industry leader. Through creating points of difference, Hormel was hitting on all cylinders while our competitors were failing and going out of business.

Before the strike began and for the second year in a row, *The Wall*

*Street Transcript* named Hormel as the best managed company in the meat and poultry industries – later known as the meat, poultry and commodity food processing industries. Was there ever a better time to step back and feel good about our progress? *The Wall Street Transcript* awarded our gold medals for several reasons, including our commitment to a program of plant replacement and modernization. "Management embarked upon an ambitious capital improvement program targeted at achieving superior operating efficiencies with a state of the art processing plant in Austin, Minnesota," the *Transcript* wrote. We had taken a genuine leadership position in the food industry – eliminating commodity product lines and outmoded labor practices. We dealt with the industry's radically new cost structure through superior technology. At a critical time, we were being recognized as an innovator of new products and processes. Now, the threat of labor strife at Hormel could well diminish our momentum.

Guyette and Rogers didn't accept this reasoning. They refused to believe that the company would be bankrupt in short order if we accepted unchanged the Local's demands I have outlined above. Their position, as we interpreted it, could be described this way:

*We read your annual report. You make money every year. You're just being greedy. Why don't we just keep going the way we've been. If you lose money, then let's talk about it.*

Their demands struck us as very unreasonable. Our counter was:

*The auto-maker Chrysler tried that very same routine. The Carter Administration and Congress finally had to come in and bail Chrysler out of disaster in 1979 with $1.5 billion in loan guarantees.*

*Chrysler would not exist today if the government hadn't done so.*[4]

We couldn't go to the edge of the same ravine, because we knew the government wouldn't bail us out. We would be gone like Swift, Armour, Wilson, Morrell and a number of others. Could we head this off in advance? We simply had to. More than employees' jobs or Hormel's future was at stake. We were talking about the fate of entire communities. Beyond Austin, there were all of those fine employees at Fremont and other Hormel plants who were complying with their newly signed contracts.

## YEAREND 1985

On October 26, 1985, we decided to operate as much of the Austin plant as we could with two-hundred Hormel supervisors and managers, one-eighth of the regular workforce size. We eliminated the pork slaughter operations. Our output in Austin was primarily shelf-stable products such as Spam, Cure 81 and other items that were produced in a highly mechanized manner. In the third quarter of 1985, because of the remarkable efforts of the Austin management team, and our outside plants, company sales rose 7% and profits bounced back. We ran this business five months without a lost-time injury to management people working on the line.

We learned that we could eliminate certain operations, particularly commodity lines at Austin and also learned that items historically produced in Austin could be made equally well in other plants. We have paid very close attention to maintaining this flexibility ever since.

---

4     *In 1998, the global powerhouse Daimler-Benz snapped up Chrysler in what they thought would be a coup. In 2007, they dumped the business, ruing their initial decision.*

There were numerous industry offers to buy the plant as well. Naturally many competitors would have loved to have had a plant with so much innovative technology and processes. It would have been unthinkable to hand over such decisive, hard-won points of difference to a competitor.

> **STRIKES ARE NEVER DESIRABLE. BUT WHEN THEY OCCUR, THEY FORCE MANAGEMENT TO ANALYZE ALTERNATIVES AS TO WHERE PRODUCTS CAN BEST BE PRODUCED.**

By November 1985, three months into the strike, most of Corporate Campaign's attention and allegations were directed toward me. Chuck Nyberg, our corporate counsel, head of communications and human resources, played a decisive role in our overall strategy during the strike. Chuck came to me and said, "Dick, you have been the lightning rod, and we have to get you out of that position. I should take on the role of the spokesman for the company." When I considered we had a total business to run, such a change was the right thing to do. Actually, we had *three* lightning rods: Chuck, Dave Larson and Deryl Arnold, who had taken over the reins of managing the Austin plant. Each of these executives made a contribution of considerable importance that paved the way for Hormel's future today. Deryl was also one of the most trusted and finest friends I've ever had. We were childhood pals. When I grew up in Crane Addition, he lived in Dutchtown – neighborhoods immediately adjacent to the old Austin plant. [5]

---

5    *Deryl passed away from cancer two years after the strike – a great loss to all of us.*

> **IN A CRISIS , IT'S KEY FOR A CEO TO FOCUS ON RUNNING THE BUSINESS AND TO HAVE A TEAM TO HELP ABSORB THE BRUNT OF PRESSURE CAUSED BY THE CRISIS ITSELF.**

When it was clear the contract negotiations with P-9 were at an impasse, I declared Hormel would be non-reactionary to the Local statements as well as to the media. We would not respond to misleading or inflammatory innuendos. Instead, we would always be ready to negotiate in good faith. Our $9/$10 offer would stand during the duration of the strike, whenever the union was willing to accept it. We couldn't do more, and we expected the Austin workforce to understand this. But, the union Local P-9 position remained unchanged to flexing on even the smallest of items. This resistance was totally out-of-keeping with mainstream collective bargaining.

My foremost responsibility was to center our attention on how Hormel was going to survive and to focus our energy on maximizing production and sales from the plants that were in full operation.

Each year, managers and their spouses would come together to celebrate the Yule season. It was a practice Nancy and I had instituted at Austin and all the other plants and was particularly appreciated by the management teams. In December 1985, with the strike underway for more than four months, we decided that the practice of holding the annual dinners should be continued. We needed to maintain the morale of our management people and to thank them for working long hours running as many operations as possible in Austin.

We still remember the quiet drive my wife and I made to the dinner for the Austin plant management team. "Nancy," I asked, "What can I possibly say that would be meaningful to our people who have gone through so much?" We both sat there in silence. Surely, striking employees were beset by many problems, but so were our managers who were working on the line, enduring threats and fearful for their families. This was a great opportunity to thank our team who were doing a magnificent job of performing in every respect. How would the managers – who were keeping the plant up and running – and their families take the considerable stress and withstand the demanding schedules? How would they bear the brunt of constant union pressure?[6] What could I possibly say at the dinner that would adequately thank them for their commitment and effectiveness?

When Nancy and I walked in the door, we were stunned when over three-hundred management team members and their spouses stood up and cheered for quite a long time on two different nights. It was moving and unforgettable! This was a rare moment of warmth among all of these tribulations. We had worried about the morale of our managers and their families. Deryl Arnold and his people were telling us they were more concerned about how *we* were holding up. They knew our family was also taking the brunt of the conflict. For Nancy and me, it was an unforgettable show of support.

## THE CONFLICT INTENSIFIES

The attempt by Ray Rogers to create a secondary boycott against the First Bank System was barred by the courts, but the campaign found new targets. We still had plants across the nation, and Corporate Campaign did

---

6     *At one point, some strike advocates even locked management in the Austin plant for two entire days.*

its best to prod employees at these sites to stage slowdowns and wildcat walkouts. With new contracts in place, we had solid relationships with union heads in other cities. Those plants had already signed the contract that Austin's Local had rejected. However, the Local's strategy led to a plant closure in Ottumwa that I will detail later.

National public opinion was another force that we couldn't disregard. The three major networks back then – ABC, CBS, and NBC – all put permanent teams on site in Austin. Media coverage made the strike a debated issue. Somehow, Rogers and Guyette were afforded the opportunity to appear on Ted Koppel's *Nightline* program, and, as I recall, they announced that Hormel was a major food manufacturer in South Africa. In fact, I had refused to approve Hormel production in South Africa until the apartheid issue was resolved. We kept asking the media to verify that Hormel was not manufacturing in South Africa – with no response. Our people countered many of the misleading statements on radio and TV talk shows and news programs in Denver, Seattle, Atlanta and elsewhere – everywhere we had the chance!

Hype abounded. All over town, Corporate Campaign had turned the chant "No Retreat! No Surrender!" into a steady theme. That message was emblazoned in gold on the back of blue P-9 jackets everywhere. Many retail establishments were pressured to show solidarity and to back the strike by showing "**WE SUPPORT P-9**" signs in their windows. I vividly recall one gas station window sign divided into three parts:

I visited with many shop owners personally and told them, 'Leave the signs up, don't worry about it – we understand the pressures you are under. You can rest assured that I and other Hormel employees won't stop shopping your stores.' A long-time friend of mine and Nancy and now, a retired Hormel board member, is Geri Joseph.[7] As Geri put it,

> *The community and the company were so much a part of each other.*
> *We could hardly believe that this was happening, after all that Hormel*
> *had done for the community and for its employees.*

Yet the flame of care – so much an Upper Midwestern tradition – never really died out. In our own backyard, we saw what could happen if our situation unraveled. Down the road twenty miles on Interstate 90 at Albert Lea, Wilson's employees and their families went through hell in the early 1980s as that company stumbled into bankruptcy. Fifty miles away in Mason City, Iowa, Armour sold one of its several relatively new plants. It was reopened at a starting wage rate of $5.80 by ConAgra. This section of the Midwest had become an economic war-zone. It seemed Austin could not be isolated from what was happening all around us.

---

7     *Geri has also served as U.S. Ambassador to the Netherlands and has been a dynamic leader on the staff of the University of Minnesota's Humphrey Institute of Public Affairs.*

However, we were determined that the same situation should not and would not prevail in Austin.

Not long after the 1985 strike began at Hormel, a union leader passed away unexpectedly. Financially, his widow was left high and dry. Hormel made sure that she got help. Even when hostilities were at their bitterest, the most basic lines of communication between Hormel and the people of Austin withstood the pressure.

Austin had known state football, basketball, swimming, baseball, and tennis championships. Austin residents were competitors – well-meaning and determined folks. I remember one striker saying, "Nobody in Austin knows how to lose." He was right. The people who belonged to the Austin union had never lost a real skirmish with the Company. *They* were winners. When you have people who have a winner's determination, *they* can take a rather strong position. *They* were not prepared to lose this one. It was hard for these people to accept a wage adjustment even though it would still make them the best paid people in the industry. . . very much like being bested in an athletic competition *they* didn't want to lose. I knew their spirit and had played on one of those state championship football teams myself.

## 1986: THE DECISION TO RESTAFF THE AUSTIN PLANT

Our management people ran production lines every day during the first five months of the strike. After experiencing unchallenged, unyielding positions and no negotiating progress for five months; we felt there would be no lasting settlement, so we decided that we should resume the operation of the plant. We would first open the gates to our employees who wanted to return and then to newly hired employees on Monday, January

13, 1986. During that week, about fifty former strikers came through. This was a start, but hardly enough to run the plant long-term.

Days earlier, just after the turn of the year, we began to run radio ads for employees to replace those who would not cross the picket lines. These employees would operate what was then the largest and most modern food processing plant in the world.[8] Their date of employment would be January 20. That date was Martin Luther King Day and a conscious choice to reinforce a respect for non-violent resistance. Hormel stayed true to maintaining a consistent but non-reactive position throughout the strike. We were doing all we could to keep every aspect of the strike free of violence. Unfortunately that hope would not prevail.

Initially our management team wanted to canvas surrounding communities and recruit new people to work at Hormel. We later rethought that approach: If someone wanted to work for Hormel, they had to drive through the gates into our plant parking lot, where our staff would take their names and give them applications which they could take home, fill out, and bring back. We wanted these people to run the gauntlet, to experience what the circumstances would be if they came to work for us. That included being taunted and regaled with obscenities . . . and having their cars rocked by picketers. Despite the harassment, more than three-thousand people from twenty states chose to drive through the gate to apply. We went on to hire only six hundred. Even as strikers smashed the windshield of his car, one new hire told network television that he would give his right arm for a job in our plant.

People asked: **WHY** would 3,000 or 4,000 people come seeking employment? First, these were the best paying jobs in the industry and in the area! In all likelihood, the working conditions were superior compared with

---

8  *Indeed, according to industry experts, it may still be.*

other firms. They also received an important assurance. Their seniority would be permanent, second only to those employees who returned by January 20th. They would have seniority ahead of any other new or returning employee after that date. This was a big plus. Applicants who came to Hormel came for a career, and we felt obliged to acknowledge their decision to join us with a clear commitment to their future. I don't want to sound like a broken record, but: They knew we were #1 in wages, benefits, and working environment which the new plant certainly offered. Beyond that, we had also established our employee profit sharing program long ago, in 1941.

On Monday, January 20, we restarted operations and opened the front gate to the plant to returning strikers and newly hired employees, many of whom saw a unique opportunity for a lifetime career. In retrospect, it is hard to imagine any management team better prepared to create a welcoming environment and to give the necessary guidance for new and returning employees. These managers had been running many of the operations themselves for all those months. Six-hundred-sixty-five new employees along with 462 of our best employees returned and passed through the picket lines. Meanwhile, these workers were all met by 150 picketing members of the striking P-9 local. It was a wrenching point of decision – at times, picket lines parted brothers. The influence and support of outside Labor activists made its mark, but the people coming back were committed.

Inside the Austin plant, we saw the beginnings of a workforce which combined the return of our most loyal employees with an impressive cadre of new people. This crescendo signaled a bold, bright future for Hormel and Austin. Deryl Arnold and his management team set up training programs and matched our veteran employees with new employees in training teams. Our returning employees were terrific. Each was a mentoring "brother" or "sister" to the new recruits on a one-on-one basis. At the end of each day, communication sessions talked out problems. We moved people to new stations if their present assignments didn't work out. The atmosphere was one of teamwork and mutual concern.

Outside the plant, the situation was reaching a boiling point. Violence and threats of violence continued to smolder. At one point, the Austin chief of police pulled his officers off the street because he felt that ***their*** safety was being endangered. Finally, I went to Minnesota Governor Rudy Perpich in St. Paul, and I laid my frustrations out on the table. With our local police unable to handle all of the out-of-towners as well as local strikers, it was a tinder box waiting to be ignited. Three days later, on January 21, 1986, the Governor called out the National Guard. Additionally, we experienced a product tampering problem and several other serious incidents.

Another tactic pursued by P-9's management at the time was an effort to create "roving" picket lines at other Hormel plants which had already signed new contracts. In October 1985, P-9 said it would support any UFCW workers who honored such 'roving' picket lines. Once again the local came up squarely against its international union. In November 1985, UFCW President William Wynn refused to sanction roving pickets at the other Hormel plants. The effort to organize wildcat strikes at those Hormel plants continued. Workers at the Fremont plant, knowing they had signed the most favorable agreement in the industry, resisted the roving picketing and continued working at regular productivity.

A P-9 roving picket line appeared in Ottumwa in January 1986. Workers at the Ottumwa plant, which had a history of wildcat labor disruptions during the years when it had been operated by Morrell[9], walked out in clear violation of its newly signed contract. According to Hormel Foods Senior Vice President and General Counsel Jim Cavanaugh:

> *In mid-January 1986, Local P-9 and the workers represented by Local 431 asked UFCW International Union for approval to extend the Austin picket line to other Hormel locations. On January 16, in a telegram to Mr. Guyette, the International Union President refused to extend the pickets . . . 'I could not in good conscience urge other Hormel members to risk their jobs to respect an unsanctioned picket line in a hopeless cause.'*

The same telegram was received by Local 431 on January 17, 1986. The telegram was reproduced on January 18, 1986 in the local Ottumwa newspaper. On January 21, 1986, roving P-9 pickets appeared at the gates of the Ottumwa plant. Local 431 employees walked out in clear violation of its newly signed contract. In response, the Company immediately notified local union leadership that it would take disciplinary action if the employees did not return to work. Later that morning, picket lines were removed and the employees returned to work.

Union officials were warned that if the pickets returned, employees were to report to work or face termination. We sent employees warning letters (attached to their checks) stating that those who honored the picket lines would face termination. On January 27, 1986, the presence of the Local P-9

---

9     *The original Morrell plant on these grounds had burned down. When Morrell management replaced it, the result was an inefficient maze of buildings, erected as a group so that they wouldn't lose their entire production if a similar fire happened in the future. Product in process had to be moved outdoors! We purchased the site from Morrell and were able to use the newly built, cost-effective sewage plant supporting this location, but this plant was only on the fringe of good hog country, and we were moving in the direction of packaged goods. So we demolished this unworkable facility and built our new plant on this site.*

picket line again shut down the plant. In the end, over 400 employees were terminated. After the Union filed a grievance, an arbitrator ruled in August 1986 that the Union's actions were in violation of the collective bargaining agreement, and the employees were subject to discipline for refusing to report for work. The arbitrator "returned these employees back to work without back pay, treating the interim period as a suspension from employment," Jim recalls. "In the end, the plant was closed in the fall of 1987 and leased to Excel[10] with an option to buy." Ultimately, the option was exercised. Excel began its operations with a starting wage of $3.00 under what the Ottumwa contract had paid. Cargill paid us more than book value.

I had already received silent offers for the sale of that plant. Nevertheless, we were disappointed to have invested so much effort into creating a well-run production operation. On the other hand, we could not go forward with the threat that such disruptions could happen again and again as they had during the Morrell years in Ottumwa. We simply lacked confidence that a realistic labor relations climate could exist at the plant.

As an indicator, after the terminations took place, defiant union leaders in Ottumwa sent us a terse message: "We'd do it again." Our response was equally concise: "Not to us you won't."

## A WELCOME RESOLUTION

In the first half of 1986, two tendencies emerged:
- First, how intensely the International union was frustrated with the leadership of the P-9 local.
- Second, how much Guyette and Rogers had marched over the line of behavior acceptable to their own international union.

---

10    *The Excel® brand is a part of Cargill Meat Solutions.*

The responsible, and at times courageous, positions of UFCW President William Wynn can't be overlooked. In January, President Wynn telegrammed other Hormel locals, "warning them that the 'Ayatollah of Austin [Ray Rogers] is making hostages of our members,'" according to Peter Rachleff in *Hard-Pressed in the Heartland.*

The National Guard withdrew from Austin on February 21, 1986, but the unrest didn't stop. In May, UFCW put the P-9 local in trusteeship. On August 27, 1986, the 13-month strike ended when a 4-year contract was announced with wages reaching $10.77 by the end of the third year in1989.

True to our word and to the commitments I had made publicly, we were proud of our technological and marketing leadership that enabled us to deliver exactly the financial terms we had promised. Still the leading agreement in the industry, the Austin employees received the same package our other plants had been enjoying a year earlier.

Did good actually come out of the strike? Although none of us wanted the strike or really won it, this dispute did have some positive consequences. First and foremost, we came together as a team and put our labor profit formula in place on a realistic basis. The Austin workforce forged on January 20, 1986 proved to be the cornerstone of an incomparably skilled and motivated team that excels to the present day. Two populations were fused – our best and most loyal longer term employees with new and highly motivated members of the Hormel family. Had we not stood firm in the strike, Hormel could not have survived competitively. The strike was a significant test that drew out of a positive can-do attitude. Our people were able to attain and establish new levels of performance.

The strike taught us we could move production from one plant to another and schedule lines to achieve maximum economy of scale. Plant management also learned a great deal about line production processes through hands-on operations for several months. Through innovations like the new employee mentoring program, we structured important working relationships and fostered new and stronger teams throughout our employee group. And, we used the workforce changes as an opportunity to introduce a much more professional Quality Improvement Process (QIP) in 1986, including Quality Improvement Teams (QITs) in 24 locations with a 'zero-defect' goal. On the quality issue, we began to recognize a very important truth. A business really has to maintain a 'zero tolerance' position on quality. You can't accept what some may regard as a 'doable' quality standard.

> **IF YOU ACKNOWLEDGE THAT A QUALITY STANDARD OF 85% IS ACCEPTABLE, THAT'S WHERE YOU'LL END UP... AND, IT COULD BE WORSE THAN WHAT YOU ALREADY HAVE.**

During the strike, our overall productivity was superb, with lost-time injuries almost non-existent and absenteeism less than 2%. Because of the intense labor relations focus of the new employee mentoring program, this approach allowed us to strengthen our safety performance.

No one in the industry had or has the safety record we do. The Austin plant has received the State of Minnesota Governor's Award several times. It has been said that we are the best operating plant in the state. Gary Ray, Hormel Foods' retired President of Protein Products, has commented:

*Our lost-time injury rate experience is now three times lower than anybody else in the industry, a published number from the American*

*Meat Institute. That can be ascribed to technology, a strict rotation of jobs, management attention, and employee recognition. We pay very serious attention to ergonomics, for example. There are certain jobs – especially those requiring knife handling – where tasks are rotated each hour. We incent the heck out of job safety. The awards program includes family vacation trips and stock shares. There is also a measurable productivity benefit for the company. Productivity suffers if you don't have the same person there every day. You're not just paying for injury avoidance but for attendance as well.*

We ended this chapter in Hormel's history stronger, more flexible and ready to take on the formidable challenge of becoming a major player in the food industry, not just the meat segment. We were now able to compete and excel with top performing plants in the modern food industry – a very different competitive setting than the one we had known for so many years.

## CRISIS MANAGEMENT POINTS-OF-DIFFERENCE TO MINIMIZE DISRUPTION

- For any business – and especially one in the process of redefining itself – it is important for the CEO to remain focused on business operations and strategy.
- Are there capable members of the management team who can perform the roles of 'lightning rods' to help the CEO by absorbing the disruption and, often, confrontation that comes with crisis?

- In a crisis, prioritize time. In a strike situation in particular, do not let precious management time be deflected by actions intended to divert or obscure management focus.

- When you ask people to become part of controversy (e.g., crossing a picket line), make sure that they are aware of the circumstances to which they may be exposing themselves and take the necessary steps to protect them.

- When involved in a confrontation receiving intense media attention; don't shirk from clear, constant and succinct defense of your position.

- Always view a disruption, such as a strike, as a situation in which managers can better learn the operating practices of the company first hand.

- Any crisis calls for flexibility. Anticipate crises by asking "what if" questions about how you might operate differently or at different locations if you were suddenly faced with a disruption. Occasionally, a crisis will even identify fundamental changes that should or can improve efficiency and should be made permanent practices.

# Building Customer Bonds

## ANNOUNCING STRATEGIC CHANGE

I n the 1980s, particularly from 1986 on, seismic strategic change was taking place at Hormel. It was essential that our retail customers understood the magnitude of the change involved. In Chicago each May, the Food Marketing Institute (FMI) holds its annual trade show. CEOs and most of their managers throughout the retail industry came to our displays at the show and made sure that their people reviewed our product line in detail.

Trade shows are not as conventional as they might seem and can be a wonderful venue to showcase innovation. In 1988, more than a few considered us the 'star' of the convention. The investment was expensive but cost-effective in making a strong statement. Our presence at the FMI trade show would be our 'coming out party.' Through an imposing display, we could inform the retail world of the collective breadth of our assortment and the overwhelming extent to which new products played a role. Unless you have a vast array of new products, this show is of limited benefit to a manufacturer; but our extensive number of new products at that time made for a high-impact presentation.[1]

One of the high points of the event is a gala dinner. For years, Coca-Cola* hosted the event. In 1988, we made a strategic decision to take on sponsoring this centerpiece and turned more than a few heads.

Dionne Warwick and Burt Bacharach were at the height of their celebrity as pop music stars and gave a glittering show to a huge audience of our customers. The event pulled considerable focus to Hormel, and we leveraged the opportunity to increase industry awareness of the dramatic change in our company. No one salesperson could have told the story that our displays did. There was little question that we had established ourselves as a leading food company, capable of generating valued points of difference on a significant scale.

Our successful presentation of new products provided us with an opportunity to strengthen our sales calls. Jim Henson, CEO of Jewel, the premier supermarket retailer at the time, said to me, "We have decided to make Hormel one of our leading suppliers based your new campaign." An image such as this really justified our important marketing investment at the time. It signaled that we had surmounted a major hurdle in redefining our identity.

---

1    *A rule of thumb regarding presentations at industry events: If you don't have something meaningful to say, overstating or exaggerating your points of difference can be a serious error. On the other hand, if your business is void of significant new points of difference worth talking about, that too is a problem of a different sort . . . and a far more serious one.*

## DEFINING THE MARKETPLACE

As we made this crucial transition in our marketing profile, we gave priority to those retail customers who visited Austin, Fremont and other facilities to grasp the full extent of our offering – including Jennie-O turkey products. We decided to make a version of this product display a permanent attraction at our Austin headquarters. That exhibit continues today and is now called *The Marketplace*. In it, we present actual shelf and refrigerator-case displays of our entire and impressive product line. *The Marketplace* has been enlarged to include a boardroom table and a full-sized, visible cooking area. If a customer wants to sample a new product or a range of options in the development of a product, our chefs can serve the dish – and modify it – on the spot. Customers, we have found, need to be able to immerse themselves in a company's marketing program. We created the setting in which they could do it.

Another advantage of *The Marketplace* is that it is right next door to our Austin plant. Commercial customers not only see the product line-up, they also directly experience the advanced technology and remarkable sanitation standards of our manufacturing facilities. These operational plants 'explain-by-doing' how we are able to couple such high quality products with exceptional cost control. One of the most discerning visitors who ever toured the plant was the late Carl Pohlad. Carl, a great friend, a successful banker, and owner of the Minnesota Twins and the largest bottler in the Pepsi-Cola beverage group, made a friendly deal with me.

"Dick, I know you are after me for a seven-figure gift to the Horatio Alger Association to fund college scholarships for deserving, needy young people. I'll do it, but only on the condition that you give me a personal tour of the Austin plant."

With great pleasure, I agreed and our plant general manager at the time, Jeff Nuytten, arranged for a golf cart to roll Carl over the million three hundred thousand square feet. In work area after area, Carl asked penetrating questions. He was carried away by the computerization, the advanced materials handling, and the precision custom-built machinery.

I remember Carl being particularly impressed with the person who did the knife sharpening in the boning area. Carl went up to him and said, "You must be the most important person in the entire plant. I can't imagine anything getting done unless you do your job first, and you do it well." His strongest impression was of the people – their positive attitude and their intensity. "I have seen a lot of plants," Carl concluded, "but I've never seen one like this." Since that tour, Carl gave 50 Horatio Alger scholarships annually to students in the Twin Cities area. Because of his remarkable generosity among many other traits, my friendship with him was special. I shall miss Carl greatly.

## HORMEL INNOVATES CATEGORY MANAGEMENT

To be the leader in an important category, you may need to help supermarket retailers ***originate*** a new category of product where no 'grouping' existed before. When we established our shelf-stable microwaveable entrées, a whole new section was created in every supermarket starting in 1987. That means you become an entrant in a range of competitors and not just the only kid on the block. The *Marketplace* display environment was our tool. Supporting the emerging heat-and-eat category, Joe Pichler – CEO of Kroger at the time and now retired – said his people really benefited from fixturing ideas they saw in our Austin *Marketplace* displays. According to Joe:

> *Hormel used the display cases to show us specific strategies and programs that Kroger could adopt regarding home meal replacement products. You can microwave these pre-cooked items and have a delicious dinner within five minutes. By using the fixtures they presented, you could centralize one place in the store with a range of branded microwaveable containers. This display could include Hormel as well as, let's say, Kroger and even competitor products. The customer coming into the store knows that they can get a delicious meal real fast. Not necessarily cheap, but delicious. The entire array would be in one place. Hormel's fixtures enabled us to present the category in an attractive and integrated fashion.*

> ## BE PREPARED TO CREATE NEW PRODUCT CATEGORIES TO LAUNCH, PRESENT, AND DEFEND STRONGLY DIFFERENTIATED INDIVIDUAL ITEMS.

Joe, a highly respected industry leader, views us as the first manufacturer to really grasp 'category management' on a scale which transcends item-by-item marketing. Our agenda: We recognized that we were being invaded by competitors – category-by-category – because we offer such a wide assortment of products. We wanted our strongest *total* categories to excel as well. Paradoxically, this might actually cut back the amount of space devoted to our own particular items, if a lack of diversity endangered the category as a whole. Our reasoning: If the category itself was weak, that couldn't help our overall strategy. But, if the category thrived, and we were the leading force in it; then we were likely to secure our objective of achieving optimum market share.

*Category management is an exciting concept,*
*and Hormel has done breakthrough work to vitalize it.*

Retailers also value category management because of the positive effect it has on shaping customer shopping behavior. Another fine friend and retail colleague, Ron Pearson – Chairman Emeritus of Hy-Vee – explains this well when he says:

> *Effective marketing and category management are central to help shoppers navigate through the modern grocery store. Today's large supermarket is more complex to shop and may offer 50,000 stock keeping units[2] versus 6-8,000 just a few decades ago. Hormel offers such dominant items, and its long-term marketing program is designed to keep bringing the customers back into those categories where such items are to be found. These could include specific Compleats° dinners or types of SPAM°, bacon, chili or many other products. Retailers value the power of lead attractions which consistently draw shoppers back into categories.*

It was our leadership in the microwave market which gave us the platform on which to build our category program, and our Grocery Products people have led the way. We have literally hundreds of products that are building blocks for this strategy that have and can be converted into microwaveable versions.

## OVERCOMING CHALLENGES BUILDS STRONG PARTNERSHIPS

Any firm that supplies other businesses must constantly ask itself: Are we doing things that interfere with our ability to serve our customers and *their*

---

2      *A stock keeping unit (SKU) is an individual item. For example, our Chi-Chi's brand of tortillas comes in a 9-inch burrito size as well as a 6-inch soft taco size. Because the item is available in two differently sized packages, each represents a separate stock keeping unit.*

business goals efficiently? Well-intended plans can often have highly undesirable side effects. Before and during the early 1970s, Hormel built a series
of distribution plants scattered across the country. Ostensibly, these centers
were designed to improve the supply of product at the local level and
enhance convenience. Consider refrigerator-case products, such as smoked
sliced-bacon, luncheon meats and ham that might have a shelf-life of twenty to thirty days. By the time the product was shipped and stocked in its
distribution center, the effective shelf-life for the retailer might be lessened
by a week. We were simply increasing our costs and reducing the shelf-life
value of the product for our retail customers. As a consequence, during
the mid-1980s we eliminated the distribution plant concept, except where
we had manufacturing operations and it made sense. Certainly another
stimulus for discontinuing these plants was that retailers were themselves
expanding their own distribution center network at this time. Not only
was redundancy multiplying, but each additional warehousing step diminished the precious shelf life of products.

Another category concept was fortified when we introduced exact weight
cuts of fresh meat in the last several years. Recently retired SUPERVALU
Executive Vice President and President of Retail Operations John Hooley
wrote me not long ago:

> *In our opinion, Hormel has been a leader in the development of*
> *exact weight fresh meat cuts. Marinated chicken, beef, pork, and*
> *hams are all available now in exact weight packaging which makes*
> *it easy for us to do a 'one free with one sale' or to just do a feature*
> *price across multiple lines of items. It also simplifies pricing recogni-*
> *tion for consumers.*

Our branding of the fresh meat counter is doubtless having a major impact on operating expense. How many butchers do you see at work in supermarkets today? John also wrote me,

> *Hormel is known in the industry as one of the first companies to venture into the value added category, with Hormel fully cooked entrées… The fully prepared category has become so popular that our store design and equipment people are now specifying additional cases to properly display this fast growing category.*

Consumers don't always do what they say, and retailers look to us to get a handle as to why. Similarly, they know Hormel is there when a trend is for real. "On ethnic foods," says Joe Pichler, Hormel was "a leader in helping us [Kroger] develop one of the fastest growing areas of our business – an authentic Hispanic foods program. There's been a lot of Tex-Mex stuff around for years, but with the rapidly growing Hispanic population, the market for authentic Hispanic products is growing rapidly."

Among all the points of difference we have been able to offer retailers, none has been more appealing than our regular ability to innovate. "If you have good new products, retailers love them," as Mike Wright of SUPERVALU would say. Mike adds:

> *If you go back thirty years ago, most meat bought in the supermarket was bought as a commodity item. Today there is a lot of value-added product on the shelves. Hormel has taken a commodity product, enhanced it, and turned it into a value-added product. This is why they are strong and surviving and continue to succeed while companies like Armour, Wilson, Cudahy, Swift and many more are gone.*

As is evident in these illustrations and others, we had built up a powerful working rapport and synergy at the senior level within the retail community. Preserving this kind of influential dialogue requires constant contact and active listening to customers on the one hand and being a reliable and continuous source of fresh ideas on the other. Providing meaningful points of difference to retailers requires active pursuit of both behaviors.

Significant business relationships are not just built on providing products and services. They are built on trust. Some of Hormel's relationships go back sixty years or more. It's essential that these contacts have a personal foundation and that they be regularly nourished at every level. Here's one dramatic illustration of the impact relationships can have: Some years ago, a major supermarket retailer ordered truckloads of frozen turkeys from Jennie-O. The chain was building up its inventory in advance of the holiday season. After being sold to the customer, these particular shipments were routed for storage in an independent freezer warehouse. The turkeys were unloaded to the dock with exacting temperature controls every step of the way. Then a snafu of unthinkable proportions occurred. Instead of being immediately stored in the refrigerated warehouse freezer, the turkeys were left on the docks for several days. During that time, the outside thermometer hit a hundred degrees! The shipments were a total loss. When finally discovered, the warehouse tried to re-freeze the spoiled turkeys without our knowledge. Worse than that, the product was delivered to the stores from the independent warehouse.

The storage problem was neither Hormel's nor the retailer's. The retailer litigated and recovered its loss from the independent warehouse. As part of the settlement, the retailer couldn't join in any action with Hormel. We were about to incur a huge financial loss. Even worse, wrangling over the settlement could have damaged or even ended a wonderful relationship with the retailer. My instinct was to meet with the CEO. I made a personal visit. He understood our position exactly. We went on to fundamentally recover our loss and struck a settlement. Hormel put together some excellent promotional programs to make a plus out of a bad situation. Rather than being the death knell for our partnership, that resolution became a milestone in building even greater trust. Had we not had a personal relationship with the retailer and the CEO, the positive solution might never have emerged. We were both determined to invest the extra effort in order to strengthen our future relationship.

> **THE SKILLFUL RESOLUTION OF ISSUES CAN BE A POWERFUL POINT OF DIFFERENCE. IT CAN ACTUALLY STRENGTHEN CUSTOMER RELATIONSHIPS WHICH DEPEND ON EARNED MUTUAL TRUST.**

## FOODSERVICE COMES INTO ITS OWN

The timing for our establishing the new Foodservice Group was perfect. It enabled us to give specific focus to the needs of our foodservice customers instead of presenting products that just duplicated our retail offering. Foodservice operators were coming into their own, realizing they had a right to pose more exacting challenges to suppliers.

"Just how many different kinds of bacon do you think your people can handle?" a restaurant operator once asked Jim Cole, Hormel's first Group Vice President of Foodservice, back in 1990 when the Foodservice Group was established.[3] "I don't know," Jim replied. "We'll have to try and see. How many do you *want*?" This would become the cornerstone to answering the specific needs of the foodservice business. It was not part of the Hormel mentality to say we can't deliver a particular way of cooking, packaging or slicing a product. Foodservice – the industry built on away-from-home eating – is a $566 billion phenomenon today and growing. Supplying the foodservice customer has been one of Hormel's great achievements. It was a constant search for points of difference that brought new focus to our foodservice business. And, it was through bacon – commonly thought of as a commodity category – that we first saw the potential significance of differentiation in the foodservice market.

When we formed the Foodservice Group, we weren't new to this market. We were already a leading supplier to many accounts, but we were not growing at the rate the overall foodservice market was exploding, because we were not organized to serve the market in an optimum way. Over the years, the core Hormel bacon product has always been our natural hardwood-smoked strips. As restaurant operators became more sophisticated in using technology to control expenses, the more their *suppliers'* technological solutions mattered.

Can you imagine a restaurateur having to pull each slice away from the overlapped-style of bacon traditionally found in retail packages? Our first major foodservice success was LAYOUT PACK® bacon, an invention that placed sliced product side-by-side on a sheet of non-burnable paper. This format allowed foodservice operators to prepare a sheet with 17-18 slices placed automatically in the broiler at one time. It was a labor-saver which still retained great flavor quality. Layout Pack bacon was an achievement

---

3      *Tom Day, Senior Vice President of Foodservice, heads this group today. His predecessor was Steve Binder who has now become Group Vice President of Hormel Foods Refrigerated Products.*

both in saving foodservice operators labor costs as well as actually improving product quality – because it allowed the operator to achieve a more consistent result in the kitchen.

*Layout Pack bacon being prepared by our chef*
*Thomas Dickhans in the Hormel Kitchen*

We designed and built special proprietary equipment to produce this bacon packaging and cooking format for foodservice. Our competitors did everything they could – including posing as repairmen – to obtain entrance to our production site. We protect that point of difference, and others like it, with considerable vigilance. Hormel Foodservice sells bacon by the truckloads, but foodservice operators aren't interested in how to sell bacon even by the pound! They're interested in selling a *slice* of bacon and focus on how a single piece of bacon performs in a given application. So we needed to think in terms of individual slices, billions of times over.

Not long after we created our special technology for pre-cooking bacon, we became the leader in pre-cooked bacon as it caught on across the country. As a follow-up to the lay-out bacon pack, we were the first company to supply a pre-cooked bacon strip for a hamburger bacon sandwich. We packaged it on burn-proof paper for restaurateurs who wanted a quick-service bacon burger. It was a finely differentiated application. What an edge it offered! While the cost to create a single automated pre-cooked bacon production line was about one million dollars, we considered that investment an excellent risk.

Our pioneering customer was Burger King. Getting my colleagues to go along with this substantial investment was built on Hormel's strong relationship with Burger King's then parent Pillsbury.[4] They were enthused about the bacon opportunity and guaranteed they would absorb our entire output. They were even more enthused about the positive consumer response. Then the bacon cheeseburger came along. That required another level of custom tailoring. And, tailoring, as you can appreciate, is central to the many different applications of bacon. Bacon on a burger may not require a difference in quality or even taste, but it might have to look different on a sandwich than it does on a plate, sided next to an order of eggs or an omelet… or used in a salad.

The microwave affected everybody – manufacturer, restaurateur, quick-service operator and end-consumer alike. For food operators who fed the public away from home, the microwave was one of several central changes happening at once. The quick-service segment brought new standards of efficiency to the restaurant business. Every part of the expense formula was

---

4    *I was later to be offered the CEO-ship of Pillsbury, which I declined. Pillsbury was ultimately acquired by General Mills, although many of the Pillsbury-branded items remain staples in modern supermarkets.*

scrutinized under the microscope. An explosion in the number of restaurants and eating alternatives intensified the competitive climate. Consumers became more demanding, and they had a host of options where they could take their business.

> ### AS THE TYPES OF COMPETITION IN AN INDUSTRY MULTIPLY, SO DO THE OPPORTUNITIES TO DEFINE AND SERVE POINTS OF DIFFERENCE.

Our various types of customers each articulated particular needs from every product, and all expected them to be met. Gone was the day when they all – consumer, restaurateur, institutional feeder, quick-service operator – could work from the same smoked ham. Variations of bacon and ham were needed for different applications. Many products we developed were variations of successful core items.

The retail Cure 81 ham won't fit everyone's foodservice program, so we make specialized Cure 81 hams just for these applications. The original version will work for an upscale hotel or restaurant, but not necessarily for coffee shops. The breakfast trade may need something that will take a bit more 'grill abuse' requiring the ham to be prepared with a higher moisture content. Then there are 'sandwich-size operators' such as submarine sandwich producers and delis. They require a different type of product performance from the package of ham slices they buy. A sub producer has to anticipate the high-speed volume of lots of customers in a concentrated timeframe. That may mean more slices in each individual package. We went on to create an "endless" Cure 81 to increase yields for the foodservice operator, since end pieces did not fit in their menu formats. Early on, we recognized that a hotel distributor might buy every one of the different versions we offered. A hotel, for example, might need one type of ham for its breakfast coffee shop and another sort for its club sandwiches served on an elegant terrace at lunchtime.

Responding to points of difference in foodservice wasn't a matter of wishful thinking. *Not only did we have to reorganize the packaging of the ham slices or bacon strips, we had to reorganize the foodservice sales team.* We had separate sales staffs in our Fresh Meat and Grocery Products Divisions, to be sure; but we needed a larger sales force specifically organized to sell to the needs of foodservice operators. Fortunately, we had many salespeople already calling on the foodservice trade. Further, we had no organization dedicated to making sure the foodservice products we were selling matched the particular needs of the operators we wanted to serve. It was a question of unifying them under a distinct banner with a specific mission. In recent years, we have continued to refine our niche presence in bacon, adding such products as HORMEL˙ applewood smoked bacon, HORMEL˙ Fresh Pantry™ peppered bacon, and CAFÉ H˙ jalapeño bacon. Doing so, we have been able to attain solid single-digit growth in Foodservice each year since 1989.

In order to create the Foodservice Group in 1990, we had to separate the responsibility from our sales and marketing base of our Meat Products Group headed by Stan Kerber. A dedicated team player, Stan supported the move, knowing that the company had to be more sharply focused in answering the needs of the fast growing foodservice market. As a result, both divisions have prospered, and we have a keener focus on the range of opportunities in both areas. For the individual consumer, the added value might be convenience. For the foodservice customer, the added value of convenience can translate into hard-dollar expense savings on a considerable scale. Each represents a unique point of difference. Our preparation technology and packaging have become an integral part of the operators' expense formula.

Under Steve Binder's leadership, Foodservice achieved its $1 billion sales milestone in 2007. The BREAD-READY° pre-sliced meats line has enjoyed double-digit growth in meeting the convenience needs of restaurant sandwich makers. AUSTIN BLUES° BBQ provides barbeque entrées to address another set of foodservice opportunities. Nor should we overlook that old mainstay, bacon. Increasingly innovative bacon products – such as applewood smoked bacon – represent an entirely new market segment.

Meeting the needs of the Foodservice customer requires ever more sophisticated solutions. One of our most exciting challenges in the last three years has been the development of the CAFÉ H° product line. (The H stands for Hormel, of course.)

We faced multiple challenges:

- We had established positions in the consumer ethnic food market through acquired brands like Mexican Herdez, and we wanted to leverage our ethnic food authority in our foodservice business in restaurants and hotels.

- Overall, distribution of our ethnic sauces needed improvement. Sales bonuses were based on tonnage and inventory turnover was low. Each of the ethnic sauces and brands incorporated bold flavors. Consequently, foodservice operators only required a minimal amount of sauce to create their finished menu concept.

- Mainstream foodservice chains were adding more ethnic dishes to their menus, but the consumer's standards for these dishes were changing. Consumers wanted 100% authenticity, and we soon realized that authenticity of individual dishes would be a significant point of difference even for mainstream restaurants.

Our mission was to make today's flavors simple for the foodservice operator. The Hormel team developed an 'ethnic protein' line for our Foodservice Division with the following attributes:

- *Fully Cooked, 100% Value Added*: Obtaining a higher margin was a significant priority from the start.

- *Difficult to Prepare*: We identified recipes that weren't easy to prepare and time consuming for foodservice operators.

- *Diverse Menu Applications*: Each product created had to incorporate menu diversity - specifically, the ability to be featured in at least three difference menu concepts. These included entrée, salad, sandwiches, appetizers, etc,

- *Pork*: Starting out, at least 50% of the products had to be pork based. We focused on the concept of "sexy pork ideas." (This is despite the fact that we have made a conscious effort to add beef items like prime rib to our offering and have done so with such a notable degree of success that two plants are now principally committed to producing beef entrées.)

- *Slow Cooked, Bold Flavor*: By concentrating on the above factors, the initial product ideas focused on identifying dishes with bolder flavors that took on average at least 4 hours to cook.

Initial products offered included Mexican dishes like Pork Barbacoa and Chipotle Chicken as well as the Italian specialty Pork Ossobucco

– all of which simply needed to be heated and served by the foodservice operator. We wanted to create an array of real food prepared with real recipes that could be found at enticing cafés the world over. The result added value for the consumer, the foodservice customer, and for Hormel.

Today we don't distribute directly to many hotels, restaurants and fast-food operations. Instead we work through massive Foodservice distributors like SYSCO Corporation, U.S. Foodservice, Gordon Foodservice, Ben E. Keith, Reinhardt, and Shamrock Foods – to name just a few. But, we have never lost touch with the quality that has to show up on the consumer's plates and in the sandwiches they buy.

The consumer's appetite for convenience continues to blur the distinction between eating out, taking out, and cooking at home. Our consumer business and the foodservice business cross-fertilize each other. Grocery stores now have a line of bacon products, and a line of ham products… and a line of Spam. The pattern is repeating itself in hundreds of other product innovations to meet the specific needs of the market. The Hormel divisions might compete with each other to see who would attain the greatest growth, but we also try to multiply opportunities for each product. We ask ourselves: How could we take this line of ham, for example, and spread it over as much of the food industry as profitably as possible? How might we multiply a core point of difference to make it even more powerful and relevant in special categories? A single breakthrough can be the source of a multitude of applications, each giving different customers a unique edge.

We think about these opportunities as we assess important directions in which we expect the food industry to continue to evolve. On the present horizon, one factor is surely an ability to anticipate and to surpass the already exacting standards that exist for food safety. Steve Binder cites the breakthroughs in high-pressure pasteurization used in our TrueTaste technology for the sliced luncheon meat category:

> *Pre-sliced luncheon meats had always been a frozen product. High-pressure pasteurization allowed us to simply refrigerate these items without preservatives. We began this proposition in foodservice with our BREAD READY® pre-sliced meats and then evolved it on the retail side with our Natural Choice line. The industry has yet to catch up to the significant point of difference our team has created.*

Applying this technology is yet another example of how advanced processes can be redeployed to create meaningful points of difference in multiple business categories.

And, we keep asking: How far can these products go to feed people . . . in whatever manner they want to enjoy the food? Everyone who shops in a supermarket eats in restaurants. Everybody who eats in restaurants also prepares meals at home. Just like the microwave, developing our foodservice business has forced us to discipline our thinking about points of difference. How can we profitably maximize the presence of our products in every important niche available to us?

> **CONSTANTLY ASK: 'WHAT IF WE APPLIED THIS POINT OF DIFFERENCE TO OTHER CUSTOMER GROUPS?'**

It's exciting to dream about possibilities, but you have to realize they don't always pan out. I remember an occasion when a major industry group recognized Hormel for ingenuity and lifestyle awareness. They presented us with an award for having developed a fat-free hot dog. When I accepted the accolade, I thanked the group as graciously as I could. Then I had to tell them the truth: "Now, I just wish we could sell some of the darn things!" We had to acknowledge the product lacked the flavor that people wanted. The idea, on the other hand, will probably go on to be yet another instance of being "prematurely right."

## CORPORATE AIRCRAFT AND CUSTOMER SUPPORT

Over the years, it's been suggested that Hormel move its headquarters to some larger urban center than Austin. For a number of reasons – many of which are mentioned in the final chapter of this book – we have declined to do that. However, when a Fortune 500 company chooses a smaller city location, some implications have to be considered. Because we are headquartered in landlocked Minnesota, corporate aircraft have offered our best means to show people the revolutionary things we were doing. If you don't place your headquarters in a mainstream location, then you have to find ways to bring customers to wherever you are. Over time, corporate jets have become part of our assets, and we make a conscious effort to maximize their practical utility. Our customers have always had first priority to use our planes. Management used the airplanes only when available; and, as CEO, I flew commercial coach on many domestic U.S. business trips and still do.

Our corporate aircraft have proved to be one of our most formidable marketing tools to reach trade customers and to establish and nurture customer relations. Our corporate planes are available to industry customers so that they can visit *The Marketplace*, tour our state-of-the-art plant, and/or meet with their Hormel counterparts. As I have stressed, we want our customers to learn about our operations and marketing concepts first hand. This has given them confidence in our assortment, our innovations, and our competitive production capabilities. It's our view that these planes are time-saving communications tools, and this dialogue with our customers may be the most important communication we undertake. Second priority is given to our management to reach those plants not located in major metropolitan areas, as well as giving our Marketing people and customers in the field a better opportunity to be exposed to our plants.

> **RECOGNIZE THE POWER OF CONTINUOUS CUSTOMER RELATIONSHIPS AND THE IMPORTANCE OF ANCHORING THEM AT ALL LEVELS OF THE MANAGEMENT TEAM. THIS INCLUDES THE CEO WHEN POSSIBLE.**

# ANCHORING BUSINESS-TO-BUSINESS RELATIONSHIPS *WITH POINTS OF DIFFERENCE*

- How is your firm regarded within your industry? If you have made a major breakthrough in your positioning, have you "announced" your new status to the industry as a whole?

- Have you presented your complete range of products to your customers? Often, customers will overlook entire categories of a supplier's offering simply because they don't know these exist.

- If your manufacturing facility is state-of-the-art, do you exploit it as a selling point with your business customers? Have you encouraged visits or presented virtual tours on your website?

- Do good CEO-to-CEO relationships exist with your most important customers? Have you offered your involvement at the CEO level when you learn that one of your customers is facing a challenge?

- Are you constantly letting customers know you care and that you are working hard to help them succeed?

- How intensely have you absorbed the business goals and profit formula of your customers? Have you studied *your customers' customers* and their specific needs? How can you help make your customers' businesses run more efficiently and more smoothly?

- Is your organization structured to respond to your customers' needs effectively and with a sense of urgency?

- Entire industries now emerge – and expire – over a business lifespan of just a few years. Are you aligning yourself with customers in an up-to-date way?

- Are you doing everything you can to make it advantageous to and convenient for your customers to do business with you?

# CHAPTER 7

# *Successful Successorship*

"**W**hat's so unique about successorship at Hormel?" "How is Hormel able to develop so much talent within its own organization that it rarely goes outside to fill open positions?" These questions are asked often. The answer is that we are fortunate to have a long-standing culture of internal *successorship*. This great organizational asset is a powerful point of difference and gives us a distinctive edge. Every organization has successorship in some form or other, and the need for a planned internal successorship program may seem self-evident; but it is woefully neglected in American industry. Job mobility has become a way of life, and outside recruitment is the convenient solution favored for far too many job openings.

The absence of thoughtful successorship strategies is a remarkable void and a real peril to the long-term survival and growth of many organizations. In contrast, the Hormel team has been built systematically with people who have had varied career experiences throughout the company.

This depth allows us to run one of the most efficient operations of its kind in the country and solidly positions us for growth. Our attention to successorship includes making sure we have plentiful advancement opportunities for our considerable talent base. However, there are periods in our long history when our commitment to successorship may not have been active to the degree it should have been.

Successorship is not a concept which can lie dormant. It must be constantly addressed and applied as an energizing principle. Having trained talent in place has been a crucial advantage in making acquisitions, where we can quickly infuse needed talent to improve operational standards quickly.

> ### THE TIME TO PAY ATTENTION TO ORGANIZATIONAL DEPTH IS *BEFORE*, NOT *AFTER*, A STRATEGIC ACQUISITION IS MADE.

Our attention to succession has paid handsome dividends in the past and promises to do so in the future, provided we continue to be vigilant about its importance.

## CONSTRUCTIVE CAREER PATHING

After becoming Hormel's president, I remember having a discussion about the future with one of our best managers. "It's unlikely either of us will be moving to a new job very soon. Still," I asked him, "who's your backup?"

He responded with a kind of blank look. I bet he was thinking: 'Why does Dick want to know who my backup is? He's not planning to get rid of me, is he?'

"We can't promote you until you have a backup," I said with a smile.

"From this day forward, one of your top responsibilities is to find and develop the manager who'll replace you. Then it's to find *that* person's backup. In fact, one of the most important jobs you have is to plan for backups *three-deep* throughout the entire organization of our production operations. Have we taught them everything they need to know and charged them with responsibility to prepare for Hormel's growth?"

Bill Hunter used to have huge organizational charts with magnetic tokens on a metallic base. When superintendents and foremen would visit a plant manager's office, the managers would remind their people, 'See that. It looks like a chess board, doesn't it? Hormel has options for all sorts of moves. That means you have options as an individual, too.' It was our way of dramatizing successorship planning and making it a top-of-mind issue. To make the system work, people must have the desire to advance. Then it's necessary to have a plan in place which will allow that to happen.

> **SUCCESSION IS A JOURNEY WHICH MUST BE CONTINUALLY PURSUED IF A COMPANY'S SUCCESS IS TO BE SUSTAINED.**

Fortunately, we had the depth of talent on which to build. It came from the combination of newly recruited individuals (industrial engineers and quality control professionals, especially) along with experienced veterans necessary to turnaround the old Austin plant starting in 1969. Systematically organizing that management depth, our successorship strategy became perhaps our most fundamental point of difference.

Gary Ray is a fine illustration of internal successorship. He started out as a foreman in our Fort Dodge, Iowa plant. He then advanced to supervisor. After serving in several further key operating positions, he became group vice president of Operations. Gary was promoted to executive vice president with full responsibility for refrigerated foods and took on the management of technology, logistics and marketing. In 2008, Gary retired as President of Protein Businesses – our largest operation – including Foodservice, all refrigerated items, and Jennie-O Turkey Store. Gary is a top-notch problem-solver who achieved a seamless coordination between Marketing and Operations. He has served on the Hormel board of directors longer than any of our other officers. Gary – like so many Hormel managers – had a steady progression through a wide variety of experiences that have both built his skills and equipped him with a comprehensive grasp of how the company needs to operate. Meanwhile these managers have gained a solid, meaningful familiarity with people throughout the firm. This practice has great strength and leadership at every group level. Gary Ray's successor, Steve Binder, is also a product of long-term internal development within Hormel.

Another one of the many illustrations of effective succession is Dr. Phillip Minerich, Hormel's Vice President, Research and Development. He started with us in 1976 after interviewing on campus at Ohio State. Phil had fond memories of Dinty Moore hash and stew from his camping days as a kid. As with many college grad new hires, he started out in Quality Control in the old Austin plant. After a year in QC, he transferred to the gelatin department and became a foreman. Phil moved from Austin to the new gelatin plant in Davenport, Iowa when it opened in 1979.

Thereafter, Phil transferred to the Austin plant as a FAST 'N EASY' bacon foreman for the microwave pre-cooked line. Then he became corporate manager of sanitation. Later he had a stint as a foreman in the ham boning area. He was one of the managers who operated the new Austin plant during the 1985-6 strike. In retrospect, Phil views these rotations and multiple assignments as a tremendous advantage. He believes:

> *The best advice I got during my career is this: Wherever you are, learn as much as you can as fast as you can. Hormel transfers people a lot – one day you could be in 'Bacon' and the next day in 'Ham' and the day after on an office assignment. In my past 29 years at Hormel, there have been some odd experiences like running boilers or figuring out certain pump mechanisms. I never expected to learn these skills. Yet, every one of these experiences has been valuable.*

> **MOVING THROUGH DIFFERENT AREAS, MANAGERS BUILD A COMPANY-WIDE HUMAN NETWORK, COLLABORATE BETTER, INNOVATE IN THEIR OWN DIVISIONS MORE CREATIVELY, AND DEMONSTRATE CLEARER COMPANY INSIGHT.**

As I see it, one of the great advantages of our rotation philosophy is that people learn the business in specific . . . and not in general. Perhaps the best example of effective rotation is seen in Hormel's current CEO and Chairman of the Board, Jeff Ettinger. Jeff started out as an attorney in the legal department. He asked to enter Marketing and went on to learn the grocery products marketing business for such products as HORM-EL Chili. His career path also included serving as corporate treasurer and then as President and CEO of Jennie-O Turkey Store, which grew from a $545 million business in 2000 to one which was $1.27 billion at the end of fiscal 2008. Jeff's diverse background gives him the necessary line experience to secure Hormel's powerful marketing advantages in the years to come.

Jeff is an excellent, but not an isolated, case of a career-rotation philosophy which has contributed great strength to the Hormel management team. A strong management team enables entering new businesses as well as growing existing categories. Contrary to what we might expect, this planned staffing of management talent actually fuels career opportunities rather than blocking them. I am a firm believer that you need to have the people in place who can develop. They are needed in advance to absorb and ready to build acquisitions for expansion, rather doing the deals or investing the capital first and then scrambling to find the talent to make the new business successful.

## THE ARGUMENT FOR INTERNAL DEVELOPMENT AND ROTATION

Companies often favor very specialized career paths. However, for Hormel and a number of other companies, there are some key limitations to this philosophy:

- Managers don't get to know the real work the company does.
- People are developed with a narrowly limited base of skills.
- Individuals don't know their colleagues and this weakens both morale and internal networking.
- Managers can't size up the depth of talent in the organization.
- The company becomes more territorial, and work units are increasingly defensive of their turf. This constrains team effort and diminishes results.

- People can't experience the business roles of various departments to find out where they can best perform.
- The company loses the ability to draw on talent from multiple sources in backing up key positions.
- Managers find themselves blocked in one career channel, with no hope of advancing until their boss moves. If movement is blocked for one person, it can have a paralyzing career effect for many others.
- When openings must be filled, management is forced to rely on one or two supervisory inputs as opposed to a whole range of them.
- People are less likely to be energized about their jobs, because they aren't learning and taking on new and exciting challenges.
- The net result: the company is far more likely to recruit from outside than to promote from within.

Job rotation must always be meaningful. For a quality talent pool to develop, individuals must have the opportunity to truly absorb and learn from the experience. Job rotation is not just training and sparring. It also means sticking around for the main event – being genuinely tested in these various assignments – before moving on to a new area.

We have been told Hormel's attitude toward organizational depth and succession is an advanced viewpoint. In fact, I would be quick to credit the fundamental thinking to our founder George A. Hormel back when Hormel was a meat-packing business. He once wrote,

*"I knew that when the business grew large and profitable enough to pay high salaries for brains, we could hire them, but I was more concerned with developing the talents of the men we already had. I wanted the coun-*

*try boys who came to work for us to be so good and efficient that when an opportunity arose, they, and not outside talent, would fill the better job."*

No doubt, if George A. were alive today, he would be as anxious to promote the careers of women Hormel already had on board as those of men. He was too dedicated to finding and deploying talent.[1] When George A. hired people for staff jobs who didn't advance "from the line," he insisted that they get to know the business from the ground up.

At Hormel, we have worked hard to instill the belief that anyone of us can go to the top. Family issues (e.g., nepotism) of whatever sort have been rooted out. There's nothing to impede a person's progress. Advanced education is important to be sure, but it never outweighs talent, proven results, and determination. Today we have senior executives in critical positions who do not have college degrees and who make tremendous contributions to the company's success. On the other hand, we have managers with master's and doctorate degrees, like Phil Minerich, who are evaluated against their respective fields. It depends on how well you put the puzzle together. In many respects for firms committed to preparing their people, the real 'graduate school' for all managers starts when they enter the company.

The strategic importance of the Hormel Foundation's ownership stake in Hormel Foods can't be underestimated. People know that no one will come in

---

1     *Since 30% of MBAs generally and 35% of Harvard's MBAs are today women, I am certain that the absence of women among the managers mentioned in this book may be disappointing to some readers. Male dominance was the bleak reality during the period when I was an active manager at Hormel, especially in the meat-packing era. Fortunately, that is changing. I say with some pride that two distinguished women, Luella Goldberg and Geri Joseph, joined the Hormel board during my CEOship. This was when many Fortune 500 companies couldn't succeed in finding just* **one** *female director . . . or ignored the issue altogether. In the community, Bonnie Rietz has been a stellar civic leader – first as mayor of Austin and now as a director of The Hormel Foundation.*

and buy this company and shatter their careers. That's another reason why we are able to keep so many talented people. You can't develop three-deep backup and a reservoir of ten to twenty years of company experience, unless people know they are building a career. Such a solid bedrock gives us the stability within which we can re-invent ourselves on a continuing basis. As I said, management of successorship may be Hormel's most decisive point of difference of all.

> **A PROPERLY STRUCTURED FOUNDATION CAN BE AN EFFECTIVE DEFENSE AGAINST CORPORATE PREDATORS WHO TAKE OVER BUSINESSES SIMPLY TO CARVE UP ASSETS AND REALIZE SHORT-TERM GAINS. SUCH PROTECTION STRONGLY FOSTERS EMPLOYEE LOYALTY.**

The kind of development process countless Hormel managers have experienced has given management a far more diverse look at the people who are ready for promotion. Instead of one or two people making the call, you can weigh the input of three or more managers in deciding on a promotion. You don't just improve people through diverse experiences, you improve the ability of the organization to judge people because you enlarge the pool of qualified managers who assess them.

> **JOB ROTATION ENLARGES THE CANDIDATE POOL FOR INTERNAL SUCCESSION. IT ALSO BETTERS PROMOTION DECISIONS WITH MORE INPUT AND A BROADER COMPANY VIEWPOINT.**

From a succession planning standpoint, job rotation gives the company more than one option. There is some risk, indeed, because you will also disappoint three or four qualified people who don't get a particular job when an opening arises, but that's something you have to accept. Any particular management position may require a different emphasis at a particular point in time – people skills, technical knowledge, organizational ability. In such an atmosphere of team play, company growth stretches people to be effective, often in unexpected ways.

> **DEVELOP A RESERVOIR OF TALENT THAT CAN GROW WITH EXPANSION AND IS READY BEFORE EXPANSION OPPORTUNITIES ARISE.**

Promotion from within is one of Hormel's strongest points of difference. While opportunities are available, senior managers are looking for people who are hungry for those chances. But, it's always under the fair premise of 'no promises.'

## HOW FAULTY STRUCTURES AND INCENTIVES CAN CRIPPLE SUCCESSION

One of the great points of difference in a successful succession program is creating the right organizational structure with properly designed incentives. Hormel's approach toward management development hasn't always been flawless. I can vividly recall one case where faulty structure and badly designed incentives nearly crippled the career of a very promising young executive. He went on to become a highly effective group vice president at Hormel, but very early in his career with the company, I nearly suggested he seek another career in a business that could better use his abilities.

When I was newly in charge of all sales for the Austin plant, about two hundred salesmen were part of the team. This young man was one of them, and I couldn't figure out why he wasn't more productive. He looked like he had all the equipment to be an outstanding salesperson and more. One day I sat down with him and had a serious chat.

"From everything I see in you," I told him candidly, "you ought to be a great salesman with management potential. But, you aren't performing at that level. I don't understand the problem. If I were you, I'd be tempted to quit."

"Dick, I'll tell you what the problem is," he answered. "It's my boss – the district manager."

"What's the matter? Can't you get along with him?" I probed.

"That's not the point," he answered. "There are only so many juicy accounts in the district, and he keeps those all to himself."

That prompted me to do some research and give thought to our management structure. Not only was our incentive system on the production line antiquated and counterproductive, but our sales management accountability and incentives were alarmingly misdirected as well. The system was constructed so that district managers were paid on the basis of their personal sales performance which resulted in self-selection of the accounts in their districts. This syndrome of district manager protectionism often develops in companies where the district manager's role is not properly understood or incented. In our case, the bonus system allowed – in fact, *encouraged* – them to be personal performers. Rather than delegating responsibility to a team and developing talent, district managers were concerned with their own bonuses – a natural response. They were competing with their own salespeople, and it's no surprise who controlled the prime accounts.

Shortly thereafter, at our annual district managers' meeting, we established new manager guidelines for their total district with overall performance determining their compensation. This situation wasn't the district managers' problem at all. It was the company's. We had positioned district managers without a clear definition of their responsibilities. The old incentive system for them didn't just hurt our sales and profit performance – it crippled our succession program. You could hire an ambitious young talent, but the recruit would then be saddled with demotivating jobs. Simultaneously we restructured the salary and incentive plans and clarified job responsibilities so managers were measured and paid for total overall district performance, including development of individual territories.

With the new district manager's program in place, productive and sustained high performance was the natural consequence. The managers themselves were visibly charged with the development of their total district. Young sales people were given proper attention, showed they were anxious to emerge, and excelled. And, the person I described earlier became a pace-setting salesman, an outstanding manager, a divisional manager and ultimately a highly successful group vice president.

> **A COMPANY PRODUCING SUBSTANDARD SUCCESSION CANDIDATES MAY SUFFER FROM FLAWED ORGANIZATIONAL DESIGN AND INCENTIVES, NOT JUST POOR RECRUITING.**

The importance of succession is paramount for me. When I was 32 years old, I had managed Austin – our largest plant sales operation. We had achieved substantial gains in sales and profits. The position of general sales manager for route cars[2] opened up. Before the new manager was named, my career had been moving ahead rapidly, and I was very confi-

---

2      *For a description of 'route cars' and their role at the time, see Chapter 3.*

dent of my ability to perform at the next level. I didn't get the job. I was so convinced that I was the right person for the job that I almost quit Hormel. In reality, the company was doing me a big favor. When I *did* get the position two years later, I was better prepared and had developed very strong support throughout the company. Moving before you are truly ready can be damaging. It's incumbent on senior managers to help younger colleagues to realize this.

## CEO SUCCESSION AT HORMEL

*4 GENERATIONS OF HORMEL CEOs IN 2008*
*Center: Jim Holton (CEO 1972-1981), Standing from left to right: Joel Johnson*
*(CEO 1994-2005), Dick Knowlton (CEO 1981-1993), Jeff Ettinger (CEO 2006-present)*

The line of succession for Hormel's presidents provides important insights into how the business changed . . . and, at times *didn't* change. The founder George A. Hormel ran the company from its inception in 1891 until his retirement. George A.'s formal education was confined to elementary school, but he was very proud of his work ethic and of what he did as both a manager and a craftsman. "I incessantly preached," he once wrote, "that we were engaged in one of the most important tasks in the world – feeding people. Nothing that contributed to the quality of their food was too much trouble." His passion for craftsmanship was inexhaustible. The employees in the smokehouse would say: "George Hormel looks over his hams the way most men look over a pretty girl." George A. never tired of teaching by example, trimming hams and exhorting employees on the line with: "If you can do one right, you can do them all right." Or, tearing up a dollar bill – back when a dollar was worth a good deal! – before a group of gasping bystanders on the plant floor to dramatize the cost of wasteful practices.

George A.'s son Jay was – as I have said earlier – an idea man and an innovator of the first order in product development, but also an exceptional marketing expert with an intense interest in labor relations. The leadership transition from George A. to Jay had an unusual twist to it. George A. 'retired' in 1927 and moved to Bel Air, California. Jay became Acting President while George A. remained CEO and continued to review weekly status reports on the business. Hormel's first stock exchange listing came in 1928. In 1929, the formal shift in operating authority was made permanent with George A. becoming chairman and Jay – president.

Tim Corey was named president in 1946, and Jay became chairman, serving in that role until his unexpected death at the age of 61 in 1954. A 26-year Hormel veteran at the time of his appointment, Tim Corey may have been president, but, according to Jim Holton, my predecessor as Hormel CEO, "Jay made all the big decisions. Someone else filled in the blanks. Jay set the direction. Others dealt with the details." Jay had gone to Princeton. Tim Corey was an All American tackle on the football team when he attended the University of Nebraska. Both men were officers in the U.S. Army and served in France during World War I. Jim Holton recalls:

*Tim Corey was a very stern and forceful leader. He was there early in the morning. He would walk through the old Austin plant every day. And, there was never any question as to who was the boss. Corey was totally dedicated to hard work and had been in the Hormel organization for more than a quarter century before he was elevated to the presidency.*

Jay, it is said, gave his three sons employment opportunities at Hormel but their interests were in other areas. After Jay's death, Hormel ceased to be a family business.

In 1955, Bob Gray was elected to succeed Tim Corey as president. Bob Gray had been with Hormel for 28 years before being named to this post. As always, Jim Holton's comments on people are especially astute:

*Bob Gray was a fine man, though he never darkened the door of a college, had a farm background, and worked in a small town bank . . . until he got a chance to drive and sell from a sausage truck for Hormel. As long as Corey was alive, Gray was much in his shadow.*

Although it may sound almost medieval today, the fact that Gray had no sons could have been a relief for the company, because Hormel – as every other business in those days – was governed exclusively by males.[3] Bob Gray was a real gentleman and an outstanding operating executive. He had

---

3     *Bob Gray and his wife were childless and adopted a daughter.*

a very strong grasp of rudimentary sales and transportation. Bob Gray also had remarkable insight. In 1958, he implemented a change which was to have dramatic consequences. He named Harold Butler the first manager of the old Austin plant. Because of the Austin plant's massive scale, it was always assumed that the president of Hormel would also run the Austin plant. The Austin plant's impact on the total company was so huge, it had never occurred to anyone to think otherwise.

While the firm had grown to a scale of national importance, Austin was still being managed as a geographic entity onto itself. As the company grew, this overloading of responsibilities at the president's office resulted in constant and formidable bottlenecks. Bob Gray saw this. He was a delegator, and he began the process of re-orienting our management thinking. But it took decades for that thinking to really filter down through the organization.

When Bob Gray established this groundwork for Hormel's corporate management structure in 1958 the company had a tough time coming to grips with the implications of what had been created. At first people couldn't grasp the need for such a separation. Nonetheless, partitioning the Austin plant from the corporate entity created an entirely new framework for strategic decision-making. In a short while, the managerial benefits became persuasively apparent.

Bob Gray had a personal effect on my career aspirations worth noting. When I was a freshman at the University of Colorado, I applied for a summer sales-rep job at Hormel. After being accepted and returning to Austin, I received a surprise phone call from Bob Gray. I was stunned. He wanted to know if I would play golf with him on Saturday. Impressed beyond words, I accepted, fully expecting that I would be part of a foursome. It turned out to be just the two of us, and we spent most of that Saturday together. This not only allowed him to assess a very junior-level job seeker; it also stoked my motivation to join an organization with such a keen interest in the career aspirations of young people. That golf outing with Bob Gray proved to be a defining moment in my life.

A solid succession program is built on firmly anchored loyalty, and loyalty is unattainable without personal contact. Hormel Foods' current CEO Jeff Ettinger is mindful of the ever-present need to personalize a large company, albeit one headquartered in a smaller community such as Austin. He regularly conducts one-on-one informal meetings with all of the headquarters professional managers. These chats last 20-30 minutes. With over 40 operations in the U.S. including subsidiaries, Jeff also visits these locations on a rotating cycle to meet with team members.

> **IF A CEO WANTS TO GUIDE THE QUALITY OF MANAGEMENT SUCCESSION LONG TERM, NOTHING BEATS REGULARLY READING THE PULSE OF ENTRY-LEVEL MANAGEMENT TALENT.**

Tommy Thompson became Hormel's president in 1965. He was the first college graduate to do so. A classic, extroverted salesman if ever there was one, he also proved to be an effective and aggressive plant operator. His background was strictly sales until Jay Hormel sent him to Fremont, Nebraska to manage the plant Jay had acquired. Hormel planned to build a new one next door to the existing Fremont site. One of Tommy Thompson's most crucial and timely contributions may have been in the expansion of the Fremont operation. During his tenure, its staff size grew from fifty to more than six-hundred. (This helped diminish Hormel's lopsided dependence on the Austin plant.) Like his predecessors, Tommy was a career Hormel employee and had been with the company well over thirty years before being named president. Unlike his predecessors, his tenure as president was relatively short. He moved into the chairman's slot in 1969. One of Thompson's sons was in the business for many years. Tommy was a man of action and certainly moved the company forward.

Jim Holton, my immediate predecessor, became Hormel's next president in 1969. While he too had been a long-time Hormel employee, his credentials were quite different. Jim was a World War II veteran, including participating in the Normandy invasion. Before joining Hormel in 1947, he received his law degree. Jim had no plans to stay at Hormel. He wanted to teach law. Knowing that law professors who never practiced earned slim regard, he intended to stick around for a couple of years and get some practical experience. Thankfully he stuck around a lot longer – initially because of his esteem for Jay Hormel. Jim became a teacher in an actual business environment. Not that there was any shortage of legal work, and that legal work also gave him considerable knowledge about the operations of the business. Jim recalls:

> *The Hormel people were employed under an exemption to the Fair Labor Standards Act because of Jay's annual wage concept. There were many legal problems, grievances, and arbitrations that resulted. I couldn't afford to be ignorant of operating knowledge to do the legal work. Then I got involved in sales contracts to learn how those were arranged. Regulation – a central concern in the food industry – also acquainted me with operations.*

Jim has some memorable recollections of how he came to be selected as Hormel's CEO:

*Tommy Thompson loved to golf, hunt, and fish. I had none of those assets. Thompson was about as much unlike me as you could get. Gray persuaded Thompson to take a chance on me. In August 1969, I had been an executive vice president for about a year-and-a-half. Bob Gray was then chairman and Tommy Thompson was president. Gray was thinking of retiring. That meant Thompson would move up, and they would need a new president. Bob Gray asked, "What would you think about becoming president?" I said I would give it a whirl, and, if it didn't work out, we could pick someone else. I knew I needed to learn a lot. We had to press on with fixing the out-of-control incentive systems which had greatly increased our unit labor costs over our competitors. A start had been made years before me. Too often individuals are solely credited with what are in fact joint efforts. Very little is accomplished by any one individual acting alone. The management team had basic operating skills. I was something of a freak to be picked for the job. Lucky.*

"On the day I became CEO," Jim remembers, "I issued rule number one: There would be no employment of the children of officers or plant managers at Hormel. I sensed a lot of silent cheers."

Jim is esteemed for his perceptiveness, especially his people skills. During his decade as CEO and later as chairman, Jim was very supportive of the Hormel management team as we continued to overhaul the company. Jim's administrative talents are formidable, and the partnership we formed was one I much appreciated. His support of building the new Austin plant in a period of great risk and uncertainty was especially valued. Clearly it was one of the most difficult decisions we both faced.

Jim Holton was once asked how he saw my succession into the CEO-ship evolve, and here is what he said:

> *Dick came up in Sales. . . . Our treasurer—Al Alsaker—was a brilliant guy. He was the first person to draw my attention to Dick. Al had an excellent grasp of people and he was a good judge of them. At the time, Dick was assistant manager of the Austin plant in charge of all plant sales and production. Al said I should take a look at Dick, and I trusted his judgment. We had some excellent senior people. But, most of them were too close in age with me.*

> *Early during my tenure as president, I felt I had a responsibility to prepare a* **corporate will**. *Through it, I informed the outside directors what I thought should be done in the event of my untimely disability. The person I identified as my backup wasn't Dick. That's not a negative on him. He wasn't ready. Each year, I privately solicited the opinion of outside directors as to who should succeed me. One by one, more of them said Knowlton. By then, Dick was sitting on the board as well. A consensus was building. A majority of the inside board members favored Knowlton. The outside directors were 100% for Knowlton. One director wanted to go outside Hormel, but we had never done that before. I felt that my successor really needed to know the organization.*

Jim Holton's wry sense of humor is also legendary. He knew what challenges lay ahead for Hormel's next president. At a Hormel meeting, Jim introduced my selection with a long pause and the words: ". . . And, the loser is – Dick Knowlton!" I came to the job in 1979 with 25 years experience as a full-time Hormel employee.

In the spirit of candor, I must say that my backup as the next president of Hormel did not come from within Hormel. Originally, I had hoped Jim Hall – a marvelously qualified long-term Hormel executive and team builder with just the right marketing sense – would take on that role. I envisioned Jim and I would operate as a team during a major transition – we had a solid appreciation for each other's abilities. For very understandable personal reasons, Jim opted for retirement.[4] I felt certain that the company was in need of strong marketing leadership once again at a critical juncture in its history. I thought the world of Bill Hunter, but he was too near to retirement and without marketing experience.

Age was also a consideration. I was looking hard at Gary Ray, but he had not yet had the necessary exposure to the marketing side of the business. Had Jim Hall stayed on, it would have been natural for Gary to develop that marketing expertise under Jim's and my guidance. Because of our management depth, we had some exceptionally qualified senior executives. None of them, unfortunately, had that critical marketing skill to the degree which, in my opinion, Hormel needed. Before I would relinquish the presidency, we conducted a painstaking executive search for a potential eventual replacement. The final candidates were all subjected to a scrutinizing

---

4       *Jim Hall is another example of a person whose career was stalled by the lack of a well defined organization structure. He spent considerable time as third in line in the Grocery Products Division and was ideally suited to bring together rival grocery products and meat products divisions as a single, unified marketing entity. Fortunately we were able to move several executives, including Jim, through a congested structure that had been tying up succession talent and not always efficiently serving company needs.*

review process by the entire board of directors. Once we had a prospective candidate, the rounds of board interviews by the outside directors as well as by myself were especially rigorous. The individual had an excellent track record in marketing. But, after he joined us and we had more than a year of direct exposure, we both knew the transition wouldn't work. We parted company amicably.

> **IN THE OUTSIDE HIRING OF TOP EXECS, THE DECISIVE FACTOR IS USUALLY CULTURAL FIT. DESPITE THE BEST PLANNING, THIS IS VERY HARD TO PREDICT WITHOUT ACTUAL EXPERIENCE.**

Hormel had never had a president with less than twenty years of experience within the company. It would have been easy for us to change our criteria, shed the marketing requirement, and pick an internal candidate. We didn't. In June 1991, Joel Johnson joined us as Executive Vice President of Sales and Marketing. Joel came to us from General Foods, where he had spent 24 years, the last five of them as EVP of Oscar Mayer. Fortunately for us, Philip Morris had yet another change of corporate CEOs, and didn't see the wisdom of moving Joel to the CEO-ship of Oscar Mayer. That gave us the opening to secure his considerable talents.

While he may not have been a Hormel veteran, Joel was steeped in knowledge about both the grocery and the meat industry, had an excellent grasp of marketing and mastered a particular expertise in branding – a point of difference essential for Hormel's continued growth. In July 1992, with the important experience of a year as executive vice president, Joel became Hormel's eighth president. We added the post of chief executive officer in October 1993, at the end of our fiscal year. During his tenure, Hormel's path of sales and profit growth continued its strong, positive course; and Joel lived up to the demanding marketing expectations that had been set for him. Among other achievements, Joel continued our expansion into international cuisine categories, advanced our program of fresh meat branding, and made important strides in contemporizing established Hormel brands in new microwaveable versions while updating our strong branded presence in shelf-stable products.

We were able to bring in a leader from the outside because we had such a strong core of internally developed management in every area of the company, from Gary Ray and his backup team in Operations to Don Hodapp, Jim Cole, Stan Kerber, Bob Patterson, Eric Brown, Forrest Dryden, Jim Silbaugh, Jim Jorgenson, and Ken Regner in other key management positions. Every one of these people was rock solid and strong enough to run any company as a team leader – as our steady advance in volume and profits demonstrated. However, at the time, Hormel needed leadership specifically attuned to marketing. Candidate age and the need for seasoned marketing expertise were two key considerations. I am pleased and proud to say that Hormel Foods has an incoming generation of operating and marketing managers that share the same hallmark for leadership. I have not necessarily mentioned them elsewhere in the book, and they include Bill Snyder, Bruce Schweitzer, Bob Tegt, Mark Coffey, and Jeff Nuytten. There are certainly others, and I'm confident that Hormel Foods will continue to produce an extraordinary flow of internal talent.

George Dahlman, a highly regarded food-industry financial analyst and now Co-Head of Investment Research at Piper Jaffray, wrote in a research report: The subsequent management team and CEO at Hormel were "dealt a good hand, and they have played it well." The rightness of the decision to pick Joel Johnson as a successor coupled with the strength of the existing executive team was borne out by Hormel's excellent performance record. In 2004, the baton was passed once again – this time to a 15-year Hormel veteran. The present CEO is Jeff Ettinger, whose background I detailed earlier in this chapter. Jeff is highly qualified and has already demonstrated the correctness of the decision to name him CEO. Hormel's succession story continues with considerable success. Succession requires constant vigilance – especially because it is at times so seemingly unimportant given a business's daily priorities.

# SUCCESSORSHIP:
# *A POINTS-OF-DIFFERENCE APPROACH*

- Build a 'three-deep' level of backup for all management jobs, but never let depth of backup paralyze job rotation, particularly at more junior levels. Optimally, managers should be backups for multiple positions both in their present departments and elsewhere in the organization.

- It's easy to become complacent about maintaining management depth at the 'three-deep' standard. However, a failure to do so will soon manifest itself as a drop-off in quality when key positions are filled internally.

- Retain talented people as long as they are hard-working but continue to rotate them to positions where they can excel. Take developmental risks on people but without career guarantees.

- The jobs for which people are prepared will change. Ready them for the added skills demanded by the jobs of the future, not the jobs of the present.
- Recognize people need passion as well as ability to master demanding assignments.
- To deliver future points of difference for the firm, forward-looking skills must be identified so that new technological innovations will continue to be developed.
- Watch how people's values evolve as well as their skills, so that they have the **character** as well as the **expertise** to do the job.
- Have a meaningful plan for business growth so your people can grow with the company. To keep talented people motivated, they have to see tangible opportunity.

## CHAPTER 8

# Citizen Hormel

## HORMEL'S BOND WITH MAYO

I n 1889, just two years before George A. Hormel opened shop with a retail store on Mill Street in Austin, Drs. Will and Charles Mayo built the first general hospital in Minnesota. It was a 27-bed facility that was to become the cornerstone of perhaps the world's greatest medical practice – the Mayo Clinic. In 1919, the Mayo brothers dissolved their partnership and invested the proceeds to create a not-for-profit foundation. From the very outset, the Mayo Clinic has been dedicated to medical care, research, and education. Physicians on the Mayo Clinic staff are salaried professionals and do not otherwise benefit from the practice financially. Their sole focus is to continually elevate the standards of medical care the world over.

It's 45 miles from Austin to Rochester. Philosophically, the road between the two communities is much closer than even this short span of interstate. In 1941, Jay Hormel created the Hormel Foundation which I'll describe in more detail later. In 1942, in partnership with the University of Minnesota, Jay launched the Hormel Institute for biological and chemical research.

As you see, Jay also had a community vision in mind for what the Hormel business could and should do. That Jay and Drs. Will and Charles were good friends is not surprising.

> **BOND WITH OTHER OUTSTANDING ORGANIZATIONS. THOSE ORGANIZATIONS MAY BE IN ENTIRELY DIFFERENT REALMS, SUCH AS MEDICINE OR EDUCATION.**

Over the decades, the partnership between Mayo and Hormel has been rewarding. It continues to evolve today. For the maximum term of twelve years, I had the honor of membership on the Mayo Clinic board of directors, and have had the privilege of serving on another Mayo board.

As the first Hormel executive to be a Mayo board member and in attending the first Mayo breakfast board meeting, I had the fun of piping up and asking "Where's the bacon?" For twelve years thereafter, the bacon appeared with regularity at our board breakfasts . . . and it was also the basis of an institutional relationship that was later to bring Mayo's unparalleled resources to Austin as the foundation of our community's unrivaled health care.

Mayo has added significantly to the quality of life in Austin. In 1988, during my tenure on the Mayo board, our local hospital became part of the Mayo Medical System. The Austin Medical Center has 74 physicians today. Just 12 years ago, there were only 15. Through today's high speed communications, access to the Mayo medical database and to its network of world-renowned authorities is instantaneous. Mayo has guided our Center in developing its technology. And, Mayo Clinic today even out-sources certain of its medical specialties *to* Austin.

For years, Bonnie Rietz was mayor of Austin.[1] Bonnie's husband is a doctor at the Austin Medical Center, and she is fond of noting that more new doctors arrived in the Austin community in the year 2004 than *resided* here in 1979, when she and her spouse first came to Austin! Until recently, the CEO of the Center has been Dr. Tim Johnson – a home-grown talent and a skilled physician whose father worked in the office of Hormel's Austin plant. It's Mayo-style to rotate administrative leadership, so Dr. Tim now works closely with the new highly respected CEO Dr. David Agerter.

> **WHEN YOU CREATE WORLD-CLASS CIVIC AND COMMUNITY INSTITUTIONS, YOU ALSO CREATE CIVIC LEADERSHIP OPPORTUNITIES TO SPUR THE DREAMS OF COMING GENERATIONS.**

During my Mayo directorship, Dr. Gene Mayberry became the first Mayo CEO to serve on the Hormel Foods board of directors. It was the first time we had a true authority on the Hormel board who could represent the voice of health issues, an increasingly important strategic concern for Hormel. His very presence prompted us to treat wellness topics with heightened attention. Gene also had strong marketing instincts and began Mayo's expansion into the Jacksonville and Scottsdale markets.

Dr. Bob Waller, President Emeritus and former CEO of the Mayo Clinic, served on the Hormel board until 2007. A gratifying experience for me is

---

1      *As I noted earlier, Bonnie became a member of the Hormel Foundation board of directors in 2008.*

how Dr. Waller – a perceptive force and a remarkable visionary in building on the work of the founding Mayo brothers – looked to firms outside of the healthcare industry to create significant points of difference. The firms Mayo Clinic studied included Hewlett-Packard, IBM, AT&T... and Hormel.

What could an organization like Mayo possibly learn from Hormel? In the mid-1980s, Mayo faced the same cost pressures that were descending on the rest of the healthcare industry. Hormel, Dr. Bob Waller says, was an excellent model that showed you could reduce cost and improve quality at the same time. In fact, Hormel was living proof that you could simultaneously be both a viable competitor in an industry and *still* possess the prestige brand. The wherewithal to do so often relies on investing in technology, operational processes, and efficient, new buildings as a first step.

Bob Waller believes that Hormel's decision to build a new Austin plant and borrow more than the market capitalization of the company had an influence on Mayo when it embarked on a major expansion in 1995. That year, Mayo decided to erect a 13-story, state-of-the-art medical facility in Rochester. This was the first new Mayo building in Rochester for "specialty patient care" since the 1950s and cost $441 million dollars. The structure – Mayo's largest and now named the Gonda Building – was financed by a series of philanthropists with pattern gifts coming from the Gonda family.[2] The board soon saw that twenty stories would be a far more realistic scale to anticipate future needs. Moreover, the building's interior was highly flexible – designed

---

2      *The Gondas are Hungarian immigrants to the US via Venezuela. They became undisputed leaders in the aircraft leasing industry.*

so that it could shift to the contours of emerging medical technology. The Gondas' gifts had a profound impact on enabling the continuing evolution of Mayo.

Back in 1986, Mayo began its expansion program into Florida and Arizona, but these initial facilities and staff were yet to mature as revenue sources and were in fact placing heavy financial pressure on Mayo Rochester. Also, Mayo needed to establish a better presence in nearby markets such as LaCrosse, Eau Claire, Albert Lea, Mankato, Decorah, Owatonna, and Austin where an increasingly competitive healthcare industry threatened to dislodge Mayo's natural advantage. The Mayo strategy to penetrate these markets was built around a series of carefully calculated tactical steps – often small ones – that multiplied Mayo's meaningful points of difference in countless ways. Mayo's management felt they could make enormous capital investments like the new Gonda Building profitable in an accomplishment similar to ours with the Austin plant – just as we methodically coupled points of difference in marketing expertise with operating efficiency. Using these same principles, the Mayo Clinic is now completing its third major addition to our Austin Medical Center – owned, operated, and staffed by Mayo.

When Dr. Waller retired from the Hormel board, Dr. Hugh Smith, CEO of Mayo Rochester, was asked to become a Hormel Foods director. He is a greatly respected and gifted addition. Working with him and observing his exceptional leadership skills have been particularly instructive and valuable for all of us at Hormel.

# THE HORMEL INSTITUTE

*The new and vastly expanded Hormel Institute
in Austin, Minnesota in 2009*

Mayo and Hormel shared and share a wide range of common values. These traits include having strong Midwestern roots and a commitment to fostering senior leadership from within. The newest development in the Mayo-Hormel association is an exciting partnership which has drawn together Mayo, the Hormel Institute and the University of Minnesota. Hormel Institute research in both cancer prevention and treatment has paved the way for a sharp increase in the number of grants to the Institute from the National Institutes of Health. In recent years, the Hormel Institute has grown rapidly to a staff of 100 – most of them highly trained research scientists and laboratory technicians – and its plans for continued expansion are being realized. While its fats and lipids research has become world renowned – in fact, Omega-3 and Omega-6 were both discovered and named at the Hormel Institute by Dr. Ralph Holman.

This Institute's achievements in skin research and oncology have also been exceptional.

Today the Hormel Institute is headed by the cellular and molecular biology expert Dr. Zigang Dong, who is Chinese by birth and did his postgraduate work at Columbia University. He has been an inspiring leader and scientist who has led the Hormel Institute to become a vital research organization earning national and international regard. He has personally collaborated with Dr. Yuan-Ping Pang of Mayo Clinic in the development of the cancer prevention and cure projects. The Hormel Institute has now attained such scientific acclaim that its principal operating funding comes from the National Institutes of Health. We are fortunate to have a sizable increase in research grants from NIH and others at a time when there's been a diminished availability of funds. The other major support for the Hormel Institute comes from the Hormel Foundation. Both the University of Minnesota and the Mayo Clinic have invested sizable grants in the Hormel Institute. This collaborative funding by leading organizations is a model for how a regional institution can be propelled to global stature.

The Hormel Institute's significant growth in reputation and the scope of its projects have led to a major expansion of the Institute's laboratories. We have just opened a new Hormel Institute building that has tripled the Institute's size, added 21 new laboratories, and permitted a substantial increase in staff.

Austin is a community of 23,000 people. It's not hard to imagine the impact that the Austin Medical Center and the Hormel Institute have had on the city. Both have brought an influx of the highest caliber professional talent. That in turn has upscaled the community's demographic base in a significant way with positive long-term consequences, providing attractive points of difference for both recruitment and quality of life.

> **COMPANIES HAVE A RESPONSIBILITY TO REVITALIZE AND BE ACTIVE IN THEIR RESPECTIVE COMMUNITIES IF THEY WANT TO ESTABLISH AN ENVIRONMENT FOR SUSTAINED SUCCESS.**

IBM has also played an important role. The Hormel Institute purchased IBM's Blue Gene/L supercomputer, which was developed in Rochester. This is a formidable piece of hardware that IBM declared to be the fastest computer in the world in September 2004.

Three great organizations – Mayo, the Hormel Institute, and the University of Minnesota comprise the new science triad in Southeast Minnesota. They are all thriving, and all possess inner strengths and cultures that have placed them in solid positions in their respective fields. And, they have joined forces to become the core of a Minnesota-based International Center of Research and Technology, positioned to become a global scientific magnet.

## HORMEL AND THE CITY OF AUSTIN

Even before Jay Hormel, George A. Hormel set the tone for the company's participation in the community. After George A. Hormel came to Austin in 1891, his brother Henry joined him in 1894 as minister of the Presbyterian church. The town had nearly 4,000 inhabitants and newcomer George A. became a community activist right from the start, joining the volunteer fire brigade. It's no surprise that the Hormel corporate culture is rich in its passion for community involvement. Austin was to evolve into a meat processing center, but George A. was determined that Austin would become nothing like the stockyards of Chicago he had known far too well earlier in his career. "The one thing that I have never forgotten [about Chicago]," he wrote once, "is the look of those half-fed, dirty children playing or fighting in the squalid streets alongside brothels and saloons."

George A. saw the need for an adequate infrastructure in Austin. "When my turn came to serve the city as alderman in 1894," he reported, "I took up the problem of water supply as my special province for its importance . . . [people] insisted that the city install fifty-two fire hydrants . . . " A system of such scope was an ambitious vision for the city at the time. Nor was George A. daunted by the expense of other serious urban investment. In 1902, the hot issue in Austin was whether to pave Main Street. Doing so would put debt on the public ledgers. "You show me a town out of debt," George A. proclaimed, "and I'll show you a dead town!"

When George A. retired to California, he left his completely furnished home in Austin "to the Y.W.C.A. to be used as a meeting place for the town, a community home within whose friendly atmosphere people could gather for social and community purposes." After his father left the business, Jay was equally passionate in his commitment to Austin and to the employees of Hormel and expanded the thinking toward the Foundation and the Institute, with the latter's primary focus toward research on fats and lipids.

After Jay's untimely and early death, Hormel's commitment to Austin didn't languish ... but, in the next quarter century, the meat industry certainly did. The desperate cost problems of the industry nearly drove

Hormel from Austin altogether. In 1977, about a year before my presidency of the company commenced, union negotiations with Local P-9 came to a halt in Austin. As I have described, the issues were elimination of the ever-problematic incentive program as well as a compilation of work rules that had accumulated since 1945. My predecessor Jim Holton took a bold step and announced the company would not build a new plant in Austin in the foreseeable future. We had a number of senior officers who believed that our best choice would have been to rebuild elsewhere. Austin was near to, but not in the center of the world's greatest pork industry region. Could the new plant be even more centrally located? Waverly, Iowa, for example, was seriously considered as an option. And, the questioning didn't stop there. Should the plant and the corporate headquarters be separated, some Hormel directors asked, with the headquarters moved to a more accessible location like Chicago or the Twin Cities? Geri Joseph recalls:

> *Initially, I thought Hormel was in too small a town. Particularly the corporate office, if not the flagship plant itself, ought to be in a larger community. Unless you had your own plane, Austin was hard to get to. Dick went along with us and had a variety of alternatives studied. But, it was clear that his heart was in Austin.*

Analyses were undertaken to address the board's very legitimate concerns. Good alternate sites had been identified where transition problems and costs could be avoided, but choosing another location would have been disastrous for the Austin community. My visits to closed plants of Swift, Armour, and Wilson in other cities – a number of them employing more than 3,000 employees – revealed a terrible economic aftermath that left the remaining community in disarray. I was especially concerned over consequences for Ottumwa when Morrell closed and the impact on Albert Lea in the wake of Wilson's demise. That motivated me and others to vow that this should never happen to our hometown and to all who depended on employment in the community of Austin. The context was simply this: The desperate problems of the industry, coupled with the lack of viable labor agreements, were on the verge of driving Hormel as we know it from Austin.

When competitor plants in the industry closed, many of these facilities were abandoned, leaving behind desolate towns teeming with problems and unemployment. Some of us believed Austin had to be an exception. Further, the Hormel Foundation's unusual ownership position in the company with voting control gave Hormel management a certain leverage in making that decision possible. Fortunately, in June 1978, the membership of the P-9 union Local – under John E. Hanson's leadership – ratified the agreement that eliminated the antiquated incentive system and assured the possibility of a new plant in Austin.

During uncertain economic times, community educational systems often begin to fail. In 1988, it became clear that Austin also lacked state-of-the-art educational facilities, devoted to the development of its young people. Our city, like so many others, needed a complete renovation of its public education infrastructure. The centerpiece of that renewal had to be Austin High School. At first the plan was to relocate the high school to the outskirts of the city. Two bond issues were put on the ballot to do so. Both were voted down. That didn't preclude the fact that something needed to happen.

Two coincidental events secured my personal involvement in the school infrastructure renewals. The first was a request that I teach a class at the high school in the former classroom of Dorothy Downs, my teacher for college-prep English.[3] (Indeed, the room hadn't been painted since the time I was a student.) In my junior year, I was hospitalized with a football injury for several weeks. Dorothy Downs came to the hospital with my lessons during that time. What dedication! I was not a great student, but I tested in the 90th percentile in the University of Colorado's admission exam in both English and math. Without the help of Dorothy Downs and other teachers, this might never have happened. I received a first-class education at Austin High. The school kids of Austin forty years later deserved the same break I was lucky to enjoy.

The second experience was a visit to Harvard in 1988. I was there to present a case study on Hormel to the faculty and graduate students of the Business School. The Harvard Case Study on Hormel had been written in 1985 extolling the major changes in the company. (It's too bad they didn't do that study 10 years later when we had the growth and the extraordinary number of new products in the marketplace.) Harvard wanted me to elaborate on Hormel's situation. During my stay on the Harvard campus, I happened to stroll past two construction sites in which venerable buildings were being fully preserved from the outside and totally gutted and renovated within. Austin High School is an imposing structure – two-and-a-half-blocks long. Why were we considering abandoning it in the first place? Why not salvage the wonderful facade and renovate the interior of this great building in Austin, just as was being done at Harvard?

---

3      *Perhaps someone maneuvered my visit so that I would end up in this particular classroom. If so, they did me a great service.*

Most school boards routinely contract-out construction work. They have little experience in construction project management. We were determined not to let that happen in Austin. We wanted real value for the investment. The renovation of the high school became a priority for us at Hormel as well as for the city. I have already described Hormel's gifted Engineering team. I assigned three of our top engineers, headed by Merlin Gutz, who conducted an extensive study. They found the best options to create a totally modern facility at minimum cost. We bought and moved some homes which opened up the surrounding space to achieve a campus atmosphere. Hormel Foods would ultimately give $4 million to Austin School System. The Hormel Foundation donated an additional $1 million to make this most important project a reality, and senior Hormel managers gave generously. Private citizens contributed additional major donations. The community voted in the reconstruction plan. Hormel engineers supervised the reconstruction, including totally gutting much of the building's interior and producing what many educators regard as both the most beautiful and the most advanced state-of-the-art high school in Minnesota.

The community received terrific value for its investment. It took three years, but the Austin High School, has become a state-of-the-art facility with the latest in information-systems technology . . . and at a reasonable cost. We also completed reconstruction of four elementary schools as part of the project. As of this writing, the middle-school, although relatively new, is being considered for renovation near-term including the proposed introduction of several new science labs at this level. Point-of-difference investment in community education is an absolute essential. As with most meaningful community investments, this one also has a direct payback for the firms who do business here. At Hormel, we know one of the most important considerations for retaining and recruiting top talent is the quality of the local school system for youngsters. That's especially true of the high school. Our renovation also gave us a basis to retain and attract first-rate teachers, the core to providing top-notch competitive education.

> **FORWARD-LOOKING FIRMS REALIZE THAT THE STRENGTH OF A COMMUNITY'S EDUCATIONAL SYSTEM IS ESSENTIAL TO WORKFORCE QUALITY.**

In the last year, I remember reading with dismay that the United States now ranked out of the top ten among industrialized nations in terms of its young people's science and math skills. We tend to think this deficit is only important in high-tech industries like information technology. In fact, the impact cuts across all aspects of economic life, because today advanced technology is a crucial component in nearly all goods and services.

For this reason, the Hormel Foundation has now completed an exciting new project addressing this challenge. It includes renovation of the total top floor of Austin High School – as I pointed out, two-and-a-half-blocks in length – into a state-of-the-art science center with laboratories and learning facilities supporting chemistry, biology, physics, mathematics and computer science. A number of graduates from Austin have returned to admire the new facilities and to report with envy that the Austin High labs are now superior to what they have at college.

Our emphasis on the sciences is being pursued with the proviso that English language skills will continue to receive full attention. Even more importantly, the comparison element of the project addresses teachers. To retain and upgrade teaching skills, nearly 100 of the community's very best teachers are attending specially designed advance-degree programs at the University of Minnesota in exchange for commitments to remain active as teachers in the community. When this educational initiative's success is proven – as I'm certain it will be – this will not be a short-term, one-time venture; but a continuing contribution on the part of the Hormel Foundation.

The renovation of the high school has paid an additional dividend. It also became the cornerstone of urban renewal for the city's central business district. For a city with 23,000 inhabitants, Austin is lucky to have seven interstate access ramps. The temptation is strong to build a city outward, but the usual consequence is to leave the central business district in shambles.

The renewed high school spurred a series of related investments. An out-of-date dime store was replaced with a beautiful, new town center building. The street lighting was renovated. A nature park system known as

Mill Pond was configured. Austin needed a new public library. Long-time Austin Mayor Bonnie Rietz was a city-council member at the time. She remembers another council member – who didn't *want* a new library and perhaps hadn't even set foot in the old library – saying: If we're going to *have* a library, then it's going to remain in a part of downtown needing renovation. A dynamic new public library was built in the city center with the city funding fifty percent and fifty percent coming from individual contributors. Jim Holton, my predecessor as Hormel CEO, was a dedicated leader in spearheading the library project.

> **RECOGNIZE THE INSEPARABLE BOND BETWEEN COMMUNITY QUALITY-OF-LIFE AND THE ABILITY TO RETAIN AND TO ATTRACT TOP-NOTCH TALENT IN OUR HIGHLY MOBILE SOCIETY.**

## MAKING THE COMMUNITY *BARRIER FREE*

The community should certainly be barrier-free for the physically challenged, but is it barrier-free in a broader sense as well? The late Reverend Bob Morgan, who was a pivotal figure in drawing together the Austin community's various ethnic populations, once articulated an important lesson Austin learned: "If community stability is a goal, then employees with families are far more preferable than employing individuals whose loved-ones are far away. But, if you want families, then you have to provide the infrastructure that will support their well-being." In 1999, it was clear that the nature of Austin's population was changing. For example, we noted important demographic shifts at both Hormel and in the Austin community.

Bonnie Rietz has a sharp eye for urban change. "Dick," she called me and asked, "how do we take advantage of the change? We need a broad-based initiative, and it should be citizen-driven, not government led." I suggested Jerry Anfinson, with whom I had worked on many community projects, would be the perfect leader. Jerry, a highly successful independent accountant, had been at the forefront of countless community projects. Three community leaders took on this new challenge as co-chairpersons – Jerry, Pat Ray (Gary Ray's spouse), and Bonnie Rietz. A group called Apex Austin was formed. Its multiple goals included creating a Welcome Center for new arrivals (many from a wide range of ethnic backgrounds), a childcare center, a major housing development, and transportation solutions. The Hormel Foundation pledged to match up to $5 million in community programs to get the project underway.

> **STAY IN TOUCH WITH CHANGING COMMUNITY NEEDS. MEETING THEM CAN BE A DECISIVE POINT OF DIFFERENCE ESPECIALLY IN CHALLENGED INDUSTRIES.**

Let me add a point that deserves more than passing mention. Austin's quality of life owes a great deal to the involvement of its spouses. Pat Ray is also now active in the restoration of the original George A. Hormel founder's home as a key community center. In addition to raising our family of five children, my wife Nancy was involved in community projects, especially for the hospital and the library. She was not alone, and this spirit of spousal involvement is evident in other locations where Hormel operates plants. Often we are the single largest and most important employer in moderately-sized towns, and the responsibility is ours to help set the tone for an active business-community partnership.

When the community constructed its new YMCA, our goal was to build the finest physical-fitness center for both men *and* women and most importantly, our youth. The facility that evolved has two gyms, two indoor tennis courts, a competition-sized indoor swimming pool, and an indoor running track – all of which are particularly prized in a state with Minnesota's climate. Through the Hormel Foundation's and Hormel Foods' funding support, the Y's most important advantage is that every Austin child 18-and-under has an annual membership for a dollar! It's not infrequently that the Y gets letters like one I received recently from an appreciative grandmother with a $6 check to pay the annual membership dues for all six of her grandchildren.

When the Austin Country Club burned down in 1988, insurance covered the one-million dollar loss. Our members thought that sum was adequate, but it soon became obvious that it wasn't. The Club may have owned the building, but the city owned the land. To improve the site of the course, Hormel made a trade for land in another area of the city. Rebuilding the Country Club cost $5 million. Today we have both a facility and a course which would be the pride of any major urban area. Not designed as a separate preserve for management, people from all economic levels can belong to the Club. We try very hard to keep the price of membership down, reaffirming our goal of avoiding a two-tier community. Excellent profits and dividends during the late 1980s allowed us to make this investment, one which has proved to be a symbol of community accessibility with a number of Hormel line employees as members.

> **BRIDGE CIVIC GAPS. OVERCOME 'THE DIVIDE' AND LOWER THE COST OF ACCESS FOR THE ENTIRE POPULATION TO KEY COMMUNITY INSTITUTIONS.**

## THE HORMEL FOUNDATION

The mechanism that has driven many of these programs in Austin is the Hormel Foundation. In 1928, Hormel stock was first traded on the New York Curb Exchange, later to be known as the American Stock Exchange.[4] While Hormel had become a company with publicly-traded stock, the Hormel Foundation was established to assure control. Jay Hormel and his father set up trusts that would take effect upon George A.'s death. These trusts made his heirs and the Hormel Foundation the principal beneficiaries. An unusual situation ensued: Few foundations vote controlling trusts for family members. The Hormel Foundation is one of them.

Concerned about the political power and agendas of certain large foundations, Congress launched inquiries challenging the status of whole categories of foundations in the 1960s. In 1969, a Congressional committee investigated so-called "dirty" foundations which enjoyed tax advantages but did little or nothing to benefit the public good. The Hormel Foundation was given a recommendation, saying that it was run appropriately and should be allowed ten years to develop a structure that would preserve the founder's intent. A change of legal structure was however necessary. The Hormel Foundation was a private foundation that became a public foundation, which it remains to this day. Today the Hormel Foundation votes 47.7% of the shares in Hormel Foods Corporation.

The Foundation's Articles of Incorporation state that at least one-third of the Foundation's board members be competent business people. Two

---

4    *Hormel began trading on the New York Stock Exchange in 1990.*

Hormel Foods directors also sit on the Foundation board. This certainly helps expedite joint funding on community projects, and it's a plus in resolving bottlenecks on timing. Drawing on the staffing of the Foundation board locally has a crucial advantage. The Foundation also assures stability and continuity in a number of important areas. I would highly recommend such a foundation structure to any business founder who would like to assure continuity for his or her heirs, employees, and communities of operation.

The Hormel Foundation channels its grants by giving to ten recipients: the Salvation Army, the YMCA of Austin, the Austin Medical Center, the University of Minnesota/Hormel Institute, the United Way of Mower County, Austin Public Education Foundation Inc., Cedar Valley Services Inc., the City of Austin, Austin Community Scholarship Committee, and the Austin Area Foundation. We don't scatter giving. We keep it focused. I have already pointed out the Hormel Institute's commitment to cancer and medical research generally. Under our present giving formula, the Hormel Institute receives approximately 51% of the Foundation's grants.

While the Hormel Foundation is able to make more robust contributions these days, this wasn't always the case. During the period Hormel was redefining itself, our funding desires outstretched what we could afford and wanted to achieve. Setting clear funding priorities was essential. It always is for companies and foundations pursuing a serious program of community involvement.

The Hormel Foundation's controlling position protects Hormel Foods Corp. fundamentally against hostile takeovers. As current Hormel management readily points out, the independence which Hormel Foods enjoys has been a great asset in managing the business. It also makes the company attractive to people looking for a career. Kermit Hoversten, who has been on the Foundation board since 1980 and serves as its vice chairman, says:

> *The Foundation has had a profound influence on the nature of the company. It's permitted management to make long-term moves rather than short-term ones to satisfy the financial analysts. The dialogue is open. Foundation directors are very candid and not at all afraid to speak up.*

The value of the Foundation has been appreciated by the union. Local labor leaders certainly saw the positive role the Foundation played in keeping Hormel Austin anchored in 1978. John Morrison, one of the most far-sighted leaders of the UFCW P-9 Local, has said:

> *The union continually factored in the Foundation as a major element. Today, it's hard to imagine that anyone living in Austin hasn't figured out that the Hormel Foundation is a benefit to the community.*

As Hormel director and Minnesota civic leader Luella Goldberg evaluates the Hormel Foundation, "It has been a fabulous source of strength for the community, but it's also a source of strength for the company."[5]

> **USE THE CORPORATE FOUNDATION AS A SOURCE OF COMMUNITY REJUVENATION, WHICH IN TURN CAN PROVE FUNDAMENTAL TO A COMPANY'S ABILITY TO TRANSFORM ITSELF.**

---

5    *Luella's other credentials are remarkable. Among them, she was the first woman to chair the board of the Minnesota Orchestra and the University of Minnesota Foundation. For over twenty years, she has been a member of the Board of Overseers of the University's Carlson School of Management, and she is a former director of ING (serving 2001-2008), one of the world's largest financial companies.*

## COMMUNITY WELL-BEING:
## A CORPORATE SUCCESS MEASURE

Come to Austin, Minnesota on a snowy February morning and you will see an inspiring sight. It's not yet daybreak, but you can watch people with leg braces . . . or white canes . . . cerebral palsy . . .or Down's Syndrome. . . or missing limbs – all entering special busses. They are headed off for a day's work . . . at *the Cedar Valley Rehabilitation Center*. There are three centers in this program employing 654 people with meaningful work, which they do for a number of companies. Projects for Hormel have included making sausage casings, clipping the ends of casings, special product packages, and building and rebuilding pallets. The individuals are evaluated as to the kinds of work they can perform and are paid accordingly. Because of the success of the Austin program, similar rehabilitation centers have been built in Albert Lea and Owatonna. The Center has been a remarkable model in fostering human self-worth. Such an undertaking is one any company or foundation would be proud to support.

"It's easy for a Fortune 500 company headquartered in a small city to view that community as irrelevant," says George Brophy, who headed economic development in Austin through 2007 and who grew up in Chicago, the home of so many Fortune 500 giants. "Hormel has taken just the opposite view."

How do the Hormel Foods' board outside directors view the Austin-Hormel partnership? According to Luella Goldberg:

> *It's vested self-interest. Hormel Foods wants a community that is first-rate in order to attract top people, especially top schools that will give*

*their kids a foundation so they can attend first-rate higher education institutions all over the world. There is tremendous attention to all of these considerations. There is a real ethic of arriving at work very early in the morning and working very hard. Nonetheless, life is neither as busy nor as complicated as it is in some larger metropolitan areas. People willingly devote themselves to community activity.*

The Hormel Foundation's housing project has been very realistic. As senior citizens become empty-nesters, they retire to smaller quarters, and younger families move into larger homes. We no longer have all the Norwegians living in one sector of the city and all the Irish in the southeast. During the beginning of this decade, 45 principally Hispanic families bought homes in Austin. And, we don't have gated communities to create a divide between labor and management. Austin is also the sort of place where the United Way sponsors a *Get Fit* program: students in the elementary schools get out and walk together to stay trim and active.

In the words of former mayor Bonnie Rietz: "Austin represents a community that has a welcoming spirit, an appreciation of its diversity, and a willingness to try new initiatives."

In many respects, Austin is identified as a company town. First, I prefer the term small city instead of town, but be that as it may. Second, Hormel people are only a limited number in a very wide base of the community's leadership. Robert Staughton Lynd's highly analytic account of Muncie, Indiana in the book *Middletown* in 1929 became a platform to debate the pros and cons of the company town. Some commentators attempted to portray the company town as a bad idea. My view is different. A company town can be a **very positive** concept when the company and the citizenry are dedicated to making it work. In Austin, I believe it has, and a number of visitors to Austin with vast urban *and* corporate experience share that view.

There are in fact a number of company towns in America where the model is a glowing success. As of this writing, they would include: Columbus, Indiana with Cummins Engine; Bentonville, Arkansas with Walmart; and Battle Creek, Michigan with Kellogg. These are just a few. Small cities like these have a spirit of common concern between the community and the company which is both resilient and positive. Large corporations often use their global role to justify being less involved at the local level, but I believe every corporation has an obligation to support their own community regardless of size. As a local city administrator described Austin a couple of years ago during the melt-down of fledgling dot-com companies: "It's not so bad to live in a town that makes a reliable staple like Spam, when all those high-tech firms are bursting like soap bubbles in Silicon Valley."

The list of small cities with large businesses is not short. A 2002 *New York Times* article subtitled "The Big Business of Small Towns" listed twenty towns where leading U.S. firms have their operations based. The diversity of businesses is impressive, from retailer L.L.Bean in Freeport, Maine, to carpet manufacturer Mohawk Industries in Calhoun, Georgia... from appliance powerhouse Whirlpool in Benton Harbor, Michigan, to jam giant J.M. Smucker in Orrville, Ohio.

> **THE MEASUREMENT OF SUCCESS FOR ANY CORPORATION MUST INCLUDE ITS ACTIVE PARTICIPATION IN ITS COMMUNITIES AS A CORE FACTOR IN PLANNING ITS FUTURE.**

Achieving civic growth through partnership is a multi-faceted challenge. A company needs to provide volunteer leadership to the foremost community institutions. It must lead by example on key civic issues and offer specialized talent (e.g., engineering and architecture) for top community projects. The company must also support a culture that makes voluntary community involvement both a model behavior and a responsibility. For one civic project after another, you'll see current and retired Hormel employees creating momentum by making personal leadership gifts – gifts of time and wisdom as well as money.

The thriving small community is one of America's great treasures. So many of our country's giants – educators, scientists, doctors, and teachers – have their roots in small communities. Horatio Alger, one of America's first masters of motivational thinking, was born and raised in tiny Chelsea, Massachusetts.[6] The Pulitzer Prize-winning poet Richard Eberhart, who passed away in 2005 at the age of 101, was the son of a Hormel vice president and grew up on the outskirts of Austin. Condon, Oregon has been home to three Nobel Prize winners.

Demographic experts Lynne Lancaster and David Stillman see "generational connectedness" as one of the great virtues of such cities. Lancaster and Stillman cite *The Wall Street Journal*'s Sue Shellenbarger's following comments on Condon, Oregon: "Intergenerational ties remain strong. When its top-ranked high-school basketball team hits the road, some Main Street stores close so adults can go to the game... teenagers engage adults here, greeting friends' parents with enthusiasm." Shellenbarger stresses the benefits of reinvesting "in community, taking time for scouting, sports and

---

6     *As a past president and chairman of the Horatio Alger Association, with its membership including four U.S. Presidents, the contribution of Horatio Alger as a motivational pioneer has been a particularly important personal cornerstone for me.*

other groups that foster adult bonds with children" and merging "work and home life, reversing the commuter exodus…"

How important is cultivating an environment which fosters a solid work ethic and a company with genuine values? "Given the current climate in corporate America, it should deal with how you run a company that has its feet on the ground. . . with its concern for employees and shareholders," says Geri Joseph, who retired from the Hormel Foods corporate board in September 2000. She comments:

> *Hormel was one of the first companies to do profit-sharing, starting with the founding Hormels, and continuing today. When people talk to me about what's going on with business, I always feel very proud that I can point to that company. It was run in a very conservative fashion. I chaired the audit committee of Hormel Foods' board for several years. I used to get terribly nervous. The outside auditors would tell the audit committee that this was one of the best run companies in terms of its financial statements. I worried: Is this too good to be true? We asked for some very specific information on how the inside auditors did their job and what they did. I can't even begin to tell you how detailed their report was . . . to the last penny! Do people really need to know this? After all, I would say, this is only a nickel! Hormel has had very good people. If you called there early in the morning, half these guys and gals were already at their desks. Hormel has a kind of work ethic that you really don't find in too many places.*

The sheer duplicity that toppled Enron, WorldCom or a Bernard Madoff could not occur at Hormel. Nor could the failed oversight that led to the collapse of Lehman Brothers and the bailout of AIG.

At a food industry event, I remember once meeting a top executive from an outstanding supermarket retailer – Giant Foods in Washington DC.

"Where do you live, Dick?" he asked.

"Austin, Minnesota," I answered.

"Austin, Minnesota!? What can you do in Austin, Minnesota?"

"Just live real good!" I answered.

Some months later, he came out for a visit to learn about our new Austin plant first hand. He saw the clean streets of the city decorated with the blossoms of freshly pruned flower baskets. He was impressed. He saw the rows of state-of-the-art personal computers in the remodeled high school. He was impressed. He walked up the elegantly carpeted stairs to the dining room of the Austin Country Club. He saw the sprawling new Hormel Austin plant and all of its technology. *And, was he ever impressed.* He began to realize how a corporation can benefit from the lack of distractions and disruptions when it is headquartered in a smaller city.

As I drove him back to the Hormel air terminal for him to board one of our planes to take him back to Washington, we approached a stoplight. My guest asked, "Dick, how long does it take you to get to work?"

I paused and said, "Well, that all depends. Either three or four minutes... depending if that stoplight is green or red."

Impressed? **That took his breath away!**

In 1978 and again in 1985, Hormel and Austin, Minnesota – inseparably tied together – stood at the brink of drastic economic peril. Both teetered at the edge of the ravine. Both retained their faith in pragmatic solutions and fundamental values. In the end, pragmatism and integrity exposed formidable points of difference compared with other companies and other communities. Both saw the opportunities to transform themselves with courage and conviction. My wife Nancy has handcrafted a particular thought with artful precision. It's framed and enjoys the place of honor in my office. It's a thought that was certainly true of Austin and Hormel. It will be doubtless true of countless other communities on the brink of forging a bona fide point of difference in urban-business relationships. That needlepoint reads:

On the edge of the ravine
you will always find
the most beautiful flowers

## CHAPTER 9

# *Doing Good... Better*

## A CHALLENGE FOR INDUSTRY

In recent decades, many American companies have done well. Even more CEOs have done better . . . but, some of them undeservedly so. The best performance deserves the best pay. I have long advocated that practice for individuals on the line as well as for senior managers. We are also proud of the fairness and integrity with which Hormel administers its compensation program for labor as well as management.

As an American CEO, I am *not* proud of the excesses I see make headlines many mornings. Fortunately they seem to be unrepresentative, but they are exceptions which have become more commonplace. A preoccupation with short-term results has contributed to the unnecessary breakup of significant firms and to the erosion of public confidence in the American system of free enterprise. One can hardly characterize this as responsible stewardship of business assets. In my opinion, it reflects an unhealthy trend. This outlook – one that emphasizes **getting** over **giving** – is bound to cause trouble for any nation's long-term future. As Winston Churchill eloquently put it:

> *"We make a living by what we get.*
> *We make a life by what we give."*

Writing in the spring of 2009, the current economic crisis facing America and the world creates a dramatic context for any book offering principles to help managers in future generations. I firmly believe the advice presented in the preceding pages continues to have great relevance and validity. Perhaps the ideas are even truer because they were tested and proven by a company in a dying industry at a time of considerable economic pressure.

That said, I don't believe any lasting attempts to preserve free enterprise and a market economy will succeed unless the following ideas are also embraced:

- We must find a way to preserve the nation's manufacturing base, not just in the food industry, but in the production of consumer durables and heavy industry as well. Other advanced economies have done so successfully, and we must, too. There is no future in an economy based solely on service industries.

- Our educational system needs an intense overhaul, pragmatically redirected to priorities emphasizing the applied sciences and technology in a world-competitive way.

- Corporate greed has been targeted in the press as a growingly destructive force. Compensation measures such as excessive stock options have come under fire. Ideally such devices are intended to encourage long-term management loyalty. What happens, however, when they result in transferring ownership of corporate assets to a small group of managers? Is it even fair to the managers to compel them to make crucial business decisions in a framework of often irresistible self-interest? I'm pleased to see many boards are taking action to prevent personal greed from prevailing.

- Mechanisms must be adopted to funnel part of the wealth corporations produce back into their home communities. Global outsourcing of much manufacturing has furthered the belief that such local relationships are passé. Because consumer brands and capital flows have become global, it has been convenient to assume that meaningful relationships no longer exist between businesses and their manufacturing roots. This is a dangerous illusion that must be dispelled.

The threats to American business are considerable, but it's also a fact that dirty linen tends to get the press. The low price of company stocks has increased the danger of further, potentially undesirable foreign ownership of U.S. assets. We stand at a watershed, and after decades of market liberalization, it seems that the U.S. could well see the future of its fundamental economic system challenged. Long-term, we will face serious issues of purpose as we wake up to the grim reality of who owns our corporate assets and who will call the policy shots as to how those assets are managed. A number of previously robust business sectors face a perilous future, if not extinction.

With Toyota's ascendance, a 'Big Three' made up of GM, Ford and Chrysler is a list of the past. In 2009, the Big Three American auto companies face the dramatic watershed I describe above, one that has become a grim potential bellwether for the remainder of American manufacturing. By the time you read this book, I earnestly hope that the American auto industry will have found answers to those constraints, particularly in both labor and management compensation agreements, which have made this industry uncompetitive even in our own domestic market. Having been a loyal General Motors customer for decades, I am particularly aghast at the rapid decline of this once stalwart pacesetter. Have we abandoned the very principles that made our auto industry great?

It's my hope that American manufacturers can forge the necessary spirit of labor-management teamwork to win back our position in the global auto market. If foreign manufacturers were simply permitted to move in and take over the American auto companies tomorrow, they would surely face challenges. However, I'm certain they would resolve obstacles that seem to be so troublesome to labor and management now. These issues include streamlining expenses and wages, installing the latest technology, and renovating the relationship between management and labor. That's because the Big Three have failed to make crucial improvements in these areas. Looking forward, that obligation to anticipate and act innovatively will include the social responsibility to retrain the workforce members inevitably displaced by advancing competitive technology. This series of steps is what the Hormel team was able to achieve, and the same opportunities are available to the leadership of America's automotive giants.

As I said earlier, we chose to keep Spam a domestically manufactured product but to do so in a competitive way that entailed investing in the most sophisticated technology, a seven-story colossus that could produce as many as 440 cans per minute. Some may say that this illustration is an oversimplification of a far more complex problem. I'm not sure I would agree, and I am certain that we as a nation cannot continue to run away from the challenge of manufacturing competitiveness simply by outsourcing production overseas.

As we learned in the food industry, there is just no substitute for strategizing a business to achieve and sustain viable long-term margins. I use the word "watershed" to describe the present crisis with full intent, because the collapse of the Big Three will certainly spell the demise of hundreds of smaller domestic suppliers to the automotive sector and could easily bring down what is left of American manufacturing industry as a house of cards. No country with the size and aspirations of the United States can survive by being simply reliant on service industries, no matter what fashionable business trend analysts may contend. If we lose ownership of our manufacturing base, the jobs may stay – some of them – but we will forego the strategic control, as well as the national security advantages of domestic ownership in lifeblood industries.

What also worries me, frankly, is a more insidious sort of infrastructural decay. It's not the infrastructure shouldered primarily by government. It's the breakdown of a proactive relationship between businesses and the communities in which they do business. Unfortunately, quality of community is too often one of the last considerations businesses weigh in making decisions about where to locate operations. What can be found in Austin and in so many other American communities represents a great reservoir of potential to foster a rebirth of American industry.

What has been achieved in Austin reflects the Hormel team's great commitment to fundamental and innovative points of difference in everything it does. That approach applies to the community every bit as much as to the business itself. I have a predictable bias that Hormel has done a better than average job of giving back to Austin and other communities where we operate. It has been in our self-interest to do so. Our willingness to make these decisions has not always been driven by the bottom-line first and foremost. However, what we did has paid, we believe, handsome dividends for our sustained growth and exceptional financial performance. The starting point was often anchored in values not visible in the bottom-line pure and simple. And at Hormel and particularly in Austin, we took a series of positions that had a profound impact on the future destiny of the community.

- We took a stand when we decided to turn around the business in a dying industry through becoming a technological and marketing leader.
- We took a stand rebuilding the firm through a base of largely internal talent.
- We took a stand when we decided to build a new plant in Austin, the most innovative and advanced in the industry.
- We took a stand when we completely renovated Austin High and the community's elementary schools to preserve this city's urban core.
- We took a stand when we installed a program to support continuing educational advancement for our community's teachers.
- We took a stand when we sought a collaboration with the University of Minnesota in enhancing the quality of our local educational system both for students and for teachers.
- We took a stand when we decided to rebuild the Hormel Institute and establish it as a global center for medical research in conjunction with the University of Minnesota and the Mayo Clinic.
- We took a stand when we merged our hospital and clinic into the Mayo system to ally ourselves with the best and most cost-efficient provider of medical care in the nation.

By no means do I seek to imply that Austin is the perfect community in all respects. The challenge for urban excellence, as with business excellence, is a never ending one. We, for example, are now tackling the particular demands of assimilating immigrants and minorities into our community. Each of these challenges not only requires continuing diligence. Civic energy has to be directed with an overall plan and constant reflection about the most important needs.

If a community's well-being is so important, where can businesses begin? Well, the situation is not unlike having an ailment diagnosed. In my opinion, an illness is best treated by quality diagnosis first. That's what gives a pace-setting institution like the Mayo Clinic such an edge. It's what makes Mayo both the technological leader and the low-cost provider. If that sounds suspicious, I recommend an article John Goodman wrote for *The Wall Street Journal* titled "Perverse Incentives in Health Care." In it, Goodman reports:

> *Research by John Wennberg and his colleagues at Dartmouth Medical School suggest that if everyone in America went to the Mayo Clinic, our annual health-care bill would be 25% lower (more than $500 billion), and the average quality of care would improve.*

Perceptive diagnosis can work for communities as well as people. In both cases, the outcome will be improved, and the long-term costs will be lower. If exacting diagnosis is the starting point for curing the ailing relationship businesses have with their communities; a self-audit such as the following can help firms identify the issues.

# A BUSINESS-COMMUNITY
# SELF-AUDIT
## *Building a*
## *Points-of-Difference Attitude*

1. **Through corporate philanthropy and/or the possible use of a foundation, are you giving back to the community in a planned and meaningful way?** These investments aren't strictly selfless. There is considerable enlightened self-interest at stake. Everything you do to improve quality of life in the community contributes to your ability to do business well, too.

2. **Are you aware of community plans and do you take an active interest in advancing them in crucial civic areas: education, medical care, housing, etc.?** Government may fill a central role in many of these areas, but business must play a major part. The failure of business to do so will result in a lower quality of life and a less attractive place to work.

3. **Does management take a leading role in community institutions, especially in the ones you financially support most vigorously?** Individual participation is as important and, in some instances, even more important than money. Personal involvement can return life-satisfying rewards for managers as well.

4. **Does your community have *infrastructural strength*?** We test the **structural strength** of buildings. We need to test for the

**infrastructural strength** of communities. For small cities, this might include highly organized health-care systems, heliports for medical traumas and emergency care, a navigable system of roadways, an up-to-date orientation to housing that matches the changing demographics of the community, and access to the arts and quality local athletic programs crucial to the needs of a community to be inspired and to excel.

5. **Is your community truly *barrier-free in all respects*?** The community should certainly be barrier-free for the physically challenged, but is it barrier-free in a broader sense as well? Are key community institutions like the YMCA, clinics, school resources, libraries, recreation facilities, etc. easily and economically accessible to all? Are they meaningful and of sufficient quality to attract people to use them?

6. **Have you built leadership alliances?** Let's say you think of yourself as a leading business in your area. What are you doing to forge relationships with other institutions in your community or your region – organizations which may not be in industry, but which excel in education, medicine, or the arts? Real leadership loves company and uses the synergy with and support of other regional institutions to maximize impact on community projects.

7. **Do you enable positive outside stimulation?** There are countless, ingenious ways to amplify day-to-day experience by bringing in cultural resources from larger cities and by ensuring that the community enjoys the highest level of Internet access.

8. **Are you keeping community history alive and relevant?** Are historical landmarks being leveraged and rededicated to modern ends? Communities need cultural continuity.

9. **Is your company's uniqueness invisible or part of the community's identity?** Hormel has visibility *plus* in Austin, and that's realized great dividends. We're not bashful, and we're creative. Austin has the only Spam Museum in the world, to cite just one instance, and it's become one of the town's greatest tourist attractions. Of more far-reaching significance is Austin's position at the forefront of community medical care through its involvement with the Mayo Clinic medical care system.

10. **Do you think about competitive relations in a positive way?** What are comparably sized companies in your community doing? Is it distinctive? Are they employing points of difference more creatively than you? What are comparably sized companies across the nation doing? What's distinctive about their approach that gives them a bigger-than-life presence?

Sadly, few businesses and communities have audited their situation thoroughly to identify what their strengths are and how they could be imaginatively exploited. Only by taking stock and addressing each of these points one-by-one will progress be made. Wall Street runs off Main Street and not vice versa. America is a nation of communities, not a trading desk on a global stock market. If we walk away from our communities and their vitality, we shrug our shoulders at the essence of our nation. We can only change our destiny by lighting up one shining point of difference after another… one community at a time.

# AFTERWORD

## DR. ROBERT WALLER

*Dr. Robert Waller is Chair, Board of Directors, Institute for Healthcare Improvement; and past President and CEO of Mayo Clinic, Mayo Foundation. Dr. Waller served on the Board of Hormel Foods from 1992 to 2006. He is retired Professor of Ophthalmology at Mayo Medical School.*

IT WAS A PRIVILEGE BEYOND MY EXPECTATIONS to serve on the Hormel Foods Board of Directors. At the outset, I was not at all certain that someone with a background in medicine would be a "fit" for the work of a board dedicated to the food industry. However, this introduction into the corporate environment from the non-profit world proved to be a very special opportunity.

I came to understand and greatly appreciate the qualities and characteristics of the Hormel culture, described in its many facets in *Points of Difference*. Over time, what became especially clear were the many similarities between the principles and values underpinning the mission of this great company and the principles and values of Mayo Clinic. Although it has expanded now to multiple locations, the Mayo Clinic's original base in Rochester is just 45 miles from Hormel headquarters in Austin, Minnesota.

Jay Hormel, the son of the founder George A. Hormel, and the Mayo brothers, Drs William and Charles Mayo, were good friends. One cannot help but wonder if, during their social contacts, they shared thoughts about core values and responsibilities to their organizations as well as to the communities where they lived and worked. It seems likely that their friendship, the geographic proximity of Austin and Rochester, and the realization that there were many cultural similarities between the two organizations were important formative influences. They all contributed to building the foundation for the Hormel-Mayo partnerships which today serve southeast Minnesota as well as the scientific community at large.

Described in detail in Chapter 8, an extraordinary collaboration recently developed among several partners: The Hormel Institute, the Hormel Foundation, the University of Minnesota, Mayo Clinic, and IBM. All have pooled talents and resources to create a spectacular center dedicated to cancer research. Located in Austin, this center will be one of the premier sites of advanced research in America. The clinic/hospital complex of the Austin Medical Center is now a significant element of the Mayo Health System, serving an ever expanding geographic base around Austin. These partnerships make a strong case that institutions in vastly different spheres can work together to add backbone to an even more vibrant America. Joining hands, the corporate and non-profit worlds, under the right circumstances, can indeed create meaningful "points of difference" for the common good.

It is becoming increasingly evident that leaders in the professions, in communities, in industry, and in education, to name just a few sectors, need to listen to each other more than ever before. We are all in a globally competitive era of great intensity. Resources are scarce. Doing more for less is the order of the day. The recent business/financial crises have made the need for improved dialogue among all sectors of society inescapable.

An excellent example of the value of listening to each other and the learning that comes from doing so was the response of Hormel to adversity in the 1980s. As Dick has described, the company borrowed more than its net worth to build a state-of-the-art plant in Austin. Hormel Foods simultaneously increased its investment in research, developed a remarkable array of value-added products, and brought customers to Austin from near and far to cultivate world-wide markets. This model of response to adversity is a case study worthy of serious consideration by any organization facing challenging times, whether structured as a for-profit or non-profit organization.

As one reads **Points of Difference**, it becomes readily apparent that the value-based mission of Hormel is non-negotiable. Dick Knowlton provides ample evidence that Hormel Foods has been willing and able to change successfully throughout the years without compromising its core values. Collegiality, civility, honesty, and trust are hallmarks of this company's culture. The people of Hormel understand and practice mutual respect for each other, their families, and their customers. They have zero tolerance for anything other than this respectful attitude. Hormel maintains a living awareness of what made their organization successful in the past and embraces a commitment to remember and respect those who laid the foundation for their success as they go forward.

Hormel has been a prime example of how best to develop leaders. They were truly blessed to have Dick Knowlton at the helm from 1981 to 1993. He continues to be a star by any measure. He left his post as chief executive in the superb hands of Joel Johnson, who in turn mentored the outstanding current leader Jeff Ettinger. What a privilege it has been for me to learn from them all.

In my view, ***Points of Difference*** describes one of the greatest stories to be told in corporate America.

*Robert Waller, M.D.*
*Memphis, Tennessee*
*May 2009*

# NOTES

······•··············•·················•·················•···········

## CHAPTER 1

**P. 3** Gallup Study: "Gallup Study of Changing Food Preparation and Eating Habits." Princeton NJ: Multisponsor Surveys, Inc., 1999

**P. 13** car seats: Nordqvist, Christian, "American Children Getting Too Fat For Car Safety Seats," Medical News Today, April 3, 2006 (http://www.medicalnewstoday.com/articles/40830.php)

**P. 13** 7-Eleven: Price, Wayne T., "7-Eleven Boosts Lineup with Convenient New Treats," *Florida Today*, March 6, 2008

**P. 13** specialty cheeses: "Americans turn on to specialty cheeses," The Associated Press as appears in http://dailymail.com/foodandliving/200803050302

**P. 14** Laurie Demeritt: Demeritt, Laurie, of The Hartmann Group, *The Morning Cup*, Messenger Communications Co., as appears in http://www.morningcup.net/MC_archives/archives-020408-monday-qwtuxqv247t439kfm359.htm

**P. 14** food processing: Katz, Frances, "Flavor Trends for 2007," FoodProcessing.com, January 9, 2007

**P. 14** eating at home: "Consumer Insight: Households combining trips, eating out less & staying home - United States, Fall/Winter 2006," ACNielsen Homescan & Spectra Panel Views Surveys

**P. 14** Bennigans: Grynbaum, Michael M., "Restaurant Chains Close as Diners Reduce Spending," The New York Times, July 30, 2008

**P. 24** inside the Box: Coyne, Kevin P., Patricia Gorman Clifford and Renée Dye, "Breakthrough Thinking from Inside the Box," Harvard Business Review, December 2007

## CHAPTER 2

**P. 27** ownership in Austin: Hage, Dave and Paul Klauda, *No Retreat, No Surrender: Labor's War at Hormel*, New York, William Morrow & Company, 1989, p. 37

**P. 31** 1937 Fortune Magazine: *The Hormel Legacy: 100 Years of Quality*, Geo. A. Hormel & Company, 1991, pp. 72-73

**P. 33** contract never expired: Hage, Dave and Paul Klauda, *No Retreat, No Surrender: Labor's War at Hormel*, New York, William Morrow & Company, 1989, p. 36

**P. 33** nine feet long: Hage, Dave and Paul Klauda, *No Retreat, No Surrender: Labor's War at Hormel*, New York, William Morrow & Company, 1989, p. 36

**P. 48** "Every day I made the rounds": Geo. Hormel, unpublished Memoir p. 233

## CHAPTER 3

**P. 62** hogs per day: Fusaro, Dave, "Hormel Foods Named 2008 Food Processor of the Year", *Food Processing magazine*, 12/1/2008

**P. 67** Surowiecki: Surowiecki, James, "The Free Trade Paradox," *New Yorker Magazine*, May 26, 2008, The Financial Page

**P. 74** 1973 oil crisis: Frum, David, *How We Got Here: The '70s. New York, New York: Basic Books. p. 318*

**P. 74** 1979 second oil crisis: as appears in http://www.wtrg.com/prices.htm

**P. 88** baggage handling: Johnson, Kirk, "Denver Airport Saw the Future. It Didn't Work," *The New York Times*, August 27, 2005

**P. 88** Denver Airport: Denver International Airport as appears in http://en.wikipedia.org/wiki/Denver_International_Airport

**P. 88** London's Terminal 5: Lam, Brian, "Why: Heathrow Airport Terminal 5's High Tech Failings," as appeared in gizmodo.com/379123/why-heathrow-airport-terminal-5s-high-tech-failings April 12, 2008

## CHAPTER 4

**P. 96** Originate, don't imitate: *The Hormel Legacy: 100 Years of Quality*, Geo. A. Hormel & Company, 1991, p. 34

**P. 96** Sugar-Cured: *The Hormel Legacy: 100 Years of Quality*, Geo. A. Hormel & Company, 1991, p. 34

**P. 97** Bob Hope Joke: *The Hormel Legacy: 100 Years of Quality*, Geo. A. Hormel & Company, 1991, p. 106

**P. 97** Monte Vista, Colorado theft: Hormel News Magazine / March 1991 p. 21

**P. 99** "prematurely right": Drucker, Peter F., *Managing for the Future*, New York, Truman Talley/Dutton, 1992, p.21

**P. 117** New products company: "Geo. A. Hormel & Co.: New Products Company of the Year," *Prepared Foods New Products Annual*, 1987

**P. 117** 1984 annual report: *The Hormel Legacy: 100 Years of Quality*, Geo. A. Hormel & Company, 1991, p. 176

**P. 118** Innovation Kitchen: as appears in http://www.nikebiz.com/contact/

**P. 124** Mister Microwave: "Mister Microwave," *Forbes*, January 11, 1988

**P. 132** leading food innovator: "Mister Microwave," *Forbes*, January 11, 1988

**P. 132** Investor's Business Daily: Elliott, Alan, "The Pigs Don't Like It, But Wall Street Does," *Investor's Business Daily*, January 18, 2002

**P. 133** Credit Suisse: Moskow, Robert and Pl Aquino, "Hormel Foods: Golden Turkey," Investment Research, Credit Suisse, November 20, 2007

**P. 133** diverse product offering: Churchill, Mark D., "Hormel Foods: Transitioning Coverage At Buy; Solid 1Q Results Across Business; Raising PT"", Investment Research, Piper Jaffray & Co., February 19, 2008

**P. 138** "prematurely right": Drucker, Peter F., *Managing for the Future*, New York, Truman Talley/Dutton, 1992, p.21

## CHAPTER 5

**P. 148** union ordered: Rachleff, Peter, *Hard-Pressed in the Heartland*, Boston, South End Press, 1993, p. 84

**P. 148** Lewie Anderson: Hage, Dave and Paul Klauda, *No Retreat, No Surrender: Labor's War at Hormel*, New York, William Morrow & Company, 1989, p. 101

**p. 155** wrested leadership: Hage, Dave and Paul Klauda, *No Retreat, No Surrender: Labor's War at Hormel*, New York, William Morrow & Company, 1989, p. 80

**p. 156** Ray Rogers: as appears in the website: http://www. corporatecampaign.org/raybio.htm

**p. 157** Tools to confront power with power: as appears in the website: http://www.corporatecampaign.org/provenfr.htm

**p. 157** Rogers had also: Hage, Dave and Paul Klauda, *No Retreat, No Surrender: Labor's War at Hormel*, New York, William Morrow & Company, 1989, p. 95

**p. 158** two-and-a-half hour speech: Hage, Dave and Paul Klauda, *No Retreat, No Surrender: Labor's War at Hormel*, New York, William Morrow & Company, 1989, p. 90

**p. 159** Dave Hage and Paul Klauda: Hage, Dave and Paul Klauda, *No Retreat, No Surrender: Labor's War at Hormel*, New York, William Morrow & Company, 1989

**p. 162-163** Wall Street Transcript: "TWST Names Knowlton Best Chief Executive Meat & Poultry," *The Wall Street Transcript*, (BR118/01)

**p. 168** *Nightline*: Rachleff, Peter, *Hard-Pressed in the Heartland*, Boston, South End Press, 1993, p. 119

**p. 173** refused to sanction: Rachleff, Peter, *Hard-Pressed in the Heartland*, Boston, South End Press, 1993, p. 117

**p. 176** "*Ayatollah*": Rachleff, Peter, *Hard-Pressed in the Heartland*, Boston, South End Press, 1993, p. 119

## CHAPTER 7

**p. 211** high salaries for brains: Hormel, George A., Autobiography (Unpublished Manuscript), 1944, p. 204

**P. 212** MBAs: Harvard Business School as appears in http://www. businessschooladmission.com/harvard-business-school/ and in Shellenbarger, Sue "The Mommy M.B.A.: Schools Try to Attract More Women," *The Wall Street Journal*, August 20, 2008

**P. 218** feeding people: Hormel, George A., Autobiography (Unpublished Manuscript), 1944., p. 210

**P. 218** pretty girl: Dougherty, Richard, *In Quest of Quality: Hormel's First 75 Years*, Austin, MN, Geo. A. Hormel & Co., 1966, p. 49

**P. 218** one right-all right: Dougherty, Richard, *In Quest of Quality: Hormel's First 75 Years*, Austin, MN, Geo. A. Hormel & Co., 1966, p. 50

## CHAPTER 8

**P. 239** stockyards of Chicago: Hormel, George A., Autobiography (Unpublished Manuscript), 1944, p. 76

**P. 239** alderman: Hormel, George A., Autobiography (Unpublished Manuscript), 1944, p. 217

**P. 239** town out of debt: Dougherty, Richard, *In Quest of Quality: Hormel's First 75 Years*, Austin, MN, Geo. A. Hormel & Co., 1966, p. 68

**P. 239** furnished home: Hormel, George A., Autobiography (Unpublished Manuscript), 1944, p. 123

**P. 242** case studies: O'Keeffe, Edmund under Ray A. Goldberg, "George A. Hormel & Company" Harvard Business School Case Study, N9-591-026, Publishing Division, *Harvard Business School*, Boston, MA, 1990

**P. 253** Muncie: Lynd, Robert S. and Helen Merrell Lynd, *Middletown: A Study in Modern American Culture*, Orlando, Harcourt Brace Jovanovich, 1957

**P. 254** Big Business: Romanko, J. R., "The Big Business of Small Towns," *The New York Times*, September 22, 2002

**P. 255** "generational connectedness": Lancaster, Lynne C. and David Stillman, *When Generations Collide*, New York, HarperBusiness, 2002

**P. 255** Condon, Oregon: Lancaster, Lynne C. and David Stillman, *When Generations Collide*, New York, HarperBusiness, 2002, pp. 333-334

## CHAPTER 9

**P. 260** Winston Churchill: as appears in: http://www.quotationspage. com/quote/2236.html

**P. 265** Goodman: Goodman, John C. "Perverse Incentives in Health Care," *The Wall Street Journal*, April 5, 2007

# INDEX OF PROPER NAMES

Printed in the USA
CPSIA information can be obtained
at www.ICGtesting.com
JSHW082151140824
68134JS00014B/179